Praise for *Bard, Kinetic*

"Sweeping and intimate, fierce and electric, Anne Waldman is seer, muse, and sage feminist, fast-speaking on all frequencies. *Bard, Kinetic* is a collection of poems; deep, sharp, and generous portraits; feminafestos; and ecstatic rants in her many voices. She notices, expounds, narrates, chants. The book is full of questions. It's urgent, physical, ancient and utterly contemporary. What to name the child of the crossroad? Poetry! Her words dance and spin through sources (the Tarot, the Tibetan Book of the Dead, Giorgio Agamben) and places (New York, Boulder, India). Words that come to mind: Sanctuary. Old growth trees. The mind and heart of poetry. What a colossal life, and what a monumental, unforgettable book."   **—Laurie Anderson**

"Anne Waldman has tirelessly cleared the path for many of us for decades. She is our epitome of the word *onward,* which means to move forward in a continuous motion, never stopping because surrender is out of the question! Waldman's extensive study of the global perception of the Sixth Extinction through the lives of poets comes to light in this powerful new book, which is a record of the cycles of cosmic transit! She writes, 'Feeling everyone's kinetics in that zone. But also all together swimming in a database. Imagine.'"   **—CAConrad**

"Kinetic, yes. Prophetic also. Boundlessly generous, of course. This is the Anne Waldman I know. What a pleasure it is to find everything here: every ancestral memory, every important question, every exhortation to stay human in an inhumane century. If you are curious about the value of poets and poetry, peer into this magic mirror, drink from this deep and wide and entirely remarkable archive."

—Lisa Jarnot

"I am tempted to describe the genius of the work in these radiant pages with a bounty of adjectives, but that would be a disservice to its restless momentum. Besides, Anne Waldman doesn't settle for nouns and their obsequious companions. More than dance in the range of numinous texts collected here, her intellect spins ferociously, shaking off the patriarchy's layers of concealment one after another. For Gertrude Stein, another towering figure in the Outrider lineage, 'writing should go on.' For Waldman it must do so as well, but further than the page and into the world. Goading us is just one of her gifts. To read her is to be humbled by the breadth of her vocation, to be jolted into alertness."   **—Mónica de la Torre**

Praise for Anne Waldman

Winner of the 2015 American Book Awards
Lifetime Achievement Award

"A major poet." **—Allen Ginsberg**

"When Allen Ginsberg passed from us it was Anne Waldman who dutifully gathered up his many burdens, continuing his work as poet, activist, and teacher. In following his example she has bloomed as an example herself. How fortunate we are to have her among us and may we all reach out and take a small amount of her burden upon ourselves." **—Patti Smith**

"Anne Waldman's voice is epic, mythic and above all, wild. She gives us direct courage from the force of her great heart. Her words: sacred text." **—Terry Tempest Williams**

"Wit, real teaching and speed all meet up here. . . . Anne Waldman's poetry being nothing but the eye and sound of prophecy itself." **—Eileen Myles**

"Reading Waldman is like being in the world today. . . . It's easy to feel drawn to this poet's idealism and generosity of spirit." **—Daisy Fried,** *The New York Times*

"The legitimate heir to Allen Ginsberg's crown as America's underground 'poet-ambassador' laureate." **—*Colorado Springs Independent***

"Waldman's epic goes splendidly on and on, mixing the shamanistic with the diaristic, the topical with the prayerful, incorporating almost everything." **—*Publishers Weekly***

"Waldman, a major force with more than 40 books of poetry and poetics, remains committed to experiment, cross-cultural and countercultural engagement, and verse that simply sings." **—*Library Journal***

"Waldman takes you by the collar and slams you down with language, image, and message, leaving you breathless and shattered in the aftermath of her incantatory vision." **—Chris Faatz, Powell's Books**

BARD,
KINETIC

Also by Anne Waldman and Published by Coffee House Press

ANTHOLOGIES

Beats at Naropa (coedited with Laura Wright)
Civil Disobediences (coedited with Lisa Birman)
Cross Worlds: Transcultural Poetics (coedited with Laura Wright)
Nice to See You: Homage to Ted Berrigan

POETRY

Helping the Dreamer
In the Room of Never Grieve
The Iovis Trilogy: Colors in the Mechanism of Concealment
Voice's Daughter of a Heart Yet to Be Born
Vow to Poetry

BARD,
KINETIC

Anne Waldman

COFFEE HOUSE PRESS
Minneapolis
2023

Coffee House Press books are available to the trade through our primary distributor, Consortium Book Sales & Distribution, cbsd.com or (800) 283-3572. For personal orders, catalogs, or other information, write to info@coffeehousepress.org.

Coffee House Press is a nonprofit literary publishing house. Support from private foundations, corporate giving programs, government programs, and generous individuals helps make the publication of our books possible. We gratefully acknowledge their support in detail in the back of this book.

LIBRARY OF CONGRESS CATALOGING-IN-PUBLICATION DATA

Names: Waldman, Anne, 1945– author.
Title: Bard, Kinetic / Anne Waldman.
Description: Minneapolis : Coffee House Press, 2023.
Identifiers: LCCN 2022028562 (print) | LCCN 2022028563 (ebook) | ISBN 9781566896696 (paperback) | ISBN 9781566896702 (epub)
Subjects: LCSH: Waldman, Anne, 1945. | Poets, American—20th century— Biography. | LCGFT: Autobiographies.
Classification: LCC PS3573.A4215 Z46 2023 (print) | LCC PS3573.A4215 (ebook) | DDC 811/.54—dc23/eng/20220909
LC record available at https://lccn.loc.gov/2022028562
LC ebook record available at https://lccn.loc.gov/2022028563

PRINTED IN THE UNITED STATES OF AMERICA

30 29 28 27 26 25 24 23   1 2 3 4 5 6 7 8

She said, What is history?
And he said, History is an angel
Being blown
Backwards
Into the future
He said: History is a pile of debris
And the angel wants to go back and fix things
To repair the things that have been broken

But there is a storm blowing from Paradise
And the storm keeps blowing the angel
Backwards into the future

—LAURIE ANDERSON

Contents

BARD, KINETIC

Sketch

Now we're gonna sing "By and by when the morning comes"
And what this is?
We're in the same boat, brother
We live together and we sing together
And that's the way to keep peace
Now we gonna sing "By and by" so you come right with me
I'm gonna sing the chorus first
Oh, by and by, when the morning comes
All the saints of God is gathering home
We will tell the story how we'll overcome
We will understand it better by and by
Now come with me, sing it loud
By and by, when the morning comes (sing it)
All the saints of God is gathering home (sing loud)
We'll tell the story how we'll overcome
We will understand it better by and by (sing it again)
Get it by and by, when the morning come
All the saints of God is gathering home
We will tell the story how we'll overcome
We will understand it better by and by (sing it a last time)
Yes it's by and by, when the morning come
We'll tell the story how we'll overcome
We will tell the story how we'll overcome
We will understand it better by and by

—LEAD BELLY, "BY AND BY WHEN THE MORNING COMES"

I sat on Lead Belly's lap as a baby. Patti Smith, my neighbor, insisted I start with this tantalizing detail in this sketch. Wear it as an amulet.

I was conceived on the Fourth of July 1944 shortly before my father, John Marvin Waldman, was shipped overseas from Fort Bragg, North Carolina, to Europe. After "Tennessee Maneuvers," his unit was conveyed secretly to Hoboken, where they joined the USS *General Walter H. Gordon* troopship headed for Marseilles. My mother, Frances, had been living in a rented room on MacDougal Street, Greenwich Village, in a house full of women—some single, others with husbands away at war. When her child was due, no relatives close by, she went to the town of Millville in southern New Jersey, where my father's family lived. My grandfather John worked at Whitall Tatum as a principal glassblower. His father, Frederick, who had emigrated from Hesse, Germany, in the 1850s, had also been a glassblower. John was a taciturn man, sober, serious. Maybe he was religious. Dona Hand, his wife, my grandmother, had a sharp tongue. I remember the time she put a ton of salt in the ice tea by mistake in those red Depression-ware glasses, serving a whole table of family and friends who grimaced but felt too intimidated to say anything. She was of Black Irish-English extraction. Her father had been a sea captain who lost his life somewhere between Cape May and Liverpool, delivering the New Jersey oak and pine they craved abroad. There's a trace on my grandmother's side of another ancestor with the last name of "Hand" who came from Britain in 1600 as a teenager, alone, working on a ship, to The Hamptons, Long Island. I met my father nine months after my birth. I was called a "little firecracker" and later told I was a "triple Aries" by some college friends.

My mother's parents, James Arthur LeFevre and Alice Baker LeFevre, had lived in York, Pennsylvania. A devout Christian Scientist, Alice had hoped to be a missionary in Africa but due to delicate health couldn't travel. Christ Science eschewed doctors, and illness was "separation from God." One had an "error" in the stomach, in the head, in the leg, in the heart, etc. Consequently my mother, without medical attention, was deaf in her left ear her whole life. Alice lived as a semi-invalid, rarely out, always loyal to her doctrinaire faith. Her husband played violin and was descended from the Huguenot LeFevres, who escaped persecution at the hands of the Catholics from northern France. He died when my mother was five years old. I remember visiting York at an early age and seeing in the local historical museum the family Bible that a devout LeFevre had hidden in a loaf of bread as they escaped. A long voyage. I wondered how this enormous tome had ever fit inside a loaf of bread.

My father played piano with accomplishment. After high school he worked at various local movie theaters accompanying "silents." He took up the peripatetic musician's life for a number of years, playing swing jazz with various bands around the East Coast and also accompanying modern dance artists such as the experimental Helen Tamiris, one of the first choreographers to use jazz and social protest themes in her work. John and Frances met in New York City at a party at the home of Isamu Noguchi in 1942. Possibly at the artist's studio in MacDougal Alley.

My mother had been an early independent young woman, sailing off to Greece at the age of 19 in 1929 upon marrying Glaukos Sikélianòs, the son of the celebrated Greek poet Anghelos Sikélianòs; having one child, my brother Mark; and living abroad for a decade right before WWII. An extraordinary time. Frances had entered the rich utopian environment of the Delphic Idea, a community created and nourished by Anghelos and his wife, Eva Palmer Sikélianòs, a brilliant groundbreaking visionary artist of New England, later New York, who had been associated with the "women of the Left Bank," a circle of lesbian artists, poets, dancers in the orbit of the magnetizing Natalie Barney in Paris. Barney and Eva had been childhood friends and lovers, summering in Bar Harbor, Maine, and had an extensive correspondence over many years. Eva, an American heiress and daughter of Courtlandt Palmer, a founder of the Nineteenth Century Club, was a director, composer, and weaver. Frances was very much under the spell and tutelage of her mother-in-law, Eva, who was an inspiring presence and force. This surrogate mother, mentor, and friend taught Frances how to weave. Frances also studied and picked up modern Greek and was busy translating some of Anghelos's poems, specifically *The Border Guards,* political poems about the Greek resistance. (I later published *The Border Guards,* by Anghelos Sikélianòs, translations by Frances Sikélianòs, with my press—one of many—Rocky Ledge Cottage Editions in 1982.) She translated Sikélianòs's *The Dithyramb of the Rose,* which was published by dancer Ted Shawn in 1939, as a Christmas card. She also helped with Eva's second Delphic Festival, a production under Eva's direction of Aeschylus's *Prometheus Bound,* and *Suppliant Women,* also by Aeschylus, a play that foregrounds a chorus of women as protagonist. As a young child I spent time with Eva in New York City after the war; my mother had stayed quite close. She wore her own handwoven Greek garb, her long once-auburn hair now gray and more often held up in a bun. She had an eccentric's stubborn charisma. She died when I was six years old. I later understood her generative feminist and artistic influence on Frances. I wore garments of cloth she had woven, a pair of the sandals my mother had made, Greek style with one continuous thong of leather, the kind I was told Gertrude Stein also wore.

My mother stayed alert to many things Greek. She had, after all, been an early novice and devotee in the cult of Sikélianòs's Ideal. Anghelos's vision was of an international brotherhood of elite artists and visionaries centered in Delphi. He also proposed the notion of it being a secular monastic community. Eva concentrated her energies on her festival, also part of the plan.

My father had had an early marriage as well, to the wild and reckless "flapper" daughter—Mary Ellen Vorse—of labor journalist and activist Mary Heaton Vorse, who wrote about women's suffrage, civil rights, affordable housing and was an important figure and legend in Provincetown. Vorse was close to the communist writer and labor activist John Reed. My father lived next to John Dos Passos in Provincetown. Both my parents and their original partners shared a circle of artistic friends based in and around Provincetown, NYC, and overseas. Some had connections to the Provincetown Playhouse on MacDougal. I intuited some of the same patterns of relationship and tight-knit artistic community playing out later in my own life in New York and also in Boulder. An ever-widening gyre.

Committed to a new marriage with Frances, having abandoned the uncertain vocation of musician and the unconventional lifestyle it implied, as well as sobered by the war, my father went back to school on the G.I. Bill, eventually receiving a doctorate from Columbia University. During this time, he took on many "hack" writing jobs, discoursing on the perils of smoking, for example, later writing articles and accessible books on reading and education, including the popular *Rapid Reading Made Simple*. He began working at Pace University in downtown New York City, was director of the reading laboratory there, served as chair of the English department (hosting guests Marianne Moore and Allen Ginsberg, among others), and also as secretary of the university.

I remember the musty scent and presence of my father's writing accoutrements in the cramped apartment at the top of MacDougal Street: yellow foolscap, messy typewriter ribbons, wheel eraser with its pert green whisk-skirt. And the obligatory cup of coffee and cigarettes close by. I was anxious to replicate this exotic "scene" which carried associations of solitude, daydreaming (one looked askance, preoccupied, when considering what to say), and daily work ritual. A clatter and peck of fingers at keys, making something out of nothing. And then you had a few typed pages to peruse, edit, read out loud. Or discard. John would show his pieces to cohort Frances, who was keen on getting into the project. She was by then the grammatical perfectionist, wrote her own "stuff" furtively in clandestine notebooks. I observed her writing letters and typing out poems she admired. The practice of writing and typing seemed valorous, important. I mostly liked the shape of the poems on yellow foolscap pages.

My mother was a self-appointed poet and translator (French of César Moro and Greek of Sikélianòs), but her practices, as said, were covert. She was hard on herself and others. Intellectual, an autodidact, never satisfied. Poetry was for her the highest art. These two persons with their particular bent and turns and passions certainly helped shape mine. There was a freedom to read widely, to write, think, talk about it, be inquisitive. Be critical. I was fortunate to have such parents.

Yet this was not an easy household and harbored certain contradictions—something almost Protestant in my upbringing which was weird considering my mother's earlier years—an expectation on the one hand to succeed, to excel, to fit in, to have people's respect. An upbringing which, for example, emphasized education and artistic brilliance (not just in the exclusive province of schools or academies). A smart person was never satisfied, always hungry for more knowledge, devoured books, asked questions, kept "at it." Rarely idle. On the other hand, both parents carried much of their earlier bohemianism and tolerance and permissiveness into this new marriage. Frances was edgy with me. She once said she would gun me down if she found me pushing a baby carriage, the implication being I had abandoned art for a man and settled down. She also asked me once if I would guide my father through an LSD journey to "conquer his anxieties"! My mother was a terrible housekeeper, scorned Mother's Day, resented and was critical of anything "phony." She threatened to leave when John and my younger brother, Carl, brought a TV home bought on an installment plan. She was really angry—"it's either me or the TV" she said, and something like "if that abomination crosses the threshold I'm leaving." They retreated back to Macy's. We were atheists, "agnostics" my mother would politely say. They had both flirted with the Communist party, my father most certainly a member at one point, like many progressive people of their generation, but this was before they met, before the war. Later, Frances attended services at the Church of the Ascension in lower Manhattan which had an excellent organist and choir. She went, she said, for the music. Older brother, Mark Sikélianòs, lived with us many of the early years. He was a gifted music student at the High School of Music and Art. An avid fan and aficionado of folk, classical music, and jazz who would later work at Broadcast Music, Inc., major music publishers in New York City. He spent many weekends with "folkies" in Washington Square Park, a few blocks away.

The tiny apartment was cramped. We were always "strapped" (my mother's term that became a mantra) for cash. I loved listening to the Saturday morning radio shows. And afternoon opera, broadcast live from the Metropolitan Opera House. We ate out once or twice a year in Chinatown. John and Frances both prioritized education and culture.

At the age of six, I joined the Children's Theater at Greenwich House, a community arts center on Barrow Street near Seventh Avenue, and participated in "rhythm classes" with Ingeborg Torrup. Theatrical director Helen Murphy was the guiding inspiration for the unusual creative theatrical productions. Her lovely gifted partner, Janet, taught pottery at Greenwich House. One show, *Americana,* told the history of the United States through song—work songs, spirituals, lullabies, Appalachian tunes, and lyrics from other folk traditions. I remember one of my lines in the voice of a would-be prospector: "There's gold in Californee and rangin' land in Texas." Largely a troupe of girls, all ages, we dressed in green cloth tunics and suede rhythm sandals à la Isadora Duncan (and Eva Sikélianòs). Christmas season found us singing carols at local banks and hospitals. And one program, *Stella di Natale,* featured young singer Maria Muldaur. Age twelve. I played Alice in *Alice in Wonderland,* enjoying the puns and magical language of those scenes.

Anne Waldman (left) playing Alice in *Alice in Wonderland,* Greenwich House Children's Theater, New York City, 1957.

The Children's Theater was a complement to the literary and theatrical activities at Public School 8—writing contests (a best poem about a tree for Arbor Day), magazines, school plays, playing character Tomboy Joe in one production and Puck in *A Midsummer Night's Dream.* Reading aloud, dramatizing the sense of the words all came naturally. Although I was never good at memorization (too impatient), I had a yen for the stage. Working with others was really stimulating. Theatre a world unto itself.

PS 8 was directly around the corner from MacDougal on King Street. A modest public school, later a Six Hundred School for wayward girls, years later a condominium, at the edge of SoHo. The school had a working-class atmosphere as well as an ethnic, racial, artistic mix: James Agee's children attended school there for a time, and we became friends. Their mother was from Austria. Another close friend was Portuguese. Many Italian immigrants had settled in this neighborhood called Little Italy (going back to the 1880s, when large settlements of Italian immigrants arrived) and attended either the neighborhood or parochial school close by. Irish, Black, Hungarian immigrant family, one Puerto Rican student. Black friend Howie and I kissed once. Several close Jewish friends with Holocaust-survivor family. Teachers were a diverse group. Inspired by an infectious neighborhood religiosity, a few of us decided we had seen the devil in the girls' bathroom. "I swear, Mrs. Mulherne, I did, I did see the devil, and he had little red horns and a barbed tail." Best girlfriend was Randa Haines (later grown up to become one of a handful of gifted female movie directors working in Hollywood starting in the 1980s), intelligent and inquisitive. I saw my first TV programs in her small apartment on Bleecker she shared with her mother, Edith, a single mom. I remember now how compelling the television was. Frances, in her disdain, seemed old-fashioned. Her Delphic Idea family were like Luddites. But my brother and I were allowed to watch a few programs at Randa's each week. My favorite was *The Millionaire.* It had an unseen benefactor as protagonist who set the dramas in motion. I wanted to be the guy who knocked on doors bestowing the million-dollar check. Rather than being rescued by money, characters were destroyed by it. A new wired universe swift with communication, live or canned laughter and applause, was taking off around a range of forms. With sponsors. First it was just something to do in the living room. And felt quite different than long hours in bed listening to the radio into the night. Radio was like poetry in curious ways, more than TV.

I liked hearing poetry out loud at school. Poets seemed to live interesting self-appointed lives. Being one was low tech, free of accoutrement, ornament. All you needed were words, larynx, imagination. The pictures were in your mind, not on a screen. Poet, the role of, linked back to a simpler time. It didn't matter what version of the world or what part of the world you lived in, poetry had gotten there first. Inextricably linked with human consciousness. Psychophysical rhythms of human mind and animalia and proprioception. "The eye altering alters all," said Blake. You could transform reality without a lot of props. I felt akin to some of the local folkies, balladeers, songsters, troubairitz. Years later I did some training with a community radio station in Boulder, CO. I also became a guardian of an extensive audio archive of a near half century of poetry and poetics.

TV became more public, available, total, like an Archive. A partner of mine was inspired to making movies initially by early television.

Movies were novels.

I was reading into the modernists and Yeats, Shakespeare's sonnets, Whitman, Emily Dickinson. Poetry, what mind or game was that? What was I getting into? I resorted to words to imagine a parallel universe. I could express the emotional subtext of all my experience by saying less. I could skip around, be elliptical, condense a day, a year, tell about a surrealistic dream or encounter. So poetry was a weave that might sound the world and myself back at itself. Where were the women? Hilda Doolittle seemed amazing. A link in my mind to Sikélianòs and Sappho, Marianne Moore, a favorite of Frances, lived in Brooklyn. There were the Greek and Latin epic poems as well as Gilgamesh/Inanna epic tales.

I grew up into the neighborhood, most definitely a parallel universe. Little Italy had the pageantry of Catholicism—language to consort in, Italian, Latin, and working-class street life, the corner Mafia "club," annual street festas—on the whole a distinctive flavor and rich cultural identity. Other layers to the Village included bohemian bars, music gatherings at Washington Square Park, jazz clubs, off-off Broadway arenas. Jean Genet's *The Maids*. Beckett at the Cherry Lane (where I worked briefly as a hatcheck girl/usher). Al Carmines (Judson Poets' Theater Off Off Broadway pioneer); productions of Gertrude Stein at the Judson Church, LeRoi Jones's (Amiri Baraka's) *Dutchman,* Edward Albee,

Ionesco. Diane di Prima's Poets Theatre. The Living Theatre's *The Connection*. All this radical work going on within the larger cosmopolitan environment of the city. My mother was eager to have me experience it all. She scrimped to pay for art classes at the Museum of Modern Art. We also went on special occasions to the NYC Ballet, classical music concerts, modern dance concerts.

In awe of, but feeling artistic life within reach, the connection, immediate, electric, so that you might vow to put yourself next to that work and the poets themselves, be reader and votary in the service of. Frances had lived in the household of poets and artists during her decade in Greece. I had my own propensities, but also caught the bug from her. John's love of fiction endured. I was a guinea pig at one point for his *Rapid Reading* book in manuscript. My problem was reading *too* rapidly.

Fighting the cultural conditioning of being "just a" girl was a burden, although I was aided by supportive parents who were sufficiently progressive. Frances a proto-feminist. Fanny Howe once commented on how much love and support I must have had from my mother. It explained who I was. I had close girlfriends, not yet sexual but definitely romantic. I liked to play the prince in dress-up scenarios. Frances wanted the best, of course, for her precocious children. I thought sometimes she might have felt cheated out of a girlhood, marrying so young and having a child. And by my seventh-grade year she had saved enough (with partial scholarship as well), and both Carl and I started going to Grace Church School, which was, I discovered later, directly across Fourth Avenue from where poet Frank O'Hara later lived. I liked leading the short, ecumenical religious services in the chantry. Always had a messianic streak, wanted to guide others to . . . what, the Peaceable Kingdom? A big revelation was during an LSD trip in 1965. I was also told by a Hawaiian shaman that I had been a spiritual leader in my last life who had led her students astray. I was involved with the school's literary activities, and some of us started meeting after school at 54 Fifth Avenue, in the large, rambling apartment of the Hourwich twins—two brothers whose parents had known the painter Norma Millay Ellis, Edna St. Vincent's sister, and had quite a few of her paintings on the walls. This was my first salon. We read plays by Shakespeare and Molière, Sasha's French with translation aloud, argued politics with Hourwich Sr., who was, in spite of his bohemianism, a conservative Wall Street broker. Gladys, mother of my schoolmates, was from the West Indies, a beautiful woman who smoked incessantly and wove gorgeous fabrics on several large looms.

From Grace I went to Friends Seminary, a Quaker school on Rutherford Place, and continued with literary activities, edited the school newspaper *The Oblivion* ("for what is a newspaper but a rag for oblivion?"—something like that as slogan), and contributed to *The Stove* literary magazine. My best friend in high school was Jonathan Cott, later journalist, critic, and poet who was loyal literary cohort, comrade-in-arms. We showed each other poetry, traded books. He turned me on to Rilke and the *Dream of the Red Chamber.* I was subscribing to the *Evergreen Review* by then, dutifully reading *The Village Voice,* and even sending out poems for rejection by the *New Yorker* and other notable magazines. I remember the pleasure, the private pleasure—kind of erotic—of secretly writing romantic love poems, sending them off unbeknownst to parents and friends, and then the thrill of the return envelope, although it presaged no great success. Jon and I possibly considered ourselves existentialists, reading Camus and Gide, among others. He was two years ahead of me at school. He and my mother became friendly. And Frances was by now actively reading contemporary poetry, in particular the New American poets. We three enjoyed talking about poetry. Jon memorized poetry brilliantly, it became part of him that way. His whole life he has had poetry springing from him. Another link to poetry at this time was Jon Beck Shank, provocative high school English teacher, erudite, Wallace Stevens fan, who read Stevens aloud with gusto and intelligence. His reading of "An Idea of Order at Key West" gave me goose bumps.

I worked for an air-conditioning firm one summer in high school, near Wall Street—dull hours, but was proud of my paycheck and the modest independence it provided. I remember when Marilyn Monroe died, August 5, 1962. I was on my way to Chock Full o' Nuts for lunch. Her image at all the newsstands. How was she unhappy, I wondered. Her death was mysterious and sad.

I put up with a few macho bosses, unwanted attentions. I think I was also by then typing all lowercase poems on a small Olivetti.

But more importantly, I started reading as a child, and as a teen thought to change my own pulse with the energy of language. I was drawn to theatre, to productions of Jean Genet, Anouilh, *The Theatre of Cruelty* by Antonin Artaud, Beckett plays. Was it that characters in prose came alive, and you could actually, in many instances, become them, get lost in them? Conflicted plot to follow, denouement, surprise, reconciliation at end. I adored that: *Jane Eyre, Lorna Doone, Wuthering Heights,* and *Little Dorrit. What Maisie Knew.* Yet more complex, puzzling as experience was poetry, more like dream life, with sharp turns, surprises, disassociation, jolts. Enjoyed the vocalizations of my texts, later. To make something and be shocking in a beautiful way, was the vow. And it felt doable. Others had done it. And later the vow was also to others in a community of collaboration that included poetry readings. And many things with poetry. And poetry did need character. Your persona, your energy, your consciousness, your imagination was the heroine of the song. All the poets I was paying attention to were such unique, interesting individuals. Characters. Songs. There was the nagging notion too of "against interpretation." Sontag's revelation. Poetry could be freer of "mess and message."

And a spiritual side was nurtured at Friends by teacher Dr. Earle Hunter, a Quaker who taught an excellent course in comparative religion, touching on fundamentals of Asian traditions.

Or maybe that is what I remember most. The praxis and notions behind Taoism, Hinduism, Buddhism. And the amazing story of Islam as well to fire further inquiry. The religions came with books! Scripture, poetry, liturgy! Appreciated the Quaker meetings in which we'd spend an hour in silence, then a few might spring up and speak on their thoughts. I liked the minutes of silence before classes started. These minutes were surprisingly helpful. A practice with simplicity and kindness toward yourself. No hierarchy. Closer, as I was discovering, to the meditative traditions I was attracted to. As we students took cover in the bomb shelters in the school basement, Quakers would be outside leafletting, speaking with conviction of banning the bomb. This was 1961.

During high school years, I had a wide circle of friends, many of them artistically pitched. Close companion was Kathy Emmett, daughter of Kim Hunter, the actress. I lived with her family one summer in Stratford, Connecticut, we were friends working backstage, age sixteen, while Kim acted in *As You Like It* and *Macbeth.* Jessica Tandy, Pat Hingle, Philip Bosco, Morris Carnovsky,

Carrie Nye, also in residence, attentive to youthful questions. I thought I would write a novel one day using Stratford as the backdrop. The summer season ended on a tragic suicide: one of the walk-on sword-bearers took his own life by sword during a performance of *Macbeth*. On the train home alone to New York, I remember staring out the window, wondering the ephemeral "All the world's a stage" when it also reflected our own existence. Was one inspired to write out of these moments of tragedy, irony, death, pain?

Years thirteen to seventeen were spent in the labyrinthian playground of New York City. And the particular playground of Greenwich Village with its attendant glamour, anarchy, experimentation, intensity. Toward the end of this high school period, I was spending more time with neighborhood friends—creative types, musicians, artists, dropouts. Kids from both the neighborhood working-class bohemian artist set and the sons and daughters of the affluent, liberal, and artistic literati. Martin Hersey, John Hersey's son, carried a well-thumbed copy of *Naked Lunch* around with him in an old, battered guitar case. John Hammond Jr. was already becoming a serious musician. I wanted to write good poetry. The Werthenbergs. All the kids were getting stranger—more interesting in the best sense. The times were contradictory. If you didn't have a focus or safety net you could even get in trouble with yourself.

Yearning to be an artist was always a good antidote. Reflecting on this period now, I appreciate how rich and unique it was as ground for developing alternative community. Realities of racism, anti-abortion, economic social inequities, and other poisons were permeating but held at bay more readily in urban NYC with its tolerance. One high school friend got pregnant. She was Catholic so that was a big deal and she was forced to have the child. I remember her having morning sickness at school, thin and frail.

Bennington, a women's college, was in many ways a continuation of some of these developing threads, although it carried an onus—tone of exclusivity and a hidden dysfunctionality of faculty predation, and one worried about the label "dilettantism" applied to the place. Because we were all "women." Could we be taken seriously? I think I wanted to do at least one thing well. So while I didn't suffer the worst idiosyncrasies and tragedies of patriarchal academia, it was a compromised situation. I've always been interested in the mechanisms of concealment as they relate to women. It was a haven from the city, and the gifted art and writing faculty expected a modicum of self-discipline and rigor from its students. I submitted poetry with my application, having been impressed by the number of poets on the faculty. Highly strung, sensitive, creative students were the norm. Howard Nemerov seemed a flawed person, yet a respected poet and inspiring teacher at times—particularly of Blake and Yeats. There were the later revelations of his own complicated incest with his sister Diane Arbus. Rumors of affairs with students were not uncommon. Acceptable behavior in most quarters of the college worlds, alas. I should have been more enraged by the toll this took on some students, who were stunted by the power dynamics and heartbreak in such relationships. But some of these students were mature (they claimed) and felt nurtured creatively by the relationships.

Howard often showed up in class rumpled and exhausted after a "night with the muse," pulling a piece of foolscap from his pocket—a new poem. He would then want to walk around the school pond holding hands! We might have words re: John Ashbery, Frank O'Hara, the Beats—particularly Allen Ginsberg, as he favored a more angst-ridden, "official verse culture" (Charles Bernstein's tag) poem with obligatory closure. I realized early then how certain lines might be drawn between the so-called academic exemplified by a kind of white male heterosexual neurosis ("Tamed by *Miltown,* we lie on Mother's bed" / Lowell)—and what I've come to call the Outrider tradition, characterized by spontaneity, digression, a less secure lifestyle, political opposition, and interconnected through projects with others that are not necessarily renumeration motivated. That's not the point. Working outside capitalism's structures.

Poets I was drawn to were not always products or proprietors of English departments. As a designated female I was increasingly interested in a breakdown of semantics, grammar, toward deconstruction of solid narrative mindsets and more toward performance and improvisation. These issues seemed close to concerns of mental grammar and experience. Gertrude Stein's work was amusing, playful, pushed on you. *Tender Buttons* moved in time and the odd juxtaposition, auditory associations Stein pulled off were unique and springy. The vernacular of William Carlos Williams was rich and startling. When I suggested Stein and Ezra Pound be taught seriously at Bennington, I was distressed by what I saw as an inexplicable prejudice. Not only dismissed as "silly," this formidable grand persona with her Picassos, Matisses, and a lively salon was the butt of unkind jokes. Pound was an anti-Semite and thereby beyond the pale. It was a lonely battle. But Bernard Malamud encouraged curiosity and explorations in modernism and contemporary poetry, and my own writing as well. The private seminar allowed for give-and-take, some critical. Apprentice formats seemed rare in other universities and colleges at the time. Thus I felt myself fortunate to come up against serious writers, and readers, who practiced their art with purpose and ambition. Opinionated, egocentric, solipsistic masters. Teaching was often a passion, but it was secondary to the true practice—the work. Also, it was fascinating to witness firsthand another alternative, albeit a somewhat academic and exclusive community. Stanley Edgar Hyman, married to eccentric, brilliant Shirley Jackson, dwelled in his dark study with his numismatic collection of glittering gold coins on the margins of the campus mandala. He taught an exciting "Myth, Ritual, and Literature" class, exposing us to the Dionysian heights in classical Greek drama, dark mysteries of Childe's ballads, and the tender delicacies of youth Parsifal in search of the goblet that would unlock the secret of life. Hyman challenged my own preconceptions about origins of language and why we make poetry. He brought text down to a primal, psychological level. He himself looked the part of a satyr—heavily bearded, wild gleam in an already mischievous eye. What were my rites of passage, my rituals? Envying the freedom of the male protagonist, the male poet, I was still a daughter yet carried a lot of male energy. Was it necessary to inebriate my father and subsequent fathers to steal their secrets? Coax them, seduce them? Or would I be virginal Athena, sprung forth from and forever indebted to Zeus's mind? It was hard to be a girl sometimes. I was competitive with men. I wanted their freedom.

Nemerov once commented, "I can't tell if you are a queen or a peasant!" Ha.

My mother had had more freedom, from another point of view, and was already a young mother in her early twenties, inside another culture and speaking its language! And exposed to the high rhythms of poetry, theatre, art making, and a sophisticated utopian philosophy. Stein, Laura Riding, H. D. were writers to study, emulate. How they had loved. How they had made their art. And I wanted to know more about their lives. I was starting to feel the torments of intense relationships and the conflict between so-called life and so-called art. It seemed a struggle to assert the work. Were our bodies the only source of women's power? I wanted more women teachers. Barbara Herrnstein

Smith was formidable in her way in her Romantics class. Her formal study of "closure" in Shakespeare sonnets was characteristically brilliant, but didn't feel like a model for new inklings of experimental poetry.

Poetic confidence was erratic. What was I good at? Trusted my ear. Some deeper rhythm in the nervous system demanded attention. It wasn't so much images I was good at. The great poems were intimidating. You loved them so much. If you listened to the men and stayed mooning over the classics, you could weaken your nerve. Were there secrets to steal, listening with the ear? The eye? I felt inept but ambitious. I thought myself a good student because I loved poetry. I was good at reading aloud but not to memorize and perform like theatre. It had to be more improvisatory. Like jazz. I wanted to do this work with other like-minded practitioners who felt as passionately as I did. I formed important alliances with the "guys," many of whom were closer to where I positioned myself. This was particularly true during my last year of school, where I had developed and cultivated some correspondence with poets of my own generation and had already travelled out to the Berkeley Poetry Conference. And I had made friends with David Amram, with Dan Wakefield, with John Hammond Jr. I was going to jazz concerts sometimes with my mother. My brother Mark Sikélianòs's first wife, Bobbie, was now married to sax player Steve Lacy and my niece lived nearby in that household. I ventured over with Frances and met Thelonious Monk one day. My mother first took me to hear Steve play at the Village Vanguard. I first heard Cecil Taylor, who came to Bennington, and I also first heard Dollar Brand with Frances. These were giants; I knew this. I heard Carla Bley a bit later, Sun Ra later. How to enter these worlds? Also the ever-dynamic visual arts worlds. Where to even begin? We knew the artist Ibram Lassaw.

The school had an out-of-residency work period. I went back to NYC the first year, taking a number of odd jobs, several in the theatre, including work at the Theatre Genesis at St. Mark's Church. I again worked at the Shakespeare Festival in Stratford the following summer, and then the subsequent winter with my mother's support I was able to take a volunteer job for several months with the American School of Classical Studies at Athens, assisting one of the leading archaeological scholars on the amphoras that held wine and oil. Dr. Virginia Grace was a rare being, another devotee of classical

Greece. There was something mythological in her situation. She had been crippled at a young age by polio. Lost a fiancée to early death. Remained single, a lame votary, passionate about her discoveries. Chained to the temple of Apollo. Her profile, to my eye, bore a striking resemblance to photographs of the seminal writer H. D. She took me under her wing. We often ate lunch together. I sat for hours in the cold Stoa of Attalos, surrounded by tiny electric heaters, reading and cataloguing the numerous amphoras that had been found during a recent dig around the Stoa. They bore striking seals that located their places of origin and helped determine ancient trade routes. The shapely amphoras carried wine to and from the islands, and further off, to Africa, to Asia Minor. Dr. Grace had catalogued nearly fifteen hundred stamps used on these ancient vessels. What remained but the stamps and the phallic handles, shards of cold runic clay in the hand? That held secrets to the Hellenistic civilization, its comings and goings by sea.

I took a side trip to Egypt by boat, felt my life charged, changed. There was the notion from Ezra Pound of "make it new." It wasn't anything goes, but finding old or neglected texts or "voice" from other places, your own ancestry, what called to you, perhaps, to resound with. To make anew, to recover. Buddhist texts had the same effect.

I got outside myself by being alone, without a restricted sense of "self." I was drawn to Greece, through my mother's experience, and to Egypt, to the hieroglyphs, old ritual texts. I had dipped into the Egyptian Book of the Dead. The sun god Ra says in the Coffin Texts: "I have created the gods from sweat and the people from the tears of my eye." I wanted to explore and describe these heightened experiences of attraction, of mystery, taking to other times and places. It wasn't about interpreting them. It was more like mythopoetics. These currents kept going, alive in your own psyche.

Also I wanted to be able to condense, crystalize the impressions. Wanted to make sense of what I saw. How else to hold it, even briefly. I was on the African continent suddenly! This seemed amazing. Never forget kissing the ground as we embarked in Alexandria (I'd been reading *The Alexandria Quartet* with some fervor). Never forget the night in a rickshaw waylaid by the Ali brothers, who wanted to take off my clothes and see a real American girl! And how could I forget camping on the shore and diving for fish, knife in my thick rubber belt, in the Red Sea, whose water was a rich blue. And how forget the kindness of the elegant Copt and his family who worked at the Benaki Museum. They took me to dinner on the Omar Khayyam house-boat restaurant with sumptuous courses of exotic edibles. I remember being extremely embarrassed by a drunken American at a table close by. And the Coptic children in Old Cairo throwing stones at me. Riding a camel at Giza and crawling on all fours through the narrow passageways of Cheops, imagining suffocation by sand. And the questions everywhere from young Arabs about the murder of President Kennedy. It must have been Lyndon Johnson! I had some questions too.

Never forget trying to sleep out in the desert near Luxor under stark bright moon, on alert, terrified of ubiquitous scorpions. Ambushed by a violent stranger as I tried to board the boat heading back up the Nile from the temple at Abu Simbel. And wrenching free. The constant *female swerve away from peril,* I remember thinking. The temple was slated to be moved further inland to avoid flooding caused by the ambitious but ill-conceived Aswan Dam, and I watched it disappear from view from the stern of the boat, a magnificent tribute to a megalomaniacal state of mind. Ramses wanted immortality at all costs. These sacred sites—the pyramids, Thebes, Dendera, Abu Simbel—resonated in imagination. They were power spots; I felt curious vibrations. I kept a journal. I wrote a long poem long since disappeared. This, surely, was what a writer was meant to do: rediscover, track power spots, travel around the world collecting images and stories, sleep in temples, feel the power of sacral architecture, conjure alien gods, comment on the folly of kings. "The lone and level sands stretch far away," etc. Met another American artist, Paul Zimmer, while travelling, a young actor, thinker, writer. And in Greece I had spent time with Jim Rooney, banjo player, later very involved with the bluegrass scene out of Nashville. Anubis, Horus, Setekh were guardian presences. As an inveterate romantic, this voyage was auspicious, enticing, signaled propensity for travel, wanderlust. Curiosity about reincarnation was sparked further. The Egyptian Book of the Dead also spoke of the royal barge rowed to the other side. Setting sun as a ball of dung being pushed across the sky by an invisible beetle. Everyone was Egyptian in a past life. Why be an exception? Greek, Roman, and Egyptian mythology often investigated by young poets. Go to this. Shine a light on.

In *The Iovis Trilogy* some decades later, this still had a hold.

In the summer of 1964, while working with an arts group in Philadelphia that included the Heath family of jazz musicians and Harvey Brown, student of Charles Olson and poetry editor of *Niagara Frontier Review* and Frontier Press, I was taken by some friends from Harvard to meet Mongolian Buddhist lama Geshe Wangyal, who had come to America on a Tolstoy Foundation grant and was residing in the small town of Freewood Acres, New Jersey. In a pink suburban house. I was nervous, knowing little about the protocol for meeting such a formidable personage, and had worn a dress and put on lipstick, which seemed natural enough to do. A close friend commented on the impropriety of the makeup, but I held my ground, sensing the conflict that might arise if one became sycophantically inclined, always trying to please, impress a teacher. "Come as you are" seemed the best motto. I had been reading some of the odd, stilted translations of prayers and texts emanating from the work with Geshe Rinpoche, mimeographed on a bright-goldenrod-colored mimeo paper. But I didn't quite understand the student/teacher relationship and to whom the prayers were addressed. Buddhism had a lot of ceremony and a lot of texts, but was not a theistic religion. This was unfamiliar territory. I remember my friends asking a lot of questions of the lama about LSD and the nature of consciousness and "cessation." I remember feeling that when I looked into Geshe's face, he reflected back my own projections of himself and my own projections of him looking at me. They were simply nonexistent, the projections. Who was he? I was intrigued by the colorful shrine with garish and exaggerated iconographies, offerings of flowers, pungent incense, slightly rancid odor and taste of Tibetan tea. Peeking into the dining room, I was a bit startled seeing a flock of young monks in their maroon robes gnawing on chicken bones. High-altitude people, they ate meat. I seemed to be one of the few women on the premises. I visited the lama on several occasions. What was the nature of this early connection to a living lineage-holder of a centuries-ancient, unbroken lineage? It seemed to be important, felt so to me, having an encounter with a being who seemed to go back centuries. How does all this, a vast knowledge, link to poetry? Some of the texts were poetry. A karma link to a spiritual past and path of some kind? *Auspicious* was a word that was used. Auspicious coincidence. *Tendrel.* The cogent impression was one of being at ease and comfortable with this tradition, whatever it proved to be.

It was also the time of the Philadelphia "riots," not the accurate word but so deemed. I lived close to some of the action. My cohorts with the community center in a Quaker building were paying attention. We saw some of the wreckage, followed the questionable racist behavior of authorities.

During the summer of 1965, I travelled across country with my younger brother, Carl, and a school friend who had a job lined up in Hollywood. We stopped in Santa Barbara to see some of the Sikélianòs kin. I held my newborn niece, Eleni, in my arms, who was later to come to study at the Jack Kerouac School of Disembodied Poetics at Naropa. Yet Berkeley—then the mecca of creative and political scholarship and action, where an important poetry conference was just about to begin—was the destination. Little did I realize how this trip would affect another major direction of my life. In retrospect, it seems miraculous that being in a particular place at a particular time should activate or propel one's life in such a purposeful way. I was perhaps already primed. I was a novice young votary who'd read the now-historic Donald Allen anthology *The New American Poetry, 1945–1960*. I was curious to hear some of the live voices of these persons I was privately emulating. Robert Duncan, Charles Olson, Ed Dorn, Ted Berrigan (Jon Cott, high school class-mate, had been sending copies of Ted and Ron Padgett's *C* magazine to me at school). Ed Sanders, Lenore Kandel (the only woman!) were political. The audience stayed tuned for Olson's meltdown. Some kind of tribal exchange taking place? Olson raged and wept more than he "read." But a poet coming apart and reintegrating was holding the stage. His friends were dismayed. The sense that one had a personal dance or motion in the world, a job to do, came to me. What sustained this big bear of a man whose feet lifted off the ground as he read, arms supporting his massive frame at the podium? Poetry.

And Robert Duncan's arms waved and danced in the air as he read too, ges-tures into ether. This was a body poetics. I go on about my vow too much, a vow that I would spend my life developing and maintaining such a poetry and its poets. Part of a compassionate human cadre of like-minded illumi-nati and practitioners of the art who could really "hear" recombinant music in their nervous systems. And who were outspoken rebels as well, challenging the status quo. And would "take the whole ride," as Ted used to say.

Psychedelia expanded the consciousness, as did liberated sexuality. Women could be empowered, more in touch with their bodies as landscapes for writ-ing, not imprisoned by hope and fear of being desirable, feminine. Language could stretch to these new parameters. Other cultures, old cultures, were being rediscovered. Mined. Some of us wanted to see newly, freshly, through pre-history eyes. Sappho's fragments suddenly modernist poems. Ethno-poetics was relevant—more relevant, in fact, than the European canon, as it studied the songs and rhythms of the indigenous people of this continent. "Projective verse." "No ideas but in things." "Exploratory poetics." "Form is no more than an extension of content." "Duende." "Personism." "Continuous present." Although I never eschewed commas, Gertrude Stein said they were only good for hanging your hat on.

The night of the Robert Duncan reading, I was introduced to a young writer-poet and novelist from New York, Lewis Warsh. Lewis had been travel-ling to San Francisco regularly during the summers to sit at the feet of Jack Spicer, Robert Duncan, Robin Blaser, others. He was incredibly knowledge-able about poetry and the French "nouvelle vague," and highly disciplined as a writer, having written several novels in high school. We were to become close friends, romantic comrades: hitchhiking to Mexico at the end of the poetry

Anne Waldman, Lewis Warsh, Kate Berrigan, Bustins Island, Maine, 1967.

conference; hitching back to New York City; founding *Angel Hair* magazine and books; living together; marrying in 1967 at St. Mark's Church in a wedding studded with poet friends) until 1970. We fed on pushing forward one another's writing, working together at the St. Mark's Poetry Project, and running a round-the-clock salon at 33 St. Mark's Place, which had regular weekly parties after the poetry events at the church. Frequently disturbed by disgruntled neighbors and cops to quiet down the scene. Energetic "cultural workers," poetry fiends; a close friend called us the "A" students for being so busy with poetry. You could always spend a night on our sofa, have a meal, a milkshake, an audience, a new *Angel Hair* magazine or Poetry Project publication thrust into your arms.

I met Frank O'Hara the spring after the Berkeley conference, introduced to him by Bill Berkson, who was teaching at the New York School. Frances, my mother, was in Bill's class, and Bill was having a party at his bachelor pad on posh 57th Street for his students—which included Bernadette Mayer, Hannah Weiner, Michael Brownstein, Peter Schjeldahl, later Patti Smith—and various accomplished New York School literati. Frank walked in—waltzed in—with the painter, sculptor, and musician Larry Rivers. They seemed metabolic brothers, led by an air of grace, pungent high talk. Gossip? Frank was friendly, insisting that upon graduating from college I should come work at the Museum of Modern Art—as a volunteer, of course, I'd learn lots. And he'd started at the bottom. Bill also introduced me to poet and dance critic Edwin Denby, who was to become a close older friend, mentor. Edwin tried to teach me, if anyone could, to stand in front of things, to simply stop and stand and look, and trust what came to mind. An off detail, odd gesture, obscure angle, being marginal, the awkwardness between buildings, people to observe. Stopping and looking. Follow your own train of thought.

Upon graduating, I'd moved into the St. Mark's Place apartment Lewis found and, after interviewing with the folks who were doing the hiring (including dynamic liberal rector Reverend Michael Allen) for the newly conceived St. Mark's Church in-the-Bowery arts projects (theatre and film as well as poetry), I was selected as a poetry assistant, a secretary to Joel Oppenheimer, who was to direct the poetry program.

I was writing nightly, completely charged by the constant activity of the Lower East Side environment. I was also free of school. I worked with tape recorders with bits of recorded phrases off the radio, street, conversations, stole lines from other books. I'd look out my window on St. Mark's Place and in the air a "revolution" going on, a new generational frequency going on—and felt part of it. People angry about the war in Vietnam, about police brutality, strict drug penalties, racism, social injustice everywhere. Felt as conduit for "my time." Reeling with all there is to do, all there is to read, all to follow—like so many of us in the sixties—from the intensity of wanting a better world and the struggle of the world. But much was so good about the developing evolving community around St. Mark's. Its tangibility, friendship, its interesting tentacles. Poets were usually concerned about the right things, or at least tuned in to where poetry was being invoked. Witnesses drawn to the flames. Were poets dangerous? The FBI thought so. And yet I never felt lost in the version of any particular time. Sometimes I would forget that we were in a version of anything, and reason said it couldn't be the only way. There were things to keep: poetry, books you love and people, the real history, not master narrative, etc. Poetic lineage went far back. In retrospect, I agreed with Allen Ginsberg: we in US were politically naive about the resolve of the "enemy," capitalism. As poets, would still work hard to save the world from itself. "The DeCarlo Lots," drawing on memory from earlier junior high school summers (Union Lake, New Jersey, near Millville, where my father's family was from), seemed an important piece. It was looser than other pieces I'd written yet organized with recurrent tangibles, details in a collage-like structure. This was written before the Poetry Project started. Having not entirely disowned my college manuscript, which included pieces like "College Under Water" and "The Blue That Reminds Me of the Boat When She Left," I still wanted to break free of a lugubrious "poetical" tone that I felt those poems had carried. Started all over again, needed to forget the boring rules of prosody. Metaphor, simile, objective correlative. Wanted the fluid person I thought I was (liberated, curious) to shine through. Persona was the clearer notion. I wanted an unbound line, physical freedom. And I wanted my passion, a kind of natural exuberance, to be in back of it. "The DeCarlo Lots" poem seemed to bode well for subsequent pieces. Nostalgia, tenderness, specificity, documentary, a place.

Of course the New American poets had explored much terrain, sharing it, not always claiming it. The poem was a field, the landscape was scary, rugged. These terrific beacon poets—also becoming vehicles and bridges for others—had by 1965 already left a legacy. And they were still around, alive, active, seemed more seasoned, wise. Not much older when you think of it. How young Frank O'Hara was when he died. Think of how Bill Berkson was friend and "pupil" too. The power of that friendship. Community felt significant, necessary. To hear, show work to, talk about it, back and forth. The contact provided by correspondence, literary magazines, and small-press work, as well as readings and workshops, was considerable. And the evolving major poetic network, unparalleled. The Project also took seriously a mission to preserve its legacy through documentation and recording and its institutional papers. As we did later at Naropa Institute/University take it all seriously. Joking with all this archive biz—it's to show some intelligent beings of the future that some of us were not just killing one another. Delphic Idea, the peripatetic community as tribal, connected by invisible poetic gossamers, mind-to-mind glints and gleaming. I felt the tremendous "mission" of the work, sense of purpose to keep the world safer for poetry.

Frank O'Hara's tragic death in 1966 at age forty stunned the art world and much of the poetry world. The New York School was grieving. He was a planet: magnetic, stimulating. We were planets. He was still a young poet! Although I'd only just met him, I'd felt his "transmission," an energy charge, his permission to have direct experience in and with art with poetry, with people. He suggested I come and work as a volunteer intern at MOMA. I needed a paying job, but his attention was a salient marker in my life.

How to appropriately honor and describe the countless events, readings, performances, first encounters with some of the most controversial and outrageous thinkers and writers of any time, New Year marathons, memorial readings, collaborations, benefits, all-night planning sessions, fundraisers, magazine collations that were to take place under the protective wing of St. Mark's Church? How to record the imprint in heart and mindstream of language? Sheer sound and beauty of vocables as they resounded ear-to-ear? How to tell here the sweetness of Charles Reznikoff, the trajectory of his work, unique, modest, tough? How to capture the menacing hilarity of Gregory Corso streaking at a Michael McClure reading? The symbolic "assassination" of Kenneth Koch with "blank" pistol during the period of Columbia University insurrection, where he was viewed as "establishment" hierarchy by poetic anarchists who stormed up the aisle in Marxist raincoats? Denise Levertov's sharp political concern during the Vietnam War, yearning and impassioned rage in her voice clear as a bell. Ken Kesey making the audience stand and "really breathe," the rafters shaking with hyper-ventilation? John Wieners's fragile and dreamy movie-star reading, one pant leg rolled up, gold lamé scarf around his head? Amiri Baraka hammering on content. Power of his prophetic song? Burroughs's "comeback" to America, with gravelly, demonic voice from an even darker side of samsara? Yoko Ono's minute of white silence during the annual New Year's benefit reading. Barbara Guest, elegant, brave, and lucid after a serious concussion. Light streaming in the church's stained-glass windows the morning we began the all-day, all-night Gertrude Stein marathon. Some of the story will never be told, held in magical interstices in secret mind-computer chambers, deeper in heart's tender spaces. How many times could you fall in love? How many times could you have your heart broken, reading after reading, event after event? I bow under the task of this description. Suffice to say it was, and continues to be as of this writing, a holy place for poetry. And continues to be a project in the sense of an outward projecting: "to direct one's voice to be heard clearly at a distance." Project as in Olson's projective verse.

Angel Hair magazine and books, along with *The World* magazine, kept us additionally occupied. We used an inexpensive printer, Ronnie Ballou in Massachusetts, whom I'd gotten to know editing *Silo* magazine at Bennington. When we couldn't afford printing or offset, we'd use the mimeo machine. Early issues of the magazine were honored with poems by Robert Duncan, Denise Levertov, James Schuyler, Joanne Kyger, and ourselves. We published lovely mimeo books by Frank O'Hara, John Wieners, Lorenzo Thomas, many others. And printed books by Bernadette Mayer, Peter Schjeldahl. Covers by generous artists: Jim Rosenquist, Jim Dine, Philip Guston, Donna Dennis, Alex Katz. We continued the press from both coasts even after Lewis moved for several years to California. We published many writers of our own generation: Jim Brodey, Larry Fagin, Alice Notley, Clark Coolidge, Bill Berkson. Charlotte Carter.

My own writing: what was going on then? I was editing the first *The World Anthology,* to be published in 1969. Two books, *Giant Night* and *Baby Breakdown,* were published almost simultaneously in 1970. Lita Hornick's Kulchur Foundation brought out *No Hassles* in 1971. I was writing to talk to myself, writing notes to myself and to my friends. Telling, spilling out the fast takes in my head. These early poems have energy, naivete, are guileless. Intimate. Dailiness is the measure. Quick, sometimes "stoned" associations.

Tangibles from my domestic world are present. Love poems. Always honoring the quasi-lyric.

During early hours of the morning of January 3, after the marathon New Year's Day event of 1970, when we were starting to vacuum the church rugs (a memorable red and a monumental task), an English fellow named Nik Douglas showed up with a film under his arm and asked to show it on the screen we hadn't yet dismantled. It was entitled *Tantra,* and as it unfolded its vivid documentation of various Hindu and Buddhist tantric rites, I was riveted. I remember the images of scrawny jackals in a charnel ground, in a place where holy rites were being performed. Eating leftovers? Or were they gnawing on bodies? This was the lure of the Tibetan tangkas with their fierce passion and aggression. This was lure to tantra. Things I'd heard of India and images I'd seen were vivid, like this charnel ground. Places of life and death, ritual initiation. I wanted to witness the burning ghats. I'd been studying Buddhism, and Indian singing with La Monte Young, who was a student of Pandit Pran Nath. I listened to recordings of Indian music, heard Ravi Shankar play, had seen various other singers and dancers from India. Satyajit Ray's *Apu Trilogy* were haunting films. How to get to India or make a deeper connection with some kind of deeper study, practice there? I wasn't attracted to the Hindu guru "scene," as I perceived it, but was extremely interested in the culture or cultures of India. The philosophy of Buddhism and my earlier encounter with the lama had suggested a different atmosphere or tone in terms of a spiritual pursuit. Many Tibetan Buddhist teachers were living as refugees in India, having escaped persecution in Tibet under the Chinese Communists during the late 1950s. That would be another reason to go there. Zen Buddhism was decidedly austere. Perhaps too austere for women? I was reading Walter Evans-Wentz, D. T. Suzuki, Alan Watts. Poets and artists I admired—John Cage, Gary Snyder—had made a connection to Buddhism. Jack Kerouac was rich with Buddhist notions, crazy notions! What was "empty"? Empty of what? Ego? I thought you needed a "healthy ego," as my mother called it, to be an artist. I'd already had an initial transmission from Geshe Wangyal, and I understood the nontheism of Buddhism. No savior, no salvation, no soul. Sentient beings were just bundles or conglomerations of tendencies. Did you have to travel across the planet to find someone to explain this to you? Did you need to sit at the feet of someone who spoke in a language you couldn't begin to comprehend, that seemed so alien to your ear? Would muttering mantras help anyone? Was personal "suffering," a revulsion with the "business" of the world, propelling me toward dharma? Or was it some other kind of inspiration? I think the ideas I was grasping from readings into dharma were consistent with ideas I already had; I was finding descriptions and words for what I already had an inkling of, propensity for. And the notion of sangha, or community, was familiar. Weren't the poets a kind of sangha? Didn't we, too, honor sacred text, practice the sacred and ancient art of poetry? Weren't some of the greatest poets in the Japanese and Chinese tradition Buddhists?

A party shortly thereafter at the loft of artist Wynn Chamberlain brought yet another messenger, another Englishman. He carried the Tibetan name Kunga Dawa and spoke enthusiastically about a Buddhist lama named Chögyam Trungpa, who was coming to America to a small meditation center in Vermont with the charming name Tail of the Tiger.

That summer poet Michael Brownstein and I, after visiting poet Kenward Elmslie and artist Joe Brainard in Calais, Vermont, found our way to the small Buddhist community in Barnet. We'd been living with filmmakers Nathaniel Dorsky and Jerome Hiler that summer of 1970 in Lake Owassa, New Jersey. I'd been invited by political-activist friends Nancy and Jerry Rubin in New York on an artists' mission to Cuba. I'd only have to find my way to St. John's, Canada, where presumably there would be a boat waiting. The trip never panned out, financing fell apart, but I was poised to go on in any case, and Tail of the Tiger was a step along the way. As we drove up to Tail, we saw a modest group of long-haired folks—college kids, dropouts, some elders. We were asked, please, since we seemed to have a functioning car (handsomely battered white Volvo), if we'd go pick up "Rinpoche" (literally "precious one"), who was just returning from Disneyland in California, at the airport. A provocative request. We drove with one of Rinpoche's students to St. Johnsbury. Chögyam Trungpa emerged from the plane inebriated, full of amused talk about the hologram of Casper the Friendly Ghost he'd seen in Disneyland. This was, in retrospect, a first odd, interesting taste of this particular teacher's mind. His delight in our crazy comic-book culture. And he'd come to America curious about the poets. Where were the poets? Take me to your poets, was how I read his inquiry.

Michael and I stayed two weeks, particularly for the Milarepa teachings. Milarepa was Tibet's great cotton-clad poet-yogin who lived on nettle leaves and composed on the tongue beautiful songs of realization, songs of devotion. I remember asking Trungpa before leaving what he thought about the direction "things were headed," meaning politically. What about the end of the world? Many friends were getting "back to the land." He suggested I stay in New York City and work even harder since it was a "holy city" and, he said, required a superhuman energy and tolerance. The city had always been an inspiring challenge. I loved my home city.

Back in New York I did work even harder, as if that were possible. My life already was subsumed by the Poetry Project and all the duty that enormous undertaking required. Ron Padgett, Joan Simon, and I had started Full Court Press. And there were magazine publications, books in the offing, more demands for my own work. And I was starting to give readings and was invited to participate in performance events. And writing with new confidence.

Performance obviously expanded text off the page. It put the work in a different time and space. I think of myself as a kinetic writer, thinker: amazed at the places writing originates from. Not just a conceptual place. Is it "voices" in the head? Emanating from all sense perceptions in concert? Is it innate psycho-physical-personal rhythm? This body's particular sound? The gestures and sounds of the phenomenal world? Is the body the bodhisattva vehicle? Where mind/heart (bodhicitta) can enter? Do I write the way I think— ungrammatically? Do I write the way I move? Found language? I'd felt, from my first reading at St. Mark's Church, where I sat with head bowed to page, that the voice coming out of me was only partial, and that I had a bigger sound to exhibit and explore. A sound that I would literally have to grow into. But I was nervous. Next time, I stood positioned to honor the poem, to let it guide me. I saw how the text demanded a particular rendering, and it was often close to how I heard it, how words sounded in my ear. A particular kind of resonance increased after chanting mantra, I noticed as well. And since I'd had some early experience with theatre, I appreciated the way voice could carry, inflect, conjure up various psychological and emotional states. How the words carried very particular and expressive energy pulses in its minutest forms, phones, phonemes. And although I couldn't pinpoint the effects of such experience of poetry, I knew I felt something "awakening" in my body, even when I was to read other poets in books. This was a kind of performance, a ritualized event in time. I wanted to be able to bring poems of my own alive. To have them sing or rage through my body, transmit them through vocal intention. And this worked best in a group context. *Parfornir:* to enact a ritual or feat in front of an audience.

"Fast Speaking Woman," a long chant poem inspired in part by the texts and recording of the shaman María Sabina, who intones chants and speaks through an all-night hallucinogenic-mushroom rite of passage, and begun during a trip to South America, was a particularly seminal piece for me. Allen Ginsberg, after hearing me read, had suggested I "write long." Kenneth Koch had praised my "vibrato like an opera singer's." I was already extending my performance pieces into longer time frames. The poem was every woman's song in a sense and hung on the very simple structure "I'm a this woman, I'm a that woman . . ." allowing, too, for improvisation. Upon hearing me read the poem on stage in San Francisco, Lawrence Ferlinghetti rushed backstage afterward to ask to see it, saying he wanted to publish the poem in a City Lights Pocket Poets edition. Childhood fantasy come true! I'd been enamored of those compact and handsome editions for years. This was the maverick publisher of Ginsberg, Mayakovsky, Gregory Corso, Diane di Prima. Ten poems appeared in the edition, which sported a glamorous photo taken by Sheyla Bakyal that had been taken during *The Palm Casino Revue,* an off-off Broadway show which featured Jackie Curtis, Candy Darling, others, and the exceptional musical poet and librettist Kenward Elmslie, a close friend. There was the sense of it being a "live" or "oral" book. A kind of performance. In retrospect, its publication in 1975 put my work and the performance of it into a wider cultural context. And I was busier from then on managing an even more active public career. Is *managing* the word? I never felt I managed myself particularly well, a tendency to drive myself beyond certain physical boundaries, get too pressured, speedy. An overachiever, workaholic. There were not only the various projects to attend to, but this more demanding travel/work schedule. And I was always up late writing after everything else had been put to bed. I snatched those precious bands of open dark time from the night. I was beginning to work in a focused way with dream and travel journals. Tracking the twilight left-hand path. Travel inspired dreams.

From 1971 to 1973 I'd done some earnest travelling. To the West Indies, in particular the unique black-sand island of Dominica, which seemed about two hundred years behind the other islands in exploitation and development. To Colombia, Ecuador, and Peru, a trip that taught me something about that extraordinarily violent history, but also about the contemporary American subculture, particularly the drug culture that spanned the Americas. These were the awful dread Nixon years. A downfall. It was interesting to perceive our country's influence everywhere, the crass materialism—infectious, insidious, and wickedly irresistible. Meeting renegades, desperadoes, smugglers, dealers, thieves. I was writing little travel stories based on these vivid folk. Reading, too, magical realism, *One Hundred Years of Solitude,* which affected how I experienced Colombia in particular. Also spent many days at extraordinary ruins and museums, musing on the origins of the unique cultures I was studying. Who made the Nazca lines? Why did those Mochica figures look as if they were meditating, as if they were in Buddhist samadhi? Finally in 1973, with poet companions Michael Brownstein and John Giorno, I made the long-awaited pilgrimage to India. I was supposed to attend a three-month Buddhist seminary in the States that fall, but all the omens (including inexpensive tickets—only $250 round-trip to Delhi) were propitious to going.

How complex, contradictory the sense, senses, of India. One experiences every possible state of mind. Emotion, as well. Feels the endless grind and turning of the immense wheel of life, as phenomena play out their flickering shadows. Witness the wheel of birth, old age, sickness, and death. I saw burning ghats by the holy Ganges, watched the construction of yet another funeral pyre, stuck my head in the Ganges. Visited rat temples, listened to ecstatic chants of sadhus and Bauls, contemplated the strange mix of myriad luminous details. Benares: one of the oldest cities in the world, biblical. People were doing things as they'd done them thousands of years ago. And yet there was a harsh modern edge at every turn, which causes a kind of schizophrenic chaos. India is never sentimental. We travelled north to Darjeeling and spent over a month taking teachings from the Tibetan lamas resident there, nestled under the splendid Kanchenjunga mountain range. There was also a very sophisticated literary, artistic, and film scene.

Did this visit change my life? It deeply enhanced it. It gave me an alternative vision, or version, of reality. India carried its old thrust into the present. Stubborn, adamantine, titillating. At the same time savagely scarred. Ennobled through suffering? Hardly, but it existed as a repository for all levels of human and inhuman expression. The lowest-caste women seemed beaten down, stoical, long-suffering. Homeless children in the cities. Yet many proud and stunning. Resourceful, quick on their feet. Children both cursed and blessed from birth. The caste system was horrific to my mind. What was the unflinching logic? How could I, logical liberal Westerner, ever understand the web, the Indra's net of this vast and complicated landscape with all its strange old yearnings and wraithlike beings? Wrathful Hindu goddess Kali seemed the totemic deity of the place: she chews up and spits out the "stuff" of life, over and over again. Gives life, takes it back. Strong connections were made with Buddhist teachers, particularly with Lama Jadral Rinpoche, a yogin who had spent many years wandering and living in caves, and whose own early teacher had been a woman he'd begun studying with at the age of fifteen. He was rugged, earthy, direct, and had a distinctly no nonsense aura about him. After I "took refuge" in a ceremony that required the aspiration to give up one's personal history as neurosis and limitation and to enter a larger vision or path where you cut your own ego or trips and begin to serve others, I was afraid he'd set me out to pasture tending cows with the Belgian nun (another student, who'd just done the same ceremony), expecting a more rigorous command. He was lenient, encouraging me to continue my practice and studies back in the States. It can be done anywhere, he said. "Achieve a certain level of practice, and I will teach you everything your mind desires."

In 1974 I was invited along with Allen Ginsberg and Diane di Prima to Boulder, Colorado, for the first summer program of the Naropa Institute, founded by Trungpa and some of his senior students. I'd spent time during several summers at Allen Ginsberg's farm in Cherry Valley, New York, approximately four hours from the city. Many friends, poets, artists, distinguished guests, Zen teachers, others would pass through. Allen was, for the most part, busy elsewhere, but his longtime companion Peter Orlovsky was in residence during most of the two summers I spent time there, tending a large and energetic vegetable garden. The summer of 1974, poet Bernadette Mayer and some other friends joined me at the farm—she and I had just completed a reading/performance in Artpark near Niagara Falls—which started me thinking how best to take some of the poetic energy out of New York and generate an alternative place in the country where poets could gather. Some way to live off the Lower East Side for a spell. We should be able to schedule writing or contemplative retreats, write epic poems under the influence of a gibbous moon. Sing to our vegetable garden. But the invitation had arrived to visit Naropa, the newly gathering, experimental Buddhist school on the spine of the continent in the Rocky Mountains, an auspicious journey which altered another wave of my life.

At a meeting, which included John Cage, Gregory Bateson, poet Jackson Mac Low, Allen Ginsberg, Diane di Prima, myself, and others, Trungpa said the Naropa Institute would be a "hundred-year project, at least." It sounds trite to say a chill went up my spine, but the experience was something like that. Shaktipat! Allen felt it too. A charge we agreed seemed to shoot beyond our own boundaries. I could feel the surge of this larger "command," as if I had heard it before. It was amazing to think of something that might conceivably continue—if it had worth—beyond our own lifetimes. John Cage was asked to speak to how Black Mountain, the experimental college in North Carolina, had worked, to which he replied, "It all came together at lunch." Allen and I were asked to design a poetics department in which poets could learn about meditation and meditators could learn about poetry. Fired up with the assignment, we went back to the apartment (we were roommates that summer) and started making lists of all the people we'd want to invite, all the chairs we'd create to honor poets. The Emily Dickinson Chair of Silent Scribbling, the Frank O'Hara Chair of Deep Gossip. We founded the Jack Kerouac School of Disembodied Poetics that same night, delighted we had a title, a moniker we both agreed upon, and giddy with the imagination of what this school could be. Kerouac, because he had realized the first Buddhist Noble Truth of Suffering and had written the spontaneous *Mexico City Blues,* an ecstatic series of choruses inspired by Buddhist thinking ("first thought, best thought"), be-bop, and his own lively poet-mind. Also a writer of both generations of peers—my own and Allen's— might give sanction to, acknowledging Kerouac's original praxis (nonstop spontaneity), tenderness of heart in the actual language, prodigious accomplishment in both prose and poetry. As well as being an influence on Ginsberg himself, a goad to William Burroughs, Gregory Corso, and others, he had influenced writers such as Clark Coolidge and Ted Berrigan, who were closer to my poetic generation. In addition, Kerouac had been not simply writer but culture hero, taking personal risks, epitomizing in his own search the yearning of the North American immigrant—for higher consciousness, or "satori": a poetic realization of the tenderness and emptiness and interconnectedness of all beings on the planet. He represented for me the genius-witness to both the decline of our Western civilization—its cri de coeur—as well as its outrageous, fraught wisdom and flawed delight. He was also to many a male chauvinist, sexist. I could see that too. I'm not an apologist for any of these guys. There was that aspect with all the Beats and most of the poet artist guys I had encountered my whole life. Cancel culture has instituted Ginsberg and Kerouac both as "symbols of white patriarchy."

People show up at Naropa who feel this way. There was a move to change the name to the Gertrude Stein School of Embodied Poetics at one point but she, too, is challenged by her Vichy compromise, etc. I threw the term *disembodied* into our school's banner to augment the notion that we were honoring a wild experimental lineage, poets that had tread the path before us, such as Sappho, Blake, Whitman, Dickinson, Melville, H. D., Mina Loy, Stein, Pound, James Joyce, W. C. Williams, James Baldwin, Lorine Niedecker, Baraka, Frank O'Hara. And women seekers such as Joanne Kyger and Diane di Prima, who arrived at the beginning. Bernadette Mayer and Alice Notley, my close contemporaries, visited many years. And our faculty was to be for the most part "at large," peripatetic. It was a bow, too, to the tantric Buddhist backdrop—the word *disembodied* sounded provocative, otherworldly?—of the Naropa Institute. I was also associated with the second-generation New York School and brought that community almost fully inside. Barbara Guest, Ann Lauterbach. The Beat Literary Generation and artists and poets such as John Cage and Jackson Mac Low, Leslie Scalapino, Mei-mei Berssenbrugge, and Eileen Myles were interested in the puzzle and science of the koan of consciousness. In meditation on these things. Is consciousness a continuum? Can it be measured in DNA?

A whole new generation showed up: Lisa Jarnot, Harryette Mullen, Will Alexander, Nathaniel Mackey, Eleni Sikelianos, Hoa Nyugen, Rachel Levitsky, Lee Ann Brown, Erica Hunt, Elizabeth Willis, Akilah Oliver, Dawn Lundy Martin, many others.

The Jack Kerouac School had its first full summer in 1975, with an impressive roster of faculty, including William Burroughs, John Ashbery, Diane di Prima, Gregory Corso, and Joanne Kyger. I decided to make a commitment to help develop the Naropa Institute as a year-round school and moved into an inexpensive apartment at the Hotel Boulderado, a turn-of-the-century mining hotel in downtown Boulder, in the fall of 1975—keeping the apartment on St. Mark's Place as well for my trips back there. I continued to work part of the time with the Poetry Project and other artists in NYC. The city was still home, family. Longer collage pieces and serial poems were published, such as *Sun the Blond Out*. Late nights found me in the tiny hotel apartment gathering together and editing a lot of the dream and travel and journal work for a book Stonehill wanted to publish, entitled *Journals and Dreams,* which was released in 1976.

Jerome Rothenberg, Anne Waldman, Peter Orlovsky, Allen
Ginsberg, Diane di Prima, Chögyam Trungpa, Barbara Dilley,
William S. Burroughs. Naropa Institute, Varsity Townhouse
Apartments, Boulder, Colorado, circa 1975.

More opportunities were arising for travel to a number of universities and
other venues to present my own work. That fall I was also invited to accom-
pany Allen Ginsberg on Bob Dylan's Rolling Thunder Revue tour as a
poet-in-residence, and to help work on the film *Renaldo and Clara,* trav-
elling through much of New England and Canada as the show made sur-
prise stops in various towns and cities. Like a nomadic caravanserai wending
its way across a cool desert, we'd often travel by night in the exotic limo-
buses. These fancy vehicles came complete with showers, bar, buckets of
ice, handy curtained cots, intense conversation, and live music through
the night. Many musicians joined in for performances in the various stops
along the way: Joni Mitchell, Eric Andersen. Friend, playwright Sam Shepard
from Theater Genesis days at St. Mark's Church was also present, writing dia-
logue for the film. The shows were phenomenal: energetic, various, unpre-
dictable. Dylan wore white face and had turkey feathers sticking out of
his felt hat. He looked like a Kachina doll. The poem-journal I kept during
the tour *(Shaman Hisses You Slide Back into the Night)* was published about a
year and a half later by a small press in Boston entitled White Raven, then
afterward in a German bilingual edition translated by Rolf Brück and Jürgen
Schmidt and published by Apartment Editions. I had a few salient ideas for
the film—one was to show Joan Baez meeting with the Shakers in Maine to

exchange songs and sing "Simple Gifts." Unfortunately, the advance team sent ahead to make the contact which I had initiated, thought the Shakers "too old." The idea for the brothel scene filmed at the Château Frontenac in Quebec City was mine also, after a glance at the château's garish red wallpaper and heavy red velvet drapes. I was also filmed in Native American costume reading from *Fast Speaking Woman* in front of Niagara Falls, a ridiculous scene mercifully cut from the movie, though several minutes of the audio survived as soundtrack for the film. I had a close look at the rock 'n' roll world, although it seemed atypical. As compelling and glamorous as the scene was and much to love in the people and their brilliant work and performances, I was yearning for the conversation of poets and spent much spare time on the telephone. When the tour came to Fort Collins, Colorado, I joined in the design for head gear (I was myself sporting what I called my "Joseph of Arimathea turban headdress" which the band wanted to imitate), for a documentary which was filmed as *Hard Rain*. It did rain hard. When the electricity was turned off, I pressured Bob to let Allen Ginsberg get up on stage to read a poem. Let the poet read in the rain! Which Allen did. "On Neal's Ashes," a tribute to desperado Neal Cassady, legendary inspiration for Kerouac's hero Dean Moriarty in *On the Road*. I came away appreciating the opportunity to have travelled with such a "wild mind" artistic community. To have been supported for the work I did, and the serendipitous romantic nature of the voyage. And feeling close to Dylan's trickster ethos and imagination. We never knew exactly where we were going to be next. The public only had twenty-four-hour advance notice. Crowds were delighted by the sudden intrusion. It was always a generous occasion. I romanticized the possibility of a similar, scaled-down poetry caravan for years.

The idea of living outside Boulder in the rugged and rocky terrain with views of magnificent snow mountains close by was attractive to one cooped up so long in New York City. Rentals were relatively cheap. I lived in four different mountain dwellings over the subsequent five years. It was difficult commuting to downtown Boulder, especially when the snows came, but poet companion Reed Bye and I braved the Boulder Canyon (heralded as the most dangerous road in the West!) many a wintry night, chains on Reed's old red International Ford truck. William Burroughs had lent us his apartment in town when he was away, convenient for days I was teaching. Fascinating students—some already poetically adventuresome—were arriving because of the alternative quality of education at the maverick school. Some also attracted by the dharmic backdrop. Teachings with dharma teachers, classes in Tibetan and Sanskrit. Teaching pushed on my writing and performance. I followed my own assignments. Collaborative work with students ensued; also publishing students' work was a priority. Women in particular seemed strong, independent, and much of their writing felt riskier than that of the men to me—more provocative, exploratory. "I'm coming up out of the tomb, men of war, just when you had me down . . ."

I had met poet Reed Bye at a poetry event in Boulder that local poet Jack Collom, old friend Lewis MacAdams, and I had organized to mix the Naropa scene with the local one. Reed had been a student at the university, dropped out to join the Merchant Marines and had settled back to Boulder modestly writing poems, doing tree work and roofing for a living. We immediately felt a powerful, bond, attraction of opposites. Reed was conservative by nature, domestic, private, and was to become a serious Buddhist practitioner. We felt we could live and work together, and did for a number of years (on our magazine and press and then through various projects at Naropa, where he was also teaching poetry and poetics). He became a popular core faculty for a number of years. More scholarly in his approach but always speaking through his own experience of what he taught. We married in 1980 and gave birth to our son, whom we named Edwin Ambrose, on October 21, 1980. I'd had dreams for many nights about a boy who would be named "our man," who would travel to me through "stormy weather." I felt the baby's nose pushing against my spine during excruciating labor. Every woman will tell how much pain and ecstasy is involved in childbirth. How you reenact the primordial birth of the first being, and how you finally recognize your body's secret agenda. Ambrose was a miracle, a blessing—I hadn't expected to have a child, being driven by a sense of poet-life and not settled enough in a relationship that could accommodate family. This was an inspiring turning point, unconditional love for the first time, and in many ways a deeper political commitment to the survival of the planet, the species. My child became a teacher.

Reed and I had started *Rocky Ledge* magazine and Rocky Ledge Cottage Editions on a secondhand mimeo press that we picked up for thirty-eight dollars in Denver. We published some lively issues of the magazine which included interviews with Diane di Prima, Peter Orlovsky, a transcript of conversations with Edwin Denby, of a class with Gregory Corso. I was writing

"Cabin," inspired also by a shot in Vermont, "Dialogue at 9,000 Feet," many of the meditative poems that appeared in the book *Makeup on Empty Space.* Handsome black-and-white covers were generously commissioned from Alex Katz, Glen Baxter, Jane Freilicher, Yvonne Jacquette, others.

We'd travelled abroad in 1978, starting in Germany on a reading trip which took us "singing for our supper" to Venice. The political intrigues, terrorist threats were everywhere. We were stopped near King Ludwig's castle outside Munich as police searched cars for members of the Baader-Meinhof Gang. Aldo Moro had been kidnapped in Italy. We boarded the Orient Express and headed for Turkey, travelled through Iran which was on the edge of revolution. Enormous portraits of the Shah and his family greeted us at the border. How long would they remain in place? Rebellion was afoot. In Tehran I boarded a train for India, and Reed elected to continue on through Afghanistan by bus. This was just before the Russian occupation there. The borders were closed shortly after he got to India. We finally reunited in Kathmandu. Some of this journey is reflected in the piece "Blue Mosque," which was written in New Delhi. We spent time in Nepal with Tibetan friends, disaffected "Ingies," spiritual seekers from all continents. We made pilgrimages to Buddhist gompas and other sacred Hindu and Jain and Newari sites. One lama spoke to me about an ancient prophecy which predicted that a third of the planet would be destroyed in our lifetime.

I returned to Boulder that summer for the Writing Program, and Reed stayed in New York to work as a consultant on the new roof at St. Mark's Church in-the-Bowery as part of the Preservation Youth Project, which gave work to neighborhood youth to renovate the historic building. July 12, 1978: I will never forget being called out of the pool at the Varsity Townhouse complex, where I was taking a swim with Robert Duncan, one of our illustrious Naropa faculty that summer, to the telephone to hear news of the devastating fire at St. Mark's Church. It had completely gutted the main sanctuary. Most probably started by an oxyacetylene torch employed to weld new copper downspout sleeves from the gutter, the fire destroyed the entire roof, second story of the church, historic beams, old wood floor. The bell had fallen down from the base of the steeple and cracked. I felt that a part of the poetry world, this Lower East Side holy spot, this artistic landmark which went beyond my own "scene," my own world, was coming apart. Luckily no one was hurt. I stood there soaking wet, feeling like a fool. Why wasn't I in New York to help out? I wrote a poem that night in the voice of the church. The Poetry church! It would take many years to rebuild its, our, ravaged "self."

We had moved back to New York City in 1981, taking a leave from Naropa, to the apartment on St. Mark's Place in order to be closer to both our families. I had a job teaching several semesters at the Stevens Institute of Technology in Hoboken. These students were so different from their Naropa counterparts, engineers for the most part, who groaned when I announced as a distinguished visiting guest professor I'd be teaching poetry. "Poetry? No!" I made them take a *vow* not to sell their books upon graduating. "Keep them on the shelf," I implored, "they might come in handy. You might need the appropriate quotation from Gertrude Stein, Djuna Barnes, Hilda Doolittle one day." Three female students sat in the front row, the males at the back, decorously sipping their beer from paper bags. It was a night class.

My mother's illness and long bout with diabetes complications kept us on tenterhooks most of the year. I cared for her, took notes by her bedside of strange verbal effusions and ramblings. She had utopian visions that included elaborate ceremonial events from many traditions—Christian weddings, Jewish seders, Native American dancing, participation of the grandchildren of William Carlos Williams and other famous poets, and last funeral rites. Bernadette put some of this account in her book *Utopia*. Grateful to be with her the moment she died—one of the most "real" moments I'd ever experienced as I felt life leave her body, take flight like a bird. I remember chanting *Let go, let go, let go* over and over again inside my own head until I made myself dizzy. Don't cling, the Buddhists recommend. We had a memorial service for her in the St. Mark's parish hall, she being well loved and appreciated by so many of the younger poets she had befriended and encouraged, as well as elders of the tribe.

Back in Boulder that summer of 1982 for the Jack Kerouac Conference at Naropa, then by fall in San Francisco for a stint at the New College of California, more readings and travels, and then a return to New York by Christmas. My son Ambrose's serious asthma and consequent hospitalizations (three major episodes) took us to Boulder to settle into a permanent domestic situation, sensible for his health. It had been an emotionally difficult, painful year, lying under the boy's crib at Bellevue Hospital all night fighting off cockroaches. Haunted by his labored breathing and panic. Still grieving my mother's death, never sleeping, writing chaotic monologues and tirades such as the piece "Drugs." Worried about everyone's mortality and suffering. Blessed by my beautiful child. But I didn't want any children to suffer! I was inspired by the ongoing work and activities at Naropa and the Poetry Project (I'd already begun editing a new mammoth anthology of work selected from issues of the Project's *The World* magazine) but worried too about the Project surviving during the Reagan years and the continued marginalization of artists in the culture. Friend and former student turned music producer Lynn Lynn produced a 45-rpm single of my song "Uh-Oh Plutonium!" with the flip side in French, as an anti-nuclear-warhead-proliferation statement. I worked with a band performing this and other songs on several occasions around the city. Utilizing exaggerated sound, intense instrumentation, I was performing/singing from the gut now. Ted Berrigan's advice was "Be like Mayakovsky." Reed and I also collaborated with dancer Douglas Dunn, friend and brilliant choreographer, on writing a text for and appearing in an ambitious dance-video production, commissioned by Boston's wGBH television station entitled "The Secret of the Waterfall." As poets, we look very strange and "lost" wandering around the various "sets" in Martha's Vineyard amongst confident and energetic dancers. Who are we? Tourists? This piece is a kind of reverie inspired by odd and beautiful gestures of the dancers.

The death of Ted Berrigan on July 4, 1983, followed by Edwin Denby's suicide just over one week later, plunged the poetry community into grief and despair. Huge losses. Ted's death was in many ways the result of poverty, poor health. He was only forty-eight years old. Edwin did not want to be a burden to anyone as his health declined. He was eighty.

Could we even take care of each other properly? Did most poets die tragically: botched health, unsung, obscure, soon forgotten?

A relief to return to Boulder as Ambrose's asthma condition lessened. The boy blossomed in the cleaner Colorado air. He could run around outside. Beautiful, bright, highly verbal, curious. His speech was entering my writing in an energetic way. I renewed my commitment to the Naropa poetics vision. In the semesters away from the school, Allen Ginsberg had "spelled" me and I hadn't missed any of the summer sessions. The summer program, which brought students from around the country and abroad, students from other schools, scholars with varying credentials, and a creative writing faculty of the highest caliber, was obviously the centerpiece of the entire poetics plan. It became the nexus for the master of fine arts degree. Naropa was now a fully accredited university and ready to enter a larger educational arena. It needed to declare itself as a contemplative college, a stronger alternative to more traditional and academic programs. There was some concern surrounding the founder Chögyam Trungpa Rinpoche; his lack of boundaries with practitioners within the dharma community had resulted in varying allegiances to him as students' root teacher (tsawe-lama). Having immense gratitude for his teachings and books and his role as one of my Buddhist teachers, and as friend to poets and artists, I decided to continue my path as a founder and teacher at the Jack Kerouac School of Disembodied Poetics at Naropa. I felt deeply my vow to the vision of a non-competitive progressive school of Poetics, to giving "place" to the experimental poetics of the New American Poetry (and beyond), and to continue the work I had begun as one of the workers/founders at The Poetry Project in New York City. Allen Ginsberg was under scrutiny, but mostly by the CIA.

I was getting more work around the country and abroad and found myself not only manifesting as poet, performer, lecturer, but as ambassador for a viable alternative community vision. In addition to the Poetry Project anthology, I had already started gathering work for a Ted Berrigan homage, *Nice to See You*. My own book *Skin Meat Bones* was released in 1985. I commuted to the Institute of American Indian Arts in Santa Fe to teach for a semester that spring, with poet Arthur Sze. I was intrigued by the writing of extraordinarily gifted Native American students who seemed outside the mainstream of white materialist culture. Their lives seemed more integrated with their art. It was important to continue to work with these exceptional students—they were from many tribes throughout the States—and a relationship began with Naropa for scholarship possibilities, particularly during the summer programs.

The opportunity arose to return to India as a guest of the Indian government to act as a consultant for the Festival of India, helping organize the visits of Indian poets to the States. My work took me to Bhopal just a year after the heinous Union Carbide disaster, where I saw firsthand some of the devastation and results of chemical leaks. Listened to stories of residents, survivors. How to bring the perpetrators, those responsible, to their knees? It would take years. The open-air festival in Bhopal, with participants from all over India representing various poetic traditions, was convened to determine what poetries might be best exported to the States. Vedic masters, trained since childhood; Baul singers and dancers; poets of different tongues, Assamese, Marathi, Hindi; Tamil and Khond tribal dancers enacting ritual human sacrifice; all took part. It would be a difficult decision. As an exchange, I read my poem "Skin Meat Bones," where the three words repeat as notes in varying registers, to a startled audience. It's a lively performance with vocal flourishes.

The following winter I travelled to Nicaragua as a guest of the Sandinistas for the annual Rubén Darío festival, which hosted poets from the States, staying with Nicaraguan poet Christian Santos, activist, mother of five, passionately in love with her country. A woman whose grandfather had been hacked to death by Samosa, whose parents had also been tried and suffered, a religious woman in many ways who had been radicalized through difficult experience. She was stronger, more active than her husband, from whom she was estranged. The women seemed generally more vocal, empowered, the stronger writers, had taken up arms, and many had broken from husbands and lovers who expected them to stay at home. Her beautiful young son was just that day bravely off to the front in well-pressed uniform, hair combed, AK rifle slung over his handsome shoulder.

We shared a light bulb, which moved from kitchen to bathroom to tiny sleeping quarters. We went without water at least two days a week. She was exceedingly generous. Her old Russian car kept breaking down. The kind of tires it required might never arrive. Everyone seemed a poet or else could recite the poetry of others by heart. Ernesto Cardenal, Catholic priest, then minister of culture, was highly visible. A moral presence, uncompromising. I had met him some years before at a festival in Berlin, where we rode together down the Wannsee. These were difficult times. How many young people had been killed by the Contras? How many missing? How many Contras dead? Families divided? The brilliant assistant to the minister of culture— also a poet—had a husband on the other side, fighting for the Contras. It was insane to see the United States pitting itself against a country with only two elevators! Insane to realize how few Americans had any picture of the tangible reality. Nicaragua: one main street, dirt roads, no toilet paper, how rare a decent cup of coffee. Encouraging, heartening to spend time with these artist-revolutionaries, articulate, tender. Daunting to think how they'd come out from under the thumb of dictatorship only to find themselves pitted against the most militarily powerful country in the world, a country they admired for many artistic and cultural reasons and yet experienced as enemy, as obstacle to economic stability, peace. I met many people there, not one of them cynical. As with many visionary revolutions, this was to change. But at the time a distinguished cadre of intellectuals, poets, living in modest apartments with extensive libraries of American literature, posters of Jack Kerouac, Malcolm X, Roberto Clemente on crowded walls. Important to have emotional solidarity with people who were fighting for a better system, regardless of how you felt about the terms of that war. And they wanted to hear poems and news from us, the norteamericanos.

Allen Ginsberg and I travelled to Czechoslovakia right after the Velvet Revolution, read to thousands of liberated young people, lectured on American poetry and poetics, met with President Václav Havel, and visited Temelín, the enormous and problematic nuclear power plant. Allen, crowned King of May twenty-five years previously, handed over his crown to a young anarchist artist in an enormous festive ceremony in the main square. We listened to stories everywhere, narrations of suffering to stop the mind. Elderly woman who had "seen it all"—a child in World War I, translator of Marx and Lenin into Czech, later harassed, husband imprisoned in last decades, and now beyond the conditions of the world. Her face glowed with a strange weathered beauty. She seemed unattached, but tremendously engaged at the same time. Stories from people my age of unbelievable oppression, staggering humiliation, backbiting, spying, double-dealing, stunted educations, careers. We were shown hiding places for samizdat publications—much-fingered copies of Allen's *Howl* in typescript, for example. People told how they panicked every time the doorbell rang, sure they were to be arrested for reading the wrong book. Merriment in the streets now, to be followed by chaos, instability, need for retribution? Havel was a visionary who wants to govern with absolute compassion. You feel this acutely in his presence, in his writings. He sported a bright-red heart decal on his windshield.

Writing had begun on the long poem *Iovis* beginning to take shape as a committed twenty-five-years-long (at least) ongoing investigation. It was to be a weave in and around and about and beyond male energy. The first-volume poem was later to be named *Iovis,* subtitled "All Is Full of Jove." Iovis being the generative of Jove. All is full of Jove, his sperm presumably to people space. Not simply an attack on patriarchy but an investigation of male energy and my experience in my own mind and poetry of its myriad forms. So I would need other languages, voices, descriptions, and words from the other sides. I began research, I travelled to "get" the work, I let everything speak to me of this theme, through this gaze. Gathered many threads, random strands, dreams together. Worked extensively with autobiographical material, memory, journals, letters, particularly those of my grandfather Waldman, who lived in a different time zone, as I perceived it, between two devastating wars. Drew on descriptions of my father's from World War II Germany, severed limbs sticking out of the sand at the Maginot Line. Travelled to Bali to work with the Naropa Study Abroad program—a country where they have no word for "art" it is so integrated into daily practices—to study religion and gamelan accompanied by my son, Ambrose, then eight years old, and returned with more luminous details, phrases that caught the ear, some in Indonesian. Seized on notions there studying music of cyclical time, how different life-forms intersect at various pitches, points of intensity and karmic fruition. Bits of Mayan, German, French, eight-year-olds in conversation in the backyard flitted through. Poem developed into an architectonic puzzle filled with chromosomal clusters, charms, spells, incantations. A poem written for the end of the millennium, end of time. That would continue to evolve. A life that would continue to evolve. Repeat and start all over again. Scribed words of others as I travelled further: an old man on a train in northern Germany who had been intrigued by Nazi uniforms, their shiny gold buttons; a brilliant transgender European who became an intimate friend. Remembered a camel driver speaking at Cheops, how many moons ago? I worked studies of Buddhist Mādhyamaka philosophy, a process of thinking that deconstructs apparent reality, into a long section of the poem. Dreams of Hegel, Wittgenstein. I honored Robert Creeley and John Cage. Should we as artists become actively disinterested instead of complaining about politics? This was something Cage wondered at one point on the idea of being disinterested, seeing how drained we get by the pain of politics, how hopeless, useless it seems. I thought about that. I couldn't stay disinterested. The degradation of the planet seemed beyond the pale of "against interpretation." It seemed finally women had more agency. And queers and trans. And the power of fluidity. And one thinks of the ancient Chinese poets taking refuge in exile and retreat during times of crisis. We could keep our writing retreat as our sanctuary of mind and words and voice. And it's interesting that here we, in our temporary shelters, have become so focused on what we are making, doing, that somehow those events out there seem mere figments, irritations but not threats to what we really do, are engaged in, how we live, and put our lives on the line. But there are too many losses! There are threats. And we act. Dangling on the precipice.

I dreamed at first we were a "words-only" world—written world—but then we started to dance. I dreamed that we had to travel all over the world to collect and perform what was precious to us, all those teachings in dusty tomes and illuminated manuscripts, all those stories whispered late at night over fires in far exotic corners of the fragile globe that we had to commit to memory, all those gestures of compassion that were obscured in a rush to avoid dying, all the last gasps of animals, humans, hungry ghosts. That we had to catch them up and gather them and take them and ourselves underground. That this was the cure, a repository for a sick planet, where everything worthy was getting lost. And that some would come later and unlock the codes, the runes, and feel vital poetry in their blood, their marrow, their genetic streams. To help reconstitute, reanimate, and see the world again. Maybe it could someday later be a safer world. That we needed to do this because "they" were burning books again. Mystery instead of "material." And this was a choiceless task, and we would go about it cheerfully. We needed to start our own country of enlightened mind.

The colors in mechanisms of concealment invoked in the subtitle of the *Iovis* project are the ways colors get deep into the body, with their own language. It's a heart movement, my dear friend Peter Warshall has said. We talk about colors as emotions, as music. It's the way we look at anything, feel anything. But they seem to transmute some esoteric knowledge about space, about existence, about communication, how we are kept alive by mechanisms we hardly understand. And how they can be manipulated. A kind of illusion. We connect to nature, to beauty way beyond the human realm. But also to deeper, darker nature, the shadows of concealment might be more appropriate.

They—the colors—the shadows—would be a goad for the lifelong investigatory poem, this mythic record of a rival government through poetry. A system for unraveling, a universe of antidote: a long epic that exists in opposition to our own worst barbarism, zones of cruelty, and ignorance. I needed to gather and scribe and compose luminous texts that had glow of true exile. How hard the human consciousness has worked to get us to where we could be. You want to let that go? I bowed to all fathers, teachers, brothers, husbands, son, lovers, friends. I wouldn't cancel you. I'd rise you to account. The full title became *The Iovis Trilogy: Colors in the Mechanism of Concealment.* As Ambrose chanted the various ways to cover up plutonium on a long car ride and I noted them down:

Let's cover up plutonium with a graveyard
Let's cover it with
one of every single stone in the world
pennies, quarters, everything
Then gold around plutonium, then diamonds, rubies, emeralds.
Then there's plaster, then linoleum,
congoleum

Thus the child in an act of spontaneous litany became the ultimate guide for the poem, how to transmute toxicity in the most extended piece I'd written up to this this point (1991). It was an attempt to catch the vibration, or patterned energy, of one being on this planet as she collides with all apparent and non-apparent phenomena.

Part I: Arche

(beginning—the sense of first things, as mind, as larynx)

I've been commanded to sleep but refuse to surrender
All of existence which is not life is time, says Seneca
I find this out later—or never

—LYN HEJINIAN

I came out of the wilderness and just naturally fell in with the beat scene . . .
There were always a lot of poems recited—"Into the room people come and go
talking of Michelangelo. Measuring their lives in coffee spoons." Jack Kerouac,
Ginsberg, Corso and Ferlinghetti—"Gasoline," "Coney Island of the Mind," . . .
oh man, it was wild—"I saw the best minds of my generation destroyed by mad-
ness": that said more to me than any of the stuff I'd been raised on . . . whatever
was happening of any real value was . . . sort of hidden from view . . . Pound,
Camus, T. S. Eliot, e. e. cummings, mostly expatriate Americans who were off in
Paris and Tangiers. Burroughs, Nova Express, John Rechy, Gary Snyder, Pictures
From the Gone World . . . it all left the rest of everything in the dust.

—BOB DYLAN

I am the lover thinking in her light
Body of the single sentence of dream
That is, what I take with me & what I carry
As I weep for lovers
And their energy and charm.

—BERNADETTE MAYER

A question (makes itself heard): How late is it anyway?
The looks all turn into the same direction; there is the sibyl's
mouth, it will speak with no make-up; It says; it's as late as
today. As late as today and always.

    —PAUL CELAN

This ocean, humiliating in its disguises
Tougher than anything.
No one listens to poetry. The ocean
Does not mean to be listened to. A drop
Or crash of water. It means
Nothing.
It
Is bread and butter
Pepper and salt. The death
That young men hope for. Aimlessly
It pounds the shore. White and aimless signals. No
One listens to poetry.

    —JACK SPICER

Prelusion

kinetic from *kinetikos,* Greek, from *kinein,* to move

relating to or resulting from motion
motion in a nation, in an ocean

(of a work of art) dependent on movement for its effect

That's what writing poetry elucidates for me. Impels. Stimulates. Moment to moment. What is it to be a poet right now, in time of every breakdown imaginable. Feeling part of a continuum and also a current community of wild purpose, love, sodality, citizens of imagination who write and read poetry. Often difficult poetry. Hidden from view.

Lives dedicated to poetry, though all your lifeline that registers as coetaneous, synchronous. Accessible. And the lifetime is a magic of accretion as you age . . . what you keep, what you shake off, discard.

It's a conundrum, its value. But you keep on, like the ocean. "Tougher than anything." Feeling everyone's kinetics in that zone. But also all together swimming in a database. Imagine.

Poetry these days feels now like a battle for "human." Ordeals of navigation. Being helots, full time. Feels like a sciamachy—a shadow war. A battle for human justice, for spirit, for alignment, for all the vehicles of art and archive that keep moving consciousness forward. How do the lines cohere? What point of contact? Want to be together in all of it: struggle, in lamentation, in joy.

More like a spiral perhaps. Not growing static as the receptacle of data flows invades the psyche system, the body, the mouth, the conversation. Not mere distraction culture here, something more scary, serious, portentous. That eradicates. Will the evolutionary journey continue without our species?

Are we even human yet? Are we a world yet? Who is even speaking? What is it to be transhuman? Will that be essential form to survival in technological universe? A thread of poetry might help, with or without us.

Are you the icon of yourself or is it more risky? This is the thinking. How to make it work, get your consciousness out from under siege, keep free and clear of fascist mind, travel beyond binaries, keep pushing for knowledge, study and *studying with,* a deeper investigation, and human justice, a deeper action. *The* action. Totally necessary. Above all, do no harm.

Poetry has always braved shifting and terrifying frequencies. There is no time in human history without poetry. Poets often go into exile in fraught times. Does it *mean* to be listened to? Not necessarily. Yet you could be locked up for a dangerous poem.

It's comfortable in the scriptorium, in the imaginary, sitting in our little divinity niches. Idols of ourselves. At other times: "house arrest." Often the city walls shake; you are in the street, another kind of combat that includes a poetics of everything you hold dear.

The multitentacular poetry scene of upheaval midsixties thru seventies was heady. I had grown up in Greenwich Village.

A constant round of readings, of writing and reading or editing small-press magazines, of working at the mimeo machine all night, major collaboration of texts and infrastructure, high talk, love affairs, cultural and political activism. Respect for elders, supplicating wise poet elders. Street work. Exploration into other cultures and a curiosity about shamanic spiritual traditions. Asia. Travel. One of the founders and directors of the Poetry Project, a historical church in the Lower East Side, co-founding a poetics school in Colorado, cross currents with other disciplines, lure of performance. Wanting to create things to my desire. I was being "called to" shape and lead. This book enfolds and continues some of these formative trajectories.

Rhizome is the often-conjured term used philosophically by Deleuze and Guattari as an "image of thought that apprehends multiplicities," and like the tuber system it moves horizontally rather than vertically. This is close to the *pratītyasamutpāda* of Buddhist philosophy, which denotes the co-arising and interconnectedness of all existence.

The rhizome, as tuber system, has no central root or logical pattern. By extension this set of potentials counters the traditional or logical approach to knowledge, which is usually represented by a tree with roots. Upwardly mobile, hieratic, patriarchal.

The rhizome having neither beginning nor end but always a middle, from which it grows and brims over. Thus the rhizome is a self-vibrating kinetic region of intensities whose development eschews orientation toward a culmination point or external goal. A feminist ecology perhaps.

I felt in my teens through age twenty, when I was coming seriously to poetry and arriving into a particular nexus of Zen and tantric Buddhism and the exciting experiments in American poetry, something was already generating, a process of resonant and concomitant interests, influence of jazz, folk music, Abstract Expressionism, experimental film, New York School, the Beats, contemporary and hybrid arts, philosophical sympathies, progressive politics, interest in Asian art forms (raga, gamelan, trance, Sufi dancing), love of ancient oral poetries, poets, books as holy objects, the little Outrider magazines and presses, from Diane di Prima and LeRoi Jones/Amiri Baraka's *Floating Bear* to White Rabbit's letterpress offerings in San Francisco. To *Locus Solus*. And Margaret Randall and Sergio Mondragón's *El Corno Emplumado* in Mexico City. This state of the art, so to speak, was a liberating tangible dynamic, an ongoing continuum with points of origin that had energy but no official agenda, a place one could enter as a willing novice. Jump into the maelstrom. In media res.

Help wake the world up to itself. A set of potentials.

The rhizome description is a rejection of traditional genealogy. You can refuse the assumptions and histories of the dominant class that seemed to rule academia. It isn't a study of culture but rather an organic continuous *effort* to free the forces that have been constrained by master narratives. You are already a feminist. You challenge assumptions about gender, about class, about race. In relation to contemporary arts practices, the restrictions make no sense. Who determines what is a literary canon that too often rejects the strange, the foreign, the woman, the fellaheen. Many of the world's radiant and radical poetic seers and visionaries work outside and protest the centers of ambition. You want to join them. The busy Outriders. Become a field poet. Kneel down on that beautiful field. Remember that no one begs you to be a poet. Not down on their knees for you to do that. You are self-anointed.

We are often living a nightmarish dystopia of our own ignorance. I tell myself, don't tarry, urge that none of us tarry. Are we equipped? To work collaboratively and collectively on all the issues threatening our humanity and the living sinews of other life-forms, plant, animal species. Are we ready? The world right now.

I often obsess over the sixth extinction, other versions of the end time: Mayan, Hindu, Christian, Gnostic, Buddhist, Indigenous. Many dark visions: but how to articulate?

"This world no longer needs explaining, critiquing, denouncing. We live enveloped in a fog of commentaries and commentaries on commentaries . . . of revelations that don't trigger anything, other than revelations about the revelations. And this fog is taking away any purchase we might have on the world," writes the Invisible Committee.

What do we need, then? What power of language? What force of poetry? What will trigger the reckoning? Who will be doing it? What kind of world? Who's listening?

Achille Mbembe in *Necropolitics* wrote of a new phase in the history of humanity of the "unremitting digitalization of facts and things." And that it might become "increasingly difficult, if not impossible, to distinguish human organisms from electronic flows, the life of humans from that of processors." And the terminal point of a "digital-cognitive turn could well be a widespread infiltration of microchips into biological tissue." How vulnerable we have become, how surveilled, manipulated.

Donna Haraway reports that the troubled time now is "turbulent, is terrifying." It will require incredible perspicacity and a practice of "the long haul." "What is a thousand-year plan for the spirit?" she asks. And, I ask, for poetry and its libraries?

When we started the Jack Kerouac School of Disembodied Poetics in 1974, we projected a hundred-year plan, *at least*. And we were very close to Rocky Flats with its leaks of plutonium. And near half-life of a quarter of a million years. We ask now of Naropa and its archive and ourselves, what is the five-hundred-year plan? The thousand-year plan? We are inside an ecological Armageddon.

Eileen Crist in *Abundant Earth* calls for nothing less than the total reformation of human civilization on this planet. One of my Buddhist teachers suggests a third of the planet could be destroyed through climate or nuclear mishap. But it might also be destroyed from within. What is our status as "human subject"? Communication in the human realm is problematic in the Kali Yuga, as everything is speeded up and empathy and compassion break down. Crist invokes the miracles of wild nature and the diversity of nonhuman awareness. She invokes a "flame of life" whose richness is self-perpetrating.

Scientists and biologists reported that the earth's seismic activity stilled as the coronavirus took hold in 2020. It was the least amount of seismic activity in recorded history. The air was clean. Oil prices were down because few were flying or driving. People could see the Himalayas from one hundred miles away for the first time in thirty years. It was reported that wild animals were happier. Humans suffered, often excruciating death, from the plague. The toll continues, morphs. It will need to be a collaboration in care, our future.

Bard, Kinetic as field of possibility, with selected texts from parts and measures of my life lived interconnectedly. A book of memory. And I want the field strewn with poems.

I enjoy Keats's sense of a "fellowship with essence" which means living in doubt and beyond binaries. I want to invoke satori's sudden flash, recognition, and honor about some of the people whose work I've loved and admired. Instances of bits and pieces over the years of witness, discourse, autobiography, and memorabilia. So many poets and artists of my generation are leaving worldly time.

And their work enters the continuum, an extraordinary spectrum.

We need to continually engage with the opening of imagination, with the trope of turning, an ongoing kinetics—of Lucretius's clinamen perhaps. The swerve as a gesture moving forward and backward, and also in a vortex of compassion. Honoring the shimmering brilliance of the past—all those cultural artist-workers who struggled to make sense of existence—and an ever-morphing cyborgian future. How may we be better guardians? Are we even an evolved world as yet? Are we really post-post-post everything?

Post-Holocaust, postcolonial, post-empire, postwar? We need to recognize our symbiosis with all living things, to honor the fabric of our alchemical and magical web of life.

In the startling present, with future severities and visions for poetry's evolution, may poets and poetry be keepers and seers and activists and archivists of past and present, and held in future memory. This is the gist. *Sarva Mangalam.*

Stepping Back

I noticed the night

I noticed a new half moon
I noticed it looked
liberated
sharp, piercing

The sky was clear

I noticed my panic

I heard remote birds
I noticed the beggar I noticed
a dancer

Hesitation

Apprehension, speed
and speed I noticed

Someone fumbling
with a slippery glove
I noticed a quarter, here's
something, something

Was money safe?
Was larynx?
Sex safe?

I noticed hesitation
And how to think invincibly

That's what it means
to be wise
Think before you touch

See what you
cannot see
you can't touch

It's invisible
I noticed

Someone was kind

I noticed efficacy
I noticed warning
I noticed signs
signaling doom

Touch of optimism
I noticed rituals

I noticed
shifts of mood
flicker
I noticed momentum

This was readiness is all
This was an almanac

I noticed closing's closure,
cloisters I wanted to
hide within
I noticed distraction

Shuttered
I noticed
Shuddered

Words closer
to action

I noticed
a book

I noticed poetry
might save
you now

Save you
if you let it
add on

It's time

I noticed
startled words
jump on
the page

I noticed my speed
to stay alive

Speed is purpose
I noticed

Stand aside
Was something there
I noticed nothing

A subway stalled
I noticed anxiety
I noticed crying
people not moving

Would I be
subject for interrogation

Was I abiding

Was I living rules

I counted them
I am behaving

What did one know?

Know this could still be
empty
Know this could
be full
I noticed breathing

I noticed someone
freaking out in the bank
What he used to be,
still elegant

But not what you see now,
he told them
He told them he used to be
one with credit

Then I was one with credit
he said
I heard I noticed

I noticed speed again
I noticed speed thinking
itself a victor

Speed is a vector

No one saying what's going on
when you are in business

Put on a face,
one with credit

I noticed how your faces are in
my vocabulary now
I am in yours too, I noticed

I noticed out of pity
I noticed unheeding

I noticed the mirror
of wisdom
All things equal
shimmering mirror
holding tight in brain

I noticed no one on the streets

I noticed the outcast
And around the world

The broadcasts in my head
I noticed walking by

I noticed remembering
how one touched a
small thing gently
and it expanded

A rail, a glass, a corner
a trigger

Button to set off a bomb

How one stayed calm

I noticed
her beautiful eyes closed
I noticed thinking
Open them please

Help me

I noticed children
I noticed obedience
Tender faces in routines

I noticed insouciance
I noticed determination

I noticed listings
What is missing

What we won't be able to
notice
I noticed hesitating
stepping back

I was in the world
I noticed it

World, world?

Parks closed I noticed

I noticed the hardship of rain
when you live on the street

I remembered Berlin before
the wall came down
I remember things opening
I noticed elsewhere
things closing down

Beirut
I noticed barriers and guns

I noticed shorter hours,
longer days

I noticed the silver
foil I dropped
afraid to pick up

Wipe it down
I noticed a cough

I remembered a conference in Wuhan
Bustling city, the lake
in happy translation

I noticed the care in transition
How far we came
and back a step

I noticed the invisible scourge,
invisible body,
unseen embrace

I noticed the child in
the hallway stepping
back
Good, good

Step back

I noticed what parts of the body
shut down
I noticed my eyes
peering into screens
Eyes awake, ears straining

I noticed my voice
next to yours
noticing
a continent away.

From "Dharma Gaze"

for Ambrose, Althea, Eva

I am putting makeup on empty space
All patinas on empty space
I am putting makeup on empty space
Painting the phenomenal world

　　　—A. W.

A "gaze" in critical theory terminology, which may be literary, sociological, or anthropological, seems to be a deeply conditional and—in some cases—an entrenched way of seeing the phenomenal world and its constituents. One in the grip of a habitual gaze sees the world's trappings, its workings, and its subjects most particularly as objects of scrutiny, and possibly disdain. This often refers to situations involving systems of surveillance and various power dynamics. It is more of a self-regulating relationship than a given from a problematic stance, but when studied and deconstructed may be a way of empowering the victim. So the idea is to analyze the power relationship and break the gaze and free the object.

We have reference to the "imperial gaze" described in postcolonial theory and the "male gaze," which originated with Laura Mulvey's essay "Visual Pleasure & Narrative Cinema" (1975), seeing women from a masculine and heterosexual point of view from behind the camera. There's the "oppositional gaze" proposed by bell hooks as a tactic of rebellion for Black women.

"Le regard" is the act of seeing and being seen and is caught up in power relations, yet in some situations that very act may be turned around.

The idea here is that the subject of the gaze generally loses autonomy. Jacques Lacan speaks of the "mirror stage," the point at which the child looks in the mirror and realizes that he or she has an external appearance. This self-gazing might well trigger a long life of self-consciousness, and reinforcement of a sense of a solid self. Neurosis in Buddhism is related to a problem with "I" and other, mind and space. With identity. Who am I? What is this bundle of conglomerations of tendencies? Where do "I" fit in with all my colorful skandhas? How do others see me?

These are the very questions dharma practice wants to re-examine. Challenge fixation on a solid "I." Thus I use "dharma gaze" as an antidote, with a touch of irony. The idea here involves an act, a process, a discipline of vipashyana (clear seeing), of panoramic awareness and appropriate sense of space. This is the practice of a field poet, citizen, spiritual practitioner. This is what particular rituals seem to ask of us: gaze thru the solid sense of "I" without attachment.

A traditional ritual entitled amrita kundali was for many years performed within the Buddhist sangha that evolved around the words of Naropa Institute teacher Chögyam Trungpa, a lama born in Tibet in 1939 who came to the US in 1970. Poet, calligrapher, and author of many books on Tibetan dharma, he founded the first Buddhist-inspired school in the USA—Naropa Institute (later University)—in 1974. I arrived with Allen Ginsberg, Diane di Prima, Jackson Mac Low, dancer Barbara Dilley, John Cage, and others in Boulder, Colorado, in 1974 to be part of and contribute to a unique vision of noncompetitive contemplative arts and education. Some of us lingered and founded what Allen and I named the Jack Kerouac School of Disembodied Poetics.

I first attended an amrita kundali ritual in 1979.

Amrita is the nectar of immortality, etymologically related to the Greek *ambrosia* that appears earliest in the *Rigveda* as a synonym for *soma,* the Vedic ritual drink. Nectar signifies mindfulness in Hinduism and Buddhism. A ritual nectar is made with alcohol and dark-brown grains, and the concoction is known as *dutsi.*

Kundali, from *kundalini,* refers to the vital source of energy at the bottom of the spine. This energy triggers the formation of the child in the womb. It coils at the bottom of the spine and holds this force in stasis until we die. It may be raised in yogic practices.

The amrita kundali is available for everyone, but especially infants, young children, and the yet-to-be-born. I was pregnant when I first participated in the ceremony.

One approaches—in a shrine room or other suitable ritual space—a large standing mirror, and at the moment of recognition of one's image in the mirror, one is lightly doused with the amrita nectar, sprinkled from a juniper bow by an attending adept. "Cut!"

The mirror is an extraordinary instrument/invention, a technology of self, of self-gazing. Did we ever contemplate ourselves in this way, so fully realized? We are finally our own scene, our own deity, our own theism, worshipper, audience, and where we once saw a shadow, or less substantial reflections and emanations rippling on surface of water, we see "me."

It is precisely this moment of recognition, particularly in the case of the child, that helps cut the attachment to egoic identity, a solid sense of "me." It seems especially useful in a culture where reification of identity, and the appearance of a solid self, is problematic. In the Buddhist view there is no solid self or soul, and best to establish this dharma gaze of impermanence from the start. We live in a time of perpetual self-curation. Image-making. And beyond that, a different kind of morphing human-hybrid is being constituted through digital technologies and new media forms. What kind of monster may evolve from this over-indulged image of self? Think of amrita kundali as an antidote. Apotropaic.

What is this to poetry? To how we use language? Being haunted by impermanence is a way to deeper compassion and tenderness for the endangered human and all the rest. A way *to see through, to think with* as poetic practice. To imagine. Perceptions, ayatanas, gates of attention, seem activated by "noticing" particulars.

Yet, one wants to conjure dharma gaze as an act of resistance. *Dharma* essentially means "things as they are." The child sees others going through the same initiation. For me it was a blessing for the nascent child consciousness and then later a ritual for my child when he was starting to ask questions, What is this, Who am I, What do I do with it all? One is gazing at emptiness in the primordial mirror. One can see all phenomena as translucent and the "self" as a fluid part of a larger web of life, a larger family, not the master or tyrant of any universe. A peacock feather is dipped in amrita and sprinkled on a young sentient being's brow.

Teen Languishing in Cove

the fable
of the small child who liked sunlight, so she pulled down the blinds, to keep it
all in for herself.

little magazine of poetry
enticing to see
flagrant,
flaunts itself
a dress of black taffeta
new norm
what cannot be seen
stitches a symbol?
nuclear particle

walk through
objects, correlations
or descent to
wandering
in reading
binary frames
ineffable displacement
a teen body, vagabond
sexual
bounding
toward little magazine
of matchsticks
twigs made vibratory

hold it up all to see
queen's horses
a ride into battle
something like that
disavows taciturn
refusal

on other side of me
valiant suitor for poetry
this side
magazine is lovely
to what agency?
poetry floats
eclipses

narrative voices
girls in temperament
gone icy
while they await
discovery
inimical
to me
lovely to read to see
when a storm
someone blind in it
in error of identity
blends in, it
bends
a comma

futurist?
people mix up in it
mind and matter
their grammar
you love
to meet and pass them
on the road

long time to be found in the mouth,
in the month more migratory
herds
then it's spring.
everyone hungrier
graduating

in poetry

like temperament,
passes in a ghost system
grasses mask urgency
legacy

*what to name child
of the crossroad?*

name her "poetry"

people continue reading
as animals first appear

she lets her vibratory weight
fall on brusque poet's intentionally
so he, elder
sees
admires
she will steal his fire
with proof
of herselves
greater valor

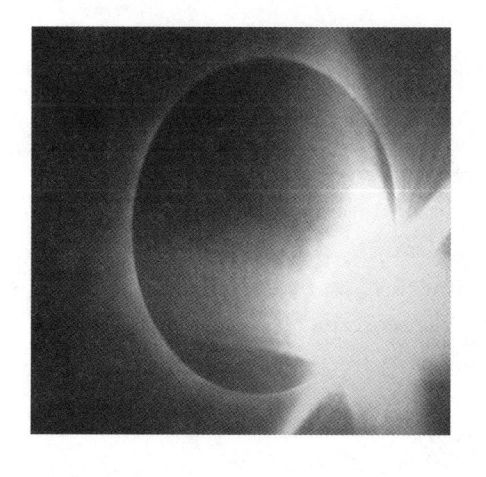

on the ground
feminist skin,
waits to be revealed
what she has chanced
in constellation
where else
get repose
poetry knows

but I am older
and truly see
wild ruses
of poetry

[1966]

Beat Roots

1

Once on the drug, we were travelling,
we were in yage land, we were in the land of brujo and bruja, someone said
"these scarabs get lost around me." It was not the shaman, it was the part-
ner of the painter who took me on a wild goose chase around the moors of
Bolinas and I lost the fancy leather coat of one Robert Creeley.

Fog, always. A sentinel for some kind of trial, tribulation, death of the psyche.
You remember Magda. Crystal ball cloudy. The heathen on the moors, like
that. Twilight.

You remember Lew Welch had disappeared by then. "A good bird always flies
like a vulture . . . / (Milarepa sang)."

Someone else had died. Many of the players were still alive. Mysterious things
were happening to her men. Lew disappeared, Jack Boyce fell off a beam.

Prayer flags around the house in the wind to vocalize Tibet in America.

Old Bull Burroughs was in his cups about scorpions, how they are clearly, he
said, *clearly*, repellent. And if anything scared him they did. Old Bull was
recalcitrant in his need for inebriants, and the bug-thing was emphatically a
part of the lore of poison, antidote, of nectar, of cum, of blood of the savior.
It's all mixed up in lethal fear I think, I said. I told of my scorpion bite out on
the Egyptian desert, and he winced. A brown recluse in the shower scared
the bejesus out of him. He could tell you all about their violin markings, and
how they only have six eyes, not eight like most spiders. And could be deadly.
He loved that they were called "recluse."

He couldn't say it enough, "brown recluse."

The coat was found in the long a.m. huddled in the corner of that witchy
woman's cave. Magda. The woman from Magdala, a high tower, one who is
elevated.

2
We were eye-to-eye in our Buddhism

with politics, which is why it made sense to mix mantra with political protest and why you could simply mimeo little slips of paper with words like "Om Ah Hum" and mingle them with "Freedom" and "Justice." This was back in the elder Mayor Daley's time. And we circled the Chicago park, ever alert for the crack of nightstick, and we took to sleeping on the wing, vigilant . . . and we sat in the courthouse and Bobby Seale gagged for the world to see.

And did it? Did it see? Did it see the fellaheen world?

You testified.

Judge Hoffman seemed to be in a play by Molière, the rhetoric was interesting. You could forget the part about manacles, jail time. You could forget that we were trying to bring that war system down. It would come down thanks to the Viet Cong resisting as we spoke. On the fringe of the park now, Allen Ginsberg effusive for the fresh air, outside in the gypsy dark, megaphones, and mantra. We would bring the world here to meditate for twenty-four hours at least and it would be a more sober clear-seeing world. Vipashyana world, all to see. This could be done. This was possible.

Earlier Allen had been brought to vatic speech by the enormity and excesses of power-mad euphemism. Pentagon wake from planet-sleep! Om Raksa Hum Hum Hum Phat Svaha! He said in so many words in a transmission mode, *You can always match their power in words, just stay candid.*

3
Gregory Corso invaded my shower one day

in the little townhouse apartment I return to in dreams as "Remember Some Apartments." It was named "Emerson Apartments." Ralph Waldo Emerson had always been an inspiration for my memory of this place although he would not have appreciated the communal arrangements and anarchist spirit. Gregory was always barging in, rooting around my toiletries, looking for valium or anything palliative and high-making, gesticulating, checking out my books—did I have any art books?—and would I ever be as good as Jane Austen? So there was that, the sense of invasion.

I was soaping my hair with lavender shampoo. We decided we would probably never sleep together. That was a good idea because he was so complicated to think about sleeping with. I mean it wasn't even an issue or much of a discussion. I was not going to get my transmissions from Beat poets, I proclaimed, by sleeping with them! I said would you be my pal? And will you behave? He hugged me as we were water rats together in the shower.

4

On the road to the contagious hospital.
It breaks me up, last days of Philip Whalen, I can't tell of it very well. In the years of war, of dark age, all the genocide raining down. Who's in charge? Philip would ask. Not I. "Them." "But them is dead!" "Them is an anachronism."

Let me say. Laguna Honda—a hospital—hospital? No, a state of mind perched high but down on its luck, better days of lovely minimally attended gardens, take a turn, all variety of cactus—is it like a Tibetan Bardo maze? Flashing on his hens and chickens, those little swirls of rubbery green succulents. And "Anne, you don't know how to speak to the chickens, let alone the hens, please, not like that . . ."

Let me say as we—Nick Dorsky and I—walk first into the empty anteroom as we might cross a magic threshold. The antechamber to death, to the part where you only have your hearing left and someone is reading the Tibetan Book of the Dead, where you fight off flickering projections back to every encounter with our dying Roshi. The time you took his hand. The time he was reading Emily Dickinson and the space got interrupted by the young man having an epileptic fit, pencil swinging madly out of control on the page where he made notes and Philip kept going, nonchalant. She (Emily Dickinson) could handle that, he said later in private . . . So all these projections arise in the antechamber. I could see Philip, thin and fragile or large and swollen. I could see him with hair and beard and I could see him enjoying food, Chinese food. Take-out. What path would he chose in the afterlife? The bright lights of food and pleasure, the dimmer light of ordinary mind? Or the most challenging blaze of all, dangerous, come back right away and save mankind.

Woe mankind, Allen sang.

And Joanne Kyger had reported in April how Philip called and said he was roaming around on Sutter Street without a cent and would someone come and pick him up?

And she said, *This now is for me how it was for you with Allen.*

One corridor, the patients reaching out to us—can you fetch a glass of water? Light my cigarette? Push my wheelchair into the sun?

It seemed to be a room of vets from the sixties war.

Lying in the hall in a bed set up temporarily with other patients while the rooms were being painted, suddenly shiny and luminous. Blind and clear and seeing us. Curtain, gauzes of discretion and intimacy set up between the dying, you hear them breathing.

5
I'd been given a gift certificate
to Bergdorf's, and John Wieners wanted it from the start as there was then a kind of sisterly competition we were playing at, which is what I am thinking now. So let's go up there now (then). He was just visiting. And about to give a reading in the gold lamé "number," a jumper, à la Liberace.

He's wadding gobs of Kleenex into the bra and the salesgirl is being very attentive, playing along, and John wants to try on a range of blouses, prolong the agony of decision. By contrast, I am a quick, impulsive shopper. Say I know the best stuff on him from the start, but he's not buying it. So we end up with a rather dowdy black thing that doesn't look any better back at the apartment on St. Mark's Place as he's primping in front of the mirror, but that means we can go back tomorrow and find another. *That would be best.* Another performance.

Then I can't remember what happened. But I think this is all precipitously before he tries to board the airplane to Rome without a passport and ends up (again) at Wingdale. And one visits the large rooms with mad people in them and he's very distracted and medicated. "Melancholy carries / a red sky and our dreams" (Wieners).

6
Where was alchemy in 1961?

Where was Freddie Herko in 1962 before he walked out the window? And the unguents and libations of velvet life and stammer and conquest and wow. How many arms can one woman have to keep a world afloat? And make babies? This bird—my dove—flies backward and in all ten directions of space.

Laboratories and ruminations of the goddess di Prima inhabit the Hotel Albert. One: a brew of herbal elixirs, good for circulation of the blood. Two: mind of the poet that warms to John Dee, occultist, astronomer to Elizabeth I, owner of the largest library of that time. Three: if you could mix sulphur and mercury you would be the perfect bisexual. Four: get on stage and act out a scream to dare the elements of invocation. Five: revolution. Six: the rotundity and science of light and cool shadow. Seven: a place in the country, preferably underground. Eight: live outside the system, and forever. Nine: barter on the side. Ten: the upside-down fool, welcome him. Understand him.

I wrote some things down for the future to bank upon, to stay the blast. My cards said "obviate," my swords said "rule," my cards said "a sun in your center," my cards said "heartbreak." I started out early to walk in the New York dawn, her stealthy Tarot on my mind.

7
Amiri urged caution . . .

We gathered for the poetry festival in Ostia, back in the seventies, the place where Fellini filmed all his beach scenes. Edge of Rome. Om-pah-pah bands marching the sand, the ubiquitous boy-child leader allegorically representing Optimism and Imagination both. Beautiful chaos set against the ebb and flow of moon, time, water, innocence, impermanence, and flicker of celluloid . . .

The audience had been camping at Ostia two days. Extremely hungry, *they might storm the stage* the organizers warned. They had been promised rock 'n' roll and food. They were hoping Patti Smith would arrive. We had several strategy meetings where William Burroughs advised, "A chair is a weapon. Stay your ground." Allen was conciliatory, remembering the savagery of cops in Chicago. He wanted to start chanting. The reading began. A somewhat magnetizing young woman came to the microphone and droned on for what seemed an eternity, story was she'd been tripping for days. Her sense of the whole world watching and she said something like that about the world watching and we are all molto bellissimo. Ted Berrigan said we should have in our psyches the voice of Mayakovsky reading to a huge stadium of nudniks. Tension in the summer night . . . the reading proceeded.

Amiri Baraka had urged caution, Amiri was the backbone of our poet cell: *there could be agent provocateurs afoot. Be cool,* he said. How would the Carabinieri react? We were being paid in lira sottobanco (under the table). Our hosts were anarchist theatre folk. Amiri's intensity transformed to a graceful animal proprioception when the crowd rushed the stage—it was surely built for this, like a movie set—and we leapt off, I caught his face—ready, resolute, alert as in *I've seen this before.* The structure collapsed.

In survival-of-the-fittest mode, Burroughs had a wooden plank ripped from the stage raised and ready for defense—or attack?

Epitaph for Octave

meet me in the park, if you love me
—FRANK O'HARA

used to get
    dressed

regularly

time shortens
impact

        of "I used to"

    MacDougal Street, used to get

shooed off, peeking into
neighborhood Mafia club
used to
                & "numbers" ring,
there, the corner

miracle to think with uses used up?

        Jon Cott,
used to

see you often, here

age thirteen

        have you heard of the Dark Enlightenment?

It's an exit

from democratic society

"with parts of the world for unregulated experiment"

Will it still be there (society?)   (used to, use it to . . .)

   use it to see our algorithmic decisions?

freedom on this planet

        the future is done

an Elizabethan pageant acknowledges that death

you light the cryonic tapers

old desk, in hope

        you wrote *Marriage: A Sentence*

once, upon
                    restless elegy, up stairs

        stirred an old wound, the wood did

get outside
    around corner's

                daily baptisms

street running from panic

        misses a "from" a "to" an "in"

disappearing

   behind
  eidetic power
    captures St. Anthony,

The saint, the church, in testament
veiling the ark of the covenant
        as if by wings of cherubim.

to answer a function of poetry
its threnody, bow down, Jon said
                to guard against pride

            need a lot of dissonance
        in your spiritual chord

all previous lovers remain at the ancient window
(Frances, *maman,* had the key)

lips and
hands

take up a different call,
  Washington Square Park

    in the singing circle
            the protest circle

    call it narcotizing nostalgia,

            an arch

over catastrophic illusion

hell call it, loss

you
                claim it. or laud it.
abolition of borders

                the beatnik night

Culture of One: Edwin Denby

I've been thinking about what Edwin Denby gives us in his work, what he writes, and how that stays vibrant, and then what he was like and consistent with. "Art is certainly even more mysterious and nonsensical than daily life. But what a pleasure it can be. A pleasure much more extraordinary than a hydrogen bomb is extraordinary." That is a radical statement. And one thinks of Adorno: can there be beauty after Auschwitz? Edwin would probably not have much truck with critical theory and ultimatums. As if humans could abandon or check their creative sensibility.

I'm a nut for ritual yet ordinary magic, ceremony and gazing into the arke, wanting to consider origins, sources, where it starts, the way back. He was willing to go there. Art origin in some ways just comes with the human who notices, doesn't have to be precious, mysterious, shrouded, but here and among us. That's what Edwin gave me. It's here, what you need from art, what you can do in art, and among us. When I sat next to him in the ballet it was, as he says in *Dancers, Buildings and People in the Streets,* like being in some imaginary family. "The amplitude that you feel you see with at your most intelligent moments." And his seeing amplified mine. Suzanne Farrell's long neck. Her odd forehead and mouth you couldn't see.

Okay, ballet, seventeenth century. But he'll go further back in the human universe. We're also needing to revalue our animals, notice them, adore them, the other denizens we share this planet with, and then there's art which sustains us and which should be, yes, an ordinary miracle. Not a fuss. Edwin shows us how a dance move—a woman's head moving—resembles the motion of a giraffe's neck, "that seems to begin below the shoulder blades."

His "Forms in Motion and Thought"—an extraordinary, vast meditation on just about everything—also has the sensible line: "There is a bit of insanity in dancing that does everybody a great deal of good."

I like that he's concerned about the greater good. He's so very civic. I'll say again he wanted art in the world, accessible but not easy and it's not daily life. I've said this. I love his amplitude. It's like Walt Whitman's "adhesive." He was happy in a diner, with simple fare.

The notion he explores here, starts with, is of taking steps and recovering balance where the only risk is rhythm, yet "the action is more fun and risk increases when the dancers step to a rhythmic beat of music." A steady beat, he says, is what dancers dream of and live for. There's a lightness there with the beat. I think of this in relationship to poetry (we start with the heartbeat), and his poetry, because there is his attention to classic prosody and containment and coming from way back. Risky balance in the *Mediterranean Cities, Sonnets:*

> I feel of night streets as of a reef, squamous
> Grotto-washed; entombed, claws loose, a Siren lies
> Who bleeds, the phosphor-drift heaps in these Naples
> Eyes, thousands of eyes, thousand and one night eyes;
>
> Fleshed, a curled swimmer's pale belly that presses
> And loosens, and moist calves, then while the charm
> Subsides, Venice secrets pleases, caresses;
> The water-like walking of women, of men
> The hoarse low voices echoes from water again

And I think of that inclination to the beat even if resisted. He loved Gertrude Stein's writing. And the sensuousness of "water-like walking" is welcome. "To be perfectly happy is to be like water" was Edwin's Taoism. The primordial element supports the human. We are, after all, most of water made. Examine the resonant lightness in Stein, her charms in *Tender Buttons,* ordinary miracles of noticing consciousness. "Venice secrets pleases, caresses."

And Edwin then goes to the Paleolithic and the cave paintings and a "developed dance sense our ancestors had fifteen thousand years ago. What are all those bison of theirs floating on, if not a steady beat?" I remembered this line, on a trip to Les Eyzies. And mused myself in cave studies the ubiquitous puzzling handprints on the walls. Those of children most likely. Were they keeping a beat? He then designates an "educated late-Paleolithic magician" perfectly at home in an air-conditioned theatre with classical ballet, with a first-class wizard conducting with a magic wand in the orchestra pit. And then a discussion about the first hints of dancing coming from wild animals. Fighting animal rituals, migrant birds in formation in a "single revolving vibrating shape which kept changing in the air—a shape that distended, that divided like an hourglass, that streamed out like a spiral nebula."

"A social celebration and a prehistoric pleasure." He goes to bees and their sign language, a "honeybee performs for her hivemates." Cats playing games. Kittens play "with no sense of a base and gradually learn to imagine." But they never mimic anyone but themselves. "Stepping to a man-made beat . . . that we alone have made." We presumably danced without a beat at first. He asks how we could have been bright enough to invent the beat? There's the current famous YouTube video of the cockatoo dancing to rock 'n' roll, stepping on the beat.

"Dance steps belong to a different species" and there's the way "classicism exhibits the body." Toe steps: "which look like tiny stilts the girl is treading on." "She can spin on them [toe shoes] like a bat out of hell." Steps that resemble a vertical balance like a butterfly.

Observational poetics. I love this natural attentiveness to the animal kingdom even as when moving to the urban centers and the waxing and waning of influence there; inventions "extending from nowadays back into a collective past" that always include the animal. There's Pound's idea that in the mind of the poet, all times are contemporaneous, and it certainly seems true in Edwin's big mind. Dante and Boccaccio dancing in village festivals (which often celebrate the harvest or the hunt). Pipers playing as tots "tried to do the steps before they could keep time." I felt dizzy reading this again, thinking of ritual, the contemporary, the difficult disconnect from our animal world, what's getting lost in how we don't notice minute particulars of life around us or examine a "pleasure in grace" as Edwin always did. Is it the artist's job to come to time? An innate thing to keep time, or shape time. What do you think? How does he illuminate our present? How does the "classic" feel now that "classicism has stretched the ancient country steps" and "ballet has kept the gift of harmony it began with." As he watched ballet, history seemed to vanish. Do you ever feel this? I still do with Balanchine registering in the archive. And what about that insanity? Where is it?

I remember Edwin told me that as he kissed Balanchine in his death casket, he felt that "dance will wane." Who could fill the master's shoes? He referred to the NYC Ballet. Has it? Was the training, Balanchine's inordinate keen eye, his beat, going to go soft? It's hard when the masters pass away, how to hold particular lineage. But we don't need dynasties either. I worry about a war on memory. I worry about corruption. He implied something would be corrupted.

Edwin was a classicist, interested in precision and discipline in ballet and in his own poetry as well. He was fond of end-rhymes and a kind of containment in spite of skewed syntactical logic. He was fastidious with his poems. He wrote sonnets primarily. But they never feel staged. William Carlos Williams makes a famous statement apropos the sonnet—really a moratorium—"You've got to cut his legs off [like a crab] to make him fit." But Edwin's sonnets never feel that way, tight as they are at times. Lush is this in its power of "longing." Edwin, the complex Romantic:

> Harbor, lost is the Greece when I was ten that
> Seduced me, god-like it shone; in a dark town, trembling
> Like a runaway boy on his first homeless night
> Ahead I rush in the fearful weep of longing

But it's this "both both" dance between the classical (at times Romantic) and the so-called modern or postmodern. His negative capability and neutrality as a viewer and participant. And the stretch of the ongoing sonnets, his perfected form, a great motion.

> Disorder, mental, strikes me; I
> Slip from my pocket Dante to
> Chance hit a word, a friend's reply
> In this bar; bare, dark avenue
> The lunge of headlights, then bare dark
> Cross on red, two blocks home, old Sixth
> The alive, the dead, answer, ask
> Miracle consciousness I'm with
> At home cat chirps, Norwegian sweater
> Slumped in the bar, I mind Dante
> As dawn enters the sunk city
> Answer a one can understand

Actual events are obscure
Though the observers appear clear

The contact, feel its motion, verbs that move: "strikes," "slip," "chance hit," "lunge," "cross," "chirps," "slumped." "Miracle consciousness" that seems to resound with the poet's, the cat's consciousness, and Dante's.

In terms of consciousness, Edwin characterizes the dancer remaining himself and not congealing to an "impersonal instrument." I am curious how current "modern" choreographers see this—how, like Balanchine, they work with specific bodies. I see contemporary work that seems more regimental, so to speak; bodies interchangeably and irritatingly obvious. It seems important to allow dancers their bodily autonomy with their particular alignments. Then inside the audience there's a grip on the imagination toward these subtle particulars.

I remember Edwin was commenting on dancers' ankles as they rested. On the perfect way the costume extended the leg. Another odd stretch of Suzanne Farrell's neck.

(Audience! Audience! Look, look, I wanted to say, see what Edwin sees!)

Edwin warmed to the occasion of the distinct balletic move in an intimate, amused way. Often smiling.

One could talk about the nonverbal meanings of "kinetic transformation." In poetry we talk about the "kinetics" of things, and "high-energy constructs," which take the pressure off meaning, message, story. A relief at times. Edwin was often kind to narrative storytellers (Martha Graham). And he embraced the narratives of Rudy Burckhardt's movies. He plays an amazing Scrooge in the film *Money:* sinister, cackling, his body postures assume the hilarious and perfect humor for complicated appetite and consumption around money. Edwin had studied "grotesque dance" in Europe, performing in Berlin.

Animating one's perceptions, indeed, was what Edwin did for me. I remember being on his rooftop once and seeing those Chelsea streets in a whole new way, all that liquid held in the water towers, we mused about that. And now as people have gotten noisier, I have to remember to appreciate some aspect of their bodies in public. The grace of a shoulder and its pause against a wall. Someone agitated in the street. The teen sprawled in a subway car. Couples embracing, couples arguing. Sometimes it's hard. I don't enjoy everyone fixated on little screens. What would Edwin say about our turning into cellular cyborgs? He also taught patience and avoidance.

And then it was wonderful when we were both introduced to Douglas Dunn. I sensed they would enjoy each other's company. It makes me cry. I remember the day in 1975 because it's in the poem I wrote for Douglas, entitled "Our Past":

> The night we met, June 6, we'd come out of the
> New York Church to observe a performer jumping
> over signposts
> I was with my friend, a mentor, much older
> You were introduced to him, to me
> You said you'd followed me out from that night where
> the continent divides, where my heart divided

I remember Edwin getting out of the cab once with Douglas and me and then our wishing we had stayed with him and gone for coffee, which he liked to do, at the all-night diner. I think watching dance animated his whole being into the night. I don't remember the party we went to. We could have been listening to Edwin.

Edwin was very attentive. He was supportive in generative ways. Towards one's creativity, what would be interesting for you to *see,* to read. I was not my frenetic self around him. Being with him calmed me, slowed me down, although my mind was racing to stay on a wavelength with his. Slowing to the details, the ordinary miracles . . . The way you need to read books and watch dance and often write poetry. I inherited his Dent edition of *Paradiso*. He read Dante slowly.

He commented on my Nova Convention (1978) reading and I can't imagine him now being at that edgy glamorous rock 'n' roll event (which was essentially honoring William S. Burroughs). He said I could be a Greek tragedian. He had this classical bent, of course, studying Greek and Latin as a teen at Hotchkiss; it's in his work. I took it as a compliment. He liked the very early poem "Giant Night." And the "stride" of other early poems, fast and breezy. He commented on *First Baby Poems*. They had some classical discipline. He was interested in Buddhism, knew quite a bit through his own study and reading of dharma texts. We spoke about Arthur Waley's *Monkey*. Alan Watts was "okay." I saw Edwin at times as the monkish aesthete. He was born in China, same time as my son's grandmother on Reed Bye's side. She was British, thin and smart and witty. They were alike in some larger generational civilized ways.

He was curious about my politics but kept his own counsel on these matters. The best political stance. I toned down my socialist, sometimes anarchist, rage around him.

He saw I had these infrastructure capabilities as director of the Poetry Project, and he knew my frustrations in particular about the sound quality in the church. It was always best if you could find the spot where the pulpit had been, the acoustics were designed to broadcast from there, without any sort of technology. But we usually missed it. Once, he told me it didn't matter: "What's important, Anne, is that people *strain* to listen. It puts them on the edge of their seats." He was sly and playful about a lot of things.

I enjoyed being around Edwin, éminence grise, during the Robert Wilson years, with the evolving magic of Bob's early pieces. The gatherings at the Byrd Hoffman School of Byrds played an important part in Edwin's life—a time of artistic hospitality as Bob so admired Edwin. He was courted and responsive in this community; the Byrds family adored him. *Einstein on the Beach* had multiple levels, layers, thirty-six performers, all extraordinary. A brilliant luminous intervention in our lives. We were so elevated, happy watching it.

But most enjoyable was having him in the next seat at the ballet. In that theatre of epiphanies! Feeling his pleasure.

About on an earlier Wilson production, Edwin said: "You can describe three images or four, or you can describe thirty or forty of them if you have the time. . . . But what you can't describe is the logical narrative connection. And the psychological connection."

He was extremely fastidious when Larry Fagin and I were working with him on *Snoring in New York,* an edition of his work, but he insistently wanted to refine the poetry until the last minute. We worried it wasn't easy for him. His perfectionism was a kind of torture.

He had self-published his first two books and had not been included in several important New York School anthologies, which seems a shocking oversight on the part of the editors. Frank O'Hara had written about his poetry for *Poetry* magazine in 1957, reviewing *Mediterranean Cities, Sonnets.* But Edwin had a scant poetry publishing record. Ted Berrigan's *C* magazine (1963) featuring Edwin was a great boon, which is where I had a first dose of his work. It was an honor, later, also to be doing the Full Court Press book. I always wanted him to read his own work at the Poetry Project, but that was anathema to him. But I think the way people have come to his work—where you have to seek it out, or come upon it surreptitiously—has been interesting. Allen would ask about his "ethereality." He's sort of "self-secret," as they say in spiritual traditions about the treasured oral teaching and transmissions. It meets his ethos in a way, not that he was playing hard to get. In a sense Edwin was a self-sufficient culture of One.

Anne Waldman with Allen Ginsberg and Edwin Denby
at the Gotham Book Mart, 1970.

Impossible Poetry?

Can we be comfortable saying that "Stanza XVI" by Gertrude Stein is arguably one of the most clunky passages ever written—a seemingly impossible text. It is part of a much longer discursive serial poem, *Stanzas in Meditation*, that Stein wrote during her "middle period," between 1929 and 1933. Considered one of the most difficult texts of her oeuvre, the whole of the mammoth book is a heroic foray into uncharted poetic territory whose only subject matter is the act of writing itself. It is not a magnetizing poem, lusting poem, or an adorable poem, it's a deadpan bastion, a battleship. It's an argument between boredom and attention and the increments of time and language. It is a wild experiment begging patience; it seems composed by a willful child or someone with a highly charged creative and insouciant sensibility. It challenges as it obscures, yet something in *Stanzas in Meditation* invites readers in—not simply to *make sense* of it all but actually to *stop making sense,* as the pop song goes. Oddly, this thrust feels generative. One looks to a stripped-down vocabulary of abstract prepositions and pronouns, cut from their moorings, and especially to the ubiquitous *they,* repeated twenty-five times in this stanza. Who are "they," and does it matter? *They* has entered the lexicon in a new way. It is a great pleasure to introduce *they* as a new identity and see through the lens of gender fluidity.

What matters to me is that the emphasis of this poem is off meaning and onto language, grammar, and modest connective words that may be obstinate and willful. As such, it suggests a new way of reading, an adventure into the stops and starts occasioned by an unfamiliar positioning of nonexpressive, nonemotional words. The process actually becomes mysterious.

I first encountered this seemingly impenetrable text when I began reading it aloud some years ago with my students in the class "Mind Gertrude Stein," a title that alluded to the rhythms of her "mind grammar," as we call it at the Kerouac School. Reading *Stanzas in Meditation* aloud was the only way "in" for me and for the students in my class. My eyes would not take in the flatness—dullness, almost—of language on the page, and I had to hear the floating pronouns to give them their proper due (although this had nothing to do with meaning). I wasn't reading this lengthy (nearly two-hundred-page) serial poem aloud to make sense; rather, I was reading aloud for the tonal logic, which had its own eccentric dance of ideas, "dance of the intellect." Suddenly the writing was a rich tapestry of dancing grammar and opacity.

In the seventies I attended and was involved with the historic all-night readings of Stein's novel *The Making of Americans* (an extremely fluid text in so many ways, especially by comparison) in New York City, which included the participation of musician John Cage, among others. Everyone read in particular inimitable and expressive ways, beautifully various. (Cage was bemused and earnest, as I recall.) But reading *Stanzas in Meditation* aloud with my students was a very different kind of experience. Its repetitions were fewer and more fractured. It was poetry, not prose, and by Stein's definition, utilized fewer verbs. It lacked the participial fervor in *The Making of Americans* and was neither as flowing nor as exotic. Where does one travel with this monster poem and its Roman numerals, which seem almost merciful in suggesting the parameters of the stanza? My students wanted some relief, a break from what seemed an arbitrary, meandering exercise. Irritating. We looked first to the patterns of meter and rhythm and the number of lines. Stein followed her own investigation into the diagramming of sentences, and we, in turn, followed her. She showed the way meditative thought could leap into language, skewing meaning. But we also "minded her," as it were, succumbing to her demand to abandon preconceptions of a normative poetry.

Next we started underlining all the repeating words in selected stanzas, hoping to create a kind of "score" for analysis. I color-coded phrases, waiting for a breakthrough. But the sense suddenly did not matter. There was a pleasure beyond getting meaning or message, of actually being able to read the words as discrete entities. It was the little words (look to the little ones, the "minute particulars," as William Blake admonishes) that Stein brought attention back to, the words we take for granted, the connective tissue that is suddenly, in her purpose, the meat and bones as well.

This particular stanza (XVI) opens with ten dull, nondescriptive, monosyllabic words. I take this as a challenge. Two uses of the word *will* (ah, there's a focus), and out of that spins a typical Steinian rhyme play: *still, until.* The word *will* is repeated ten times and recalls Shakespeare's wordplay around his own name, Will, in the sonnets. As an exercise, I suggest reading

Shakespeare's "Sonnet CXXXV" aloud, then reading Stein's "Stanza XVI" and listening for a resemblance in the tonal qualities, a delightful flurry in the meaning and message of the poem. It presents a conundrum and a close reading, in any case.

Stein's stanza repeats. There's that word *they* numerous times. *They* is the not-so-secret character or mover of the text. The initial *I* of the first line completely drops away, and this brings to mind the question of Stein's improvisation and the dynamics of an "I" and an all-encompassing "they." She plays out all the qualities and possibilities of a word that for most represents the mass of humanity or, in some cases, a paranoid sense of that mass. She positions this panoply of *they* up against the opening, "Could I think." Such a gambit for a writer. It's as if language had assumed ownership of itself. There is a wonderful solipsism in this approach, this uniquely Steinian stance. And the poem starts to feel fluid liquidity yet all the while eschews transparency.

A key line for me in this regard is also "Often left to them to come to arrange this," which is self-referential to the use of the writing and arranging of the word *they,* and suggests metatext underpinnings, one of the great pleasures of reading her. Vocabulary simple, constructs complicated, the emotion readers might feel in response is conflicted.

But in the embarrassing search for meaning, which is a terrible habit, is the line, "It is an estimate of ferocity," which really leaps out for its tangibility. It seems to sum up the thrust or force of her in the work and in the world. That she—as artist—in her calculation, in her *judging of the value,* the "estimate," is what we are left with. For this reader, it *is* a "ferocity," a stubborn willfulness to reconfigure language and imagination. And she is willful and obstinate yet compromised in her politics and in her big annoying ego. She had to survive, stay alive: both as a lesbian and a Jew. One feels her urgency but makes no excuses for her shameful compromise (survival mechanism) with Vichy. But may admire a stanza. May make her a hero of her own cause for writing. Her "collaboration," more of a friendship, with Bernard Faÿ during the Vichy France regime has sullied her reputation. He was helpful to her needs and continued residency. She did not speak out against Vichy and its horrors. Readers draw lines here. She is nevertheless one of the most influential and gustatory, voluminous writers of our time. A sacred monster.

"Stanza XVI" by Gertrude Stein, from *Stanzas in Meditation*

Could I think will they think that they will
Or may they be standing as seated still
For which they will leave it make it be still
That they will reach it for which they will until
They should be said to be planned for which they will
Not which they need not plan not more than will
It is an estimate of ferocity which they would not know
Not with surprise nor from the wish
That they would come at all
May they be mentioned
For which they can not be only lost
For which they will may they may they come in
For which they will not but very likely
But they can not be there from which they will
For they may be with that kind that is what is
When they can like it as they do
But which they can not be for them
All made as they are not without it
Often left to them to come to arrange this
More than they can at most
It was not only that they liked it
It is very kind of them to like it.

Architecture of Breathing

I am the first and the last
I am the honored one and the scorned one
I am the whore and the holy one
I am the wife and the virgin
I am the mother and the daughter
. . .
I am the solace of my labor pains.
I am the bride and the bridegroom
And it is my husband who begot me
I am the mother of my father
And the sister of my husband
And he is my offspring

      —FROM THE NAG HAMMADI CODICES

"The thunder, perfect mind,"
he will say . . .
  and then I'll interrupt
(concerns a strange eye—
      fixity of illusion
  one eye seemingly wider than other)
but can you see me, poet,
    in the garden
a seedling, wild
    in form of attention?

  then later another he,
he will say nothing
but hours later:
"to name is to destroy"
look at me, trawling
or say something

he being another:
"bubble of idle chatter"
from below
　with alternate visual foci . . .
　　　investigate my split infinitives
why are they always *saying* at me?
　polarity, echolocation, *eyeing* me
　　　　　no reconciliation for art

I get it I get
it: desire
investigate this, X says
　　useful quizzical animation
perpetual or
　　　　below motion,
a cross-border artist
what does their exile look like?

moan how difficult those guys are
the men the men the men
suffering idle stars?
labyrinthine zones with attar, musk,
　wasp nest, earwigs, nouns, nouns, nouns,
we had bouncing up the ground
　and a roof on planet Mercy
we had and I was done their telling me
　　　　　what to do
and needed ways in which to communicate
　　grapple, back off

might I invent sounds created from poems
unrelated to breathing?

"Biggest Possible Assortment of Available Things"

I met John when I was twenty years old, still in college getting a different dose of American poetics. A more hetero model with anguished (white) men who had served in the military and were "tamed by *Miltown,* we lie on mother's bed." I had been to readings by Robert Lowell, Richard Wilbur, John Berryman, Howard Nemerov, all at experimental Bennington College, where Pound was verboten, Gertrude Stein was considered "superfluous" and Williams and Stevens and Moore not much taught or "contextualized." And yet I was able to invite Robert Kelly and Stan Brakhage to campus. And Jonas Mekas and his brother Adolfas travelled to show films and make one: *Hallelujah the Hills.* But I already had an alternative life in poetry through the Donald Allen anthology, little magazines, and from attending the Berkeley Poetry Conference in 1965 (Ted Berrigan was holding up the New York School banner in this alien territory) and my mother's letters to me from her Bill Berkson workshop at the New York School. Frank O'Hara was unavailable to come to Berkeley, and John was living in France. We wanted John Ashbery to come home from France! The second-generation NYC School would soon be crashing in the railroad apartment on St. Mark's Place.

The title "Whiter Shade of Pale" from Procol Harum comes to mind, keeps returning since John died. I remember it was a favorite line of John's, and I also remember that when he saw the Bob Dylan movie *Renaldo and Clara* some years later, he was amused with my brief appearance and moment where I say, "I'd rather be home reading a good book." John seemed oddly au courant with the pop times. A kind of hip insouciance, quick-witted parlays, always kindly. Everything was fair game for his curiosity.

We moved through many of the same scenes, parties, occasions, ritualistic holidays together in the midsixties into the early seventies. Flirting at a Lita Hornick party. He might have been at the party where Kenneth Koch stripped off his shirt. The first Angel Hair book Lewis Warsh and I published was by Lee Harwood, love poems dedicated to John, with a Joe Brainard cover: *The Man with Blue Eyes.*

I had worked briefly at WRVR radio on a work-study semester at Riverside Church in 1965, where I was able to help create a few poetry shows, and John recorded there. Then it was suddenly summer and Frank O'Hara had died and that was devastating. We were reading him always and he was the saint, the secret hero of all the ruses. And the Poetry Project was born, I always felt, out of the transition, this weird gap, of losing Frank O'Hara; born out of his ashes.

It was an oddly spiritual poetry time. I was an eager child of poetry and John Ashbery was a breakthrough poet, having riveted an ever-growing number of friends, artists, readers, strangers, young poets to an elevated shift of frequency. We would work harder. The apocalypse had taken place with *The Tennis Court Oath* (1962), with its mystical dream fragment cut-ups / non sequiturs, shaped to intellect and sound: shimmering language. Also plainspoken, matter-of-fact, colloquial. Its title the flashpoint of the French Revolution.

Even as you lick the stamp
A brown dog lies down beside you and dies

John's poetry didn't seem to own, cling to, or identify with its experience, didn't beg on emotion and ponderous content. Things were symbols of themselves, not pointing toward weightier meaning and conclusion. "The real subject is its form," Ashbery had said of Raymond Roussel. I remember sitting with *Rivers and Mountains* when it came out in 1966, on the black-and-yellow-patterned sofa on St. Mark's Place, trembling with excitement and anticipation.

Perhaps we ought to feel with more imagination . . .
You were my quintuplets when I decided to leave you

You could take anything from the words. Beauty. Truth. Existence. Ambiguity. It was the elegant arrangement and attention and sound of wild mind. The mind was the subject, a haven free of baggage and usual referents, you made friends with it. It could expand all sensibility, stab your heart. You didn't know where you were going when you latched to the poems. "The Skaters" was like a dream. The surface as smooth as ice, dazzling.

And there was "A Blessing in Disguise" that still makes me cry, a poem to read to lovers. One of the beautiful poems from some long-ago world.

The text below is from an interview John and Kenneth Koch concocted that first appeared in *The World,* the mimeo magazine from the Poetry Project. There's reference to Cleanth Brooks and obsession with ambiguity. In the air with William Empson too. They were all about "ambiguity."

John had the right take.

ASHBERY: I was just wondering if ambiguity is really what everybody is after, but if it is the case, why?

KOCH: People seem to be after it in different ways. Actually one tries to avoid the Cleanth Brooks kind, no? It seems an essential part of true ambiguity that it not seem ambiguous in any obvious way. Do you agree?

A: I don't know. I'm still wondering why all these people want that ambiguity so much.

K: Have your speculations about ambiguity produced any results as yet?

A: Only this: that ambiguity seems to be the same thing as happiness—or pleasant surprise, as you put it. (I am assuming that from the moment that life cannot be one continual orgasm, real happiness is impossible and pleasant surprise is promoted to the front rank of the emotions.) Everybody wants the biggest possible assortment of all available things.

Shadow Behind Eclipse

for John Ashbery

When he died, a temperature went down
Trees in the sky above Flatirons, tremor there
Oh didn't, then did   See?
We were driving in the canyon moons ago
    when he had said then "closing in"
Fool for this love
He was our drumming ritual if you were a
    a berserker
    and willed by constellations
He was our prize for being born
This world through school time, through bliss
through saltiness in the question
Can gentlemen do without?
Never retreat from scrutiny
    or miss the enemy, burnt leaf smell like resin
He was our fear of a sentence half-dreamed
    if we couldn't seize the whole
He was our vessel
    cave and boot
    train ride to the province
    meandering by river
Panic to be left out of this
Landscape, a picnic
Whole tome memorized, many colors
He was our vanguard of nonself,
    scent and doubt
Of deep carriage into the unknown
What do you know of it
    if you know him not?
When he did laugh he did and muse
That was a blue eye special
He was putting things

next to one another
    you too somehow included
They you it—things—didn't have to bond
    but in poetry happen
And now listen to his voice with
    eyes gone wild for flowers
Scratchy reel-to-reel, 1966
Sacred fury of a primordial world
Half mannish garb on the sentence
    a profile in the hallway
    across all crystal neuro pathways
Mirror, mirror?
Up to nature and we had a glimpse
He was our respite,
Midnight excursions off limits
Sometimes a candle at the brain wondering "fallen star"
What rhymed with it?
"Espoir," hope?
Blood in the heart, held supine
He was our cosmography in a better world
    you could count on, relief, release

Nostalgia

for Jane Freilicher

To you, muse who
rocked the brains of
so many of my heroes
You a hero too
for wise quip bon mot and
panoramic eye
And stand up all-around-beauty
enters the room
our own Barbara Stanwyck
glamorous, slender, assured,
Always gracious if not a bit impatient
Why aren't these people wittier?
Perky word-monger wonder
Figure of a liberated tongue
Not miss a beat
Voice distinct in the ear
It was your classy parties,
with drink and din
Kinetics of best talk in town
Morris, Barbara, John,
Yvonne
Alex, Joe LeSueur, Kynaston
Rudy, Red, Ada, Ned,
Larry, Harry, Mimi, Maxine
Kenneth's smile,
hubby Joe's hospitality
But always a bit of intimidation
'round you
with your aura,
Those staggeringly great poems
writ in your honor
amplifying the head

You turn crazy Jane of poetic trope into
upscale glowing modish madcap Jane
Legendary gossip's elegance
mounting around you, star,
La Freilicher
formidable and by contrast
although you were never loud
the quietest paintings
as if noise forever absent
or transmuted into
compressed tension
And arrangement-transfer
was perfectly natural
John Ashbery calls "tentative"?
Could we dare say "egoless"
in this tribute?
Spaces between objects
come onto this window ledge
this table, center of the world,
a hearth to mute a button on the roar
Hush here before your
stroke and palette
Can't thank you enough
ingenious painter
for these and continuity
But back back come back again
Can't get enough of the parties
of yesteryear
Terrific Fifth Ave apartment's readiness,
gleam, of us shining too
Happy to be in your realm
a moment and
Jimmy showing up in what
Kenward called
his Lub period
with biker chains around his neck
and Joe Brainard lanky
innocently louche

and people still smoked
I remember being haunted indelibly:
how get so lucky to be *here*?
High tone and that inimitable
talk again
will never be the same
in purgatorial New York
Caught on time spiral, Jane
helping many of us late arrivistes enter
the Academy of the New York School future
which opened its doors to us

Tenderness & Gristle: Joe Brainard

I remember daydreams of being a singer all alone on a big stage with no scenery, just a spotlight on me, singing my heart out, and moving my audience to tears of love and affection.

——JOE BRAINARD

Joe Brainard had a delicate, nuanced, loving, amused, frustrated way with paint. He was frustrated but he had a way. He would start up and start up, he had his hero de Kooning not in mind but above his head, he would start and not fail, but he was thinking big in a small frame and all the de Koonings could writhe inside Joe's wide spirit. And he found a big way in drawings and collage and commentary, *memoir* is too weak, a pedestrian word for the insouciant, brilliant, shimmering honest line breath in memory, "takes" of memory he's amused by and remembered in all their gristle. How entertaining that is. You were in referent to what? Poetry, love, hybrid with another. In "I Love You de Kooning," he draws a hint of woman, a referent that is funny, that is flattering, and the words are Bill Berkson's of his fabled friend de K. Look, that is like furniture and woman that is a mountain, an alembic of energy. Bold black line = a woman's breasts. A mark on the void, a joke: "You bet!" In "de Kooning Nancy," Nancy comes to birth in a cloud of chaos. He drew me in a formal drawing portrait once—young, worried, I look like a teen male pop star I won't name. Static of face, frozen for time. But the other drawings; best sense of what my body might be looking like to him. Light and shadow. And he tried me in paint, naked. That worked best. I remember how he wrecked it, took out the face, there was some red paint, I remember frustration. I would suggest, beg, maybe try again? Painting was the challenge of the big gesture of saying I am here. *I know what I am doing,* masterfully. Paint was a trickster always slipping off, a thief, and I was saying to both of us, tender and vulnerable, I'll be a better poet, but assuredly you, Joe, can paint. You *are* painting. And then paint was getting in the way. Talk about Jasper, about Andy, about Alex Katz, about Man Ray about Jane Freilicher. What is the equivalent in poetry? If you loved them you became intimidated,

I said. I said you are the eye that could see the little things so much better, not always big sweep. You are a genius. They seemed to vibrate even more. About Joan Mitchell. I remember thinking how being a woman in big paint would need even more nerve; we talked about nerve. Her tough badass talk, smart truck driver mouth. Big, her reach. Joe a saint of modesty. Self-portraits (his) (of himself) sweet beauties. *Know thyself well before you start singing.* "I remember in Dayton, Ohio, the art fair in the park where they made me take down all my naked self-portraits." And in another guise nude, head hidden, odalisque, and remember trust felt in being seen, being caught glance of, being loved by Joe Brainard. I felt like I was making it alongside him. Was I really sleeping? He caught me many times in life, hidden, was hiding my love in him, many ways you catch a person's heart. Joe Brainard, had grace and innocence with words, you could never stop the way he got it right, the flavor of the time, the ethos caught mind—stream of time—sweep and minutia of time, mood, and let us be honest, this is Joe Brainard no one else who remembers this way, speaking. Joe would work a tan, lathered with oil in the summer grass, he would work at it and then it wouldn't matter so much staying inside reading, or going pale with books, and book afire in his steady hand could be an attention span, then reading and before lying in the grass and on a chaise longue that too, another side of reading and writing outside, a piece of a turf integrated with memory and dailiness, outside and inside-the-house ritual. And screen door bangs for a cigarette, a drink of soda with ice, you hear it in the glass. Summer is ice in a glass. Correspondence, Ron and Pat, collaboration. *The Vermont Notebook* with John Ashbery. We are in a house, it is the largess of lover and friend. Then you go in, get pale in the winter, in a city. Joe Brainard said he would forget what he read but it was the doing of it, ritual salvation, practice to be somewhere else being that description and with all the anatomy of persons and their psychology. An entertainment, heartbreak, in the moment, in the hours. I understood later how you didn't remember what you wrote in the unattachment of Joe. But you were on to something as you wrote me re: "I Remember." You said you had assurance and you were having a vision in that, and like unconditional thinking it is coming along, pouring out from you. When you find it, how generous to freely associate. Funny to be another person, amused by persons, contradictory, how unconscious you become inside another person, then unreal. And the peculiar mores and details of all you notice and hiding queer and then discovery, curiosity, and it is sex you are thinking of. They are our puppets in art and we are safe. They are "so real" and you can be sad with them. The body as desire. You spend more days lasting in books, a kind of cover for melancholia or purpose, because in books you have purpose, you are going to be the mechanism that meets halfway. A spring and a lock. Reading books by English lady authors, way to follow the day is through an English lady author and her weathers. And wit and self-deprecating melancholia. One-way conversations. What was the pressure to be and what rippling never to brag about it. I have a portrait of Kenward Elmslie's dog Whipoorwill painted in a cloud of confetti and that is the mind of this hound, a heavenly confetti. It bounces and it is the thought of a dog bouncing as he meditates, resting to leap. Painted like a dream creature. And with the gristle of a master. We are all the dog here in a pasture of fantasy. We are all dogs in a small portrait painted in a summer in Vermont. I call the painting "Whipoorwill Buddha." It is July. Restless and stammering and gift bearing.

LET GO

for Lewis Warsh

I said we started it

We founded it *then*

Angel Hair

That very night.
The Robert Duncan reading in Berkeley
1965

The conference
Night we met

Robert Duncan commanded we make a magazine

You always said no, later, it was . . . it was the car ride

In a car we founded it

How do you exactly found something in a car?

It showed the temper of our various minds

Talking in a car is a magazine I suppose

I wanted it to be falling in

Love was also this idea

That night we were falling in love and we would

Be really good together making something good

You never just fall in love with a person

And make love with them

That we make something that's the whole point

That we are inside poetry and that Robert Duncan

Commanded this

I know he did

And he is a magus

Poetry was love for us

Poetry is mysterious

How could he not have cast a spell?

You were conversant in the most exciting poetry

And the gossip about Jack Spicer hating the Beats

He wouldn't be part of the conference & then he died

Too young to think of a house,

What did we think when falling in love

There is no future

We are right now

What I liked was being in this crowd of poetry

Want to make together another reality now

(There would be babies with others,

That's making time enough or no time for that)

A magazine is a paper window, also a car window

Keep opening the papery curtains or

Let the air in

And maybe you need a windshield wiper

And music and someone else driving

To make a magazine

A bedroom of strange bedfellows (Williams)

We were the next night somewhere on Nob Hill

A fancy part of town

You were kind and very beautiful, slender gentle body

I'd never been there but you had a story with the people in the apartment

Beautiful young men

I was a new tangle

I remember standing in front of a mirror

On lysergic acid going though all my lifetimes and especially this one

I had a vision of all the persons I knew and

How we had passed through some ancient anxieties but it was important

That we were all still together, changing how we looked, morphing

Something radically changing us, fast from infant

But we were all feeling urgent about knowing something

Together and doing something

What was it?

Why were we all looking up?

My vision was look up, all of it, the people I loved

Mother Frances, look up

And you there too, my new friend

I needed an assignment for them because of love

I thought what an egomaniac

If I could just get one assignment from "up there"

From the quiet stars

I could take it on to help

Everyone take on each other for everything

They also wanted to make something together in the vision

That was what I was supposed to make, maybe it would work for everyone

What to do, thinking

And watched my face age and turn to dust. Poof!

That was the point that I disappear

It was a wandering day, did I carry / have that idea about

A magazine from the day before?

I can't remember but I wanted to be around words

And remember struggling to get over the bridge to

Allen Ginsberg reading, the conference it felt important.

And we were stopping and sitting down and

Lost in the lines on our hands, and streetlamp light

And undulation . . .

Lines of undulation . . . galaxies

I felt very light and drawn to this fluid person next to me

We were poets we were going to be poets together

And make something, syllables coming in the air

The street

That was a feminine plan

A path through parks and other places, a wandering line, a femme plan

Manicured parts but action in a garden

And plants and trees, very luscious, soft, and when

They were not

They were reminders of plant intensity

Vibrating, striking

Out

Pushing you away, then embrace

Very animate plants

We, then erotic

If you sat with them you were with them, thinking with them

I didn't know this city San Francisco at all but

It was many rays of light coming through a night

And sitting by water

Where could that have been

Like velvet

Sometimes a building looking up

Walking up hills, my insides are ribbons of light

Scent of jasmine, I am thinking

And we couldn't get over the bridge

And later I thought this was like karma,

This was action, this was where you learn about action

Whether or not you get across a bridge to hear

Allen Ginsberg for the first time is action or not

And when you don't because you think it is important

And you think you missed it

Then it's karma, it will come back to haunt you

Where you meant to fall in love, or a poetry reading

Fall in love

What we could do and did, what we didn't couldn't do

How far we could go   years

Never let go

Letter from Ted Berrigan

19 July 71

Dear Annie

You're getting to be the Sonia Sanchez of the NY school! What a tough broad!

Alas, I don't have any Chas Rezinkoff tape, tho I did play it yr ex-house. Probably Harris sold it for money to buy smack. Last I saw it it was on a footlocker in the corner near the window next to a syringe with blood in it.

I do have a tape by me and you, but I need it to listen to all the time so I can be great. However, when I go to Bolinas Weds. (two days from now), I'll take it along and copy it via my tape recorder and Tom's. I hope I send the tape, but if I don't (you know me & mail), I'll hand it to you personally when you and the star of ANOTHER WORLD wander out to here. O.K.? Don't curse, now you know I love you, it's not my fault I'm a shiftless ne'er do well irresponsible lackadaisical dreamer. Love is what counts.

I loved the last WORLD, & my goofy collaboration with the spaceman. His poems are certainly getting terrific. Larry's, too.

Tomorrow I read with Robert Cyclops at the SF smalltime star scene. We will freak their balls off, as we did at "The National Poetry Festival" where the stars were No. 1 Philip Whalen, and No. 2 Me. I'm getting to be a regular Elmer Gantry of the public platform. But best of all (there) was me running a seminar on collaborations, and making Phil, Bob C., Joel, Paul Blackburn (incidentally a great star himself), Anslem etc., and 20 students write one "I wish" line each. Phil Whalen wrote in his impeccable scribble, "I wish Lasange Verde." Joel wrote, "I wish unlimited bar credit." I have all the pages here. If you are doing another WORLD I could type all up as a poem: they read terrifically, about 25 lines.

Bob Creeley & Phil said, "what this poetry festival needs is Anne Waldman!" Alas, what it had was Diane Wakoski. Anne, you should push a little and horn in on such things, like I do. Me & Phil were the two guys who asked in to that scene, and we hogged a lot of the action once there. I told Phil, "you're the president now, babe," and he said, sadly, "it's true. Chas Olson told me the same thing two years ago." How about that!

After Whalen's reading Anselm, who was also terrific (and come to think of it who also buttd his way in) turned to me and said, "well we came here to be told and now we've been told." Whoopee!

I wish you were here to frown at me and make me giggle.
Love and kisses,
Teddy

Practical Thunder

for Cedar Sigo

I remember phone calls to Diane after a breakup
she like Joanne would advise that you keep the domicile
somehow
that was more important than heartbreak
a domicile was
somehow tangible
where will you work, set up your shrine?
living is too expensive it's not economical
can't someone live in the closet in a garage
in a shed?
work it out, take turns
don't
be privileged about this
nightmare of survival . . .
not wise ecology
but the *pain* you'd say
stay friends and there would be that
lovers to brothers
get out from under what burns you about Kerouac School
your great vow
they say it's not a school without a building
an endowment
supposed to get more academic? don't spend all the time resisting
but of course all the time, resist
make shape of your own imagining for it
what you would like to envision
if you split with that, a school you make, think about how
they'd have to deal with the load you lifted
panic about the archive maybe
someone would wake up but maybe not
if you're so damn wide awake no one will think they have to be
too scared to let go

hmmmm. guess so
but promised Robin Blaser
we'd all be in archive heaven together
& Amiri said don't let them, our poets, get buried
don't forget, moonset,
the upside-down left-hand path
ulatbamsi (topsy-turvy)
who's in who's out
we're all the scandal
never be an apologist for anyone
not the godforsaken Beats, please
we will have our Beat day in court
her third-eyed high concern
out from inside was checking me out
through the wires
maybe feeling a pulse
inside
sympathy
how hand pulls hair back out of your eyes
what you taught me, wipe your eyes
ease, Anne not worry not so uptight
let things unfold of their own volition
don't push to study every
whichway of which of the magik arts
take a symbol—stay with it a witchy way
visualize as it moves through you
they'll come requesting you
the bodhisattvas I promise
the perfect symbol for Anne
the perfect yidam
inner deity's secret
I know I say *these things are symbols of themselves*
but don't you miss it?
it's always with me
you don't want to stop?
what about Bobby Dylan . . .
lucky to have seen him play live all those times
whatever the Thunder . . .

nice time nothing to cling to
how can poets live that luxury?
why can't rock and roll do more for the cause?
it's some kind of god-realm thing
what kind of music is it anyway?
I guess for the pleasure-god realm, deva loka
could you be jealous of the god realm?
I'll never be able to define that soft indulgence
& Ginzy? he wasn't there . . . with you when you met
Ali? at the Garden? backstage
& he said so you're a poet and you know it
then having to deliver a spontaneous poem
intersections for consociational map
with his bodyguards in pastel . . .
not more unlikely contenders
& the night Bob was purposely confusing
W. S. Burroughs with Tennessee Williams
and we were going to meet Raúl Castro
at a party where?
I'd say William and he'd say Tennessee?
I sometimes wanted to get to a monastery
you want to indulge, wait till the seat gets too hot and you crash
get back on stage for "Idiot Wind"
syndrome like a stone rolls
home is no direction
more like a tambourine scatters
it's the sexy subvocal of all the songs
when you hear the man talking
beyond himself
like Glenn Gould
humming with Bach

the inner tune

Part II: Techne

(craft, operative, episteme)

These poems are hangers   the assembly of suns
Velcro was invented in such a way
a swan song for sirens and beaded mulch
the poems will grow from time to time
poems of the hulking sack   poems of nebula
A whale tooth residue then a tissue
the poems constitute   ode to brute force
a prism height? the whole examination questionable
a scraping of chair legs across the rookery
an ausable automobile?   it would happen this way
the poem to its knees   there is no such person
poem like a false break in the weather
Poem like a village full of arms
never a snow like on this poem

—CLARK COOLIDGE

From the sparrows I've learned this and that,
from Germanic tribes, to gather thoughts in herds,

From the window blinds, from the sun decayed,
from the heart, a brimming record braised and turned.

—LISA JARNOT

Push, Push Against the Darkness:
The Iovis Trilogy:
AN INTERVIEW WITH JIM COHN

Part 1: *Stylus, Weapon, Scythe*

JIM COHN: You began work on *Iovis* Book I in the mid-1980s. Book I appeared in 1993. What were the circumstances that gave birth to your writing *The Iovis Trilogy: Colors in the Mechanism of Concealment* (Coffee House Press, 2011)? Did you conceive it as a trilogy all along?

ANNE WALDMAN: The plan went way back, was always a trilogy, the classical triad. Outer, inner, secret. Heaven, Earth, Man principle (which is the triad of the haiku), nirmanakaya, sambhogākaya, dharmakaya (realms of form, light, and emptiness—a Buddhist triad); and so on. Aeschylus's *Oresteia,* Dante's *Commedia.* Endless complicated triads. H. D.'s war trilogy as well, a deep bow of gratitude in my project to the power of her epic, written against a backdrop of war. I was also thinking in terms of a feminist plan of *explicating* the male, *usurping* with the female and the hermaphrodite, and then *resolving* in something transcendent beyond gender, perhaps. And personally there is first: imagination; second: the act of writing; and third: the act of vocalizing. The subtitle *Colors in the Mechanism of Concealment* came with "Book III: Eternal War" but seemed to serve the entire project with its implication of unmasking layers of "concealment." I wanted an expansive form that would make a demand on my time—tithe my time—at least a quarter century. That would be a record—a slice of history—for my son and his generation. It was interesting to publish *Iovis* gradually, as it unwound and progressed. *Iovis* is the generative of Jove, Zeus, and I was seeing how everything is *of* the Patriarch. The title came from a line of Virgil's "Iovis omnia plena," *all is full of Jove.* A trilogy was needed to cover, to pace the subject. And it is already possibly moving into Book IV.

JC: The physical production of your one-thousand-plus-page epic poem, as an object, a relic, is no small achievement. With its highly visual formal arrangement of words and images on the page, the sheer duration of the technical ink-based performance pushes the envelope of printing. How involved were you in the actual book's layout and design?

AW: I like the idea of the object, the relic. And I see it as a time machine too or a device you plug into a socket that activates a sound and light show. I was involved with the design and production. I wanted the Balinese figure dancing on the front cover. It's as I envisioned it, actually, once I knew they would not be able to afford a three-volume book set. I was both amused and horrified by the sheer size and heft at over one thousand pages and decided to embrace it, rather than feel embarrassed. The tome feels like—and carries the burden of—twenty-five years, the years spent on writing it and the actual documentary time frame of the poem, which is very different, say from *Manatee/Humanity* (Penguin Poets, 2009), an ecological narrative, which is meant to take place over three days, although it took three years to write. I was extremely fortunate to have, in my editors at Coffee House, a very supportive base and editing team. I was pleased they supported the image of the "plutonium pit" from Rocky Flats. And the drawings. And the skewed spelling. And all the rest: circles, triangles, stars, musical notation.

JC: What is the relationship between the "abstracts" or "narratives" that begin each section of *Iovis* and the "poem" that follows? How did you come upon that format? What models, if any, did you follow in doing that?

AW: Essentially it was meant as a guide for the reader through the tangles and turns of the poem, to locate place, site, event, state of mind. I always appreciate the prose abstracts or summaries to Dante's cantos, not his, I believe, but preparatory maps, and then wanting to include other events and details important to the poem but in a different mode or genre, somewhat like the alap in an Indian raga, where all the themes are laid out first. Victorian and other period novels carry heady explanations in their chapter headings. Perhaps a didactic thrust, but I felt essential to guide myself as well as the reader though this long montage-trajectory (as one reviewer said, *Iovis* is "not for the feint of heart"!) and have a kind of documentary "voice," as it were, which is another path of the rhizome. As in the *Commedia,* I used the first person with all its avatars and split personalities and doppelgängers, and the abstracts helped ground whoever the consciousness of the poem is. Clearly an amalgam.

JC: In the opening prose section at the beginning of "I Am the Guard" (269), you write of your cofounding of the Kerouac School and note your Jovian intention regarding the male poets you admired: "The challenge of the elder poet-men is their emotional pitch she wants to set her own higher than." Do you think *Iovis* achieved the "emotional pitch" that you measured your life and work against?

AW: I would hope so. It goes higher in pitch because of the advantage of distance, and of a feminist outrage. And my vocal chords reach the high notes. Of "coming after," so to speak, in the multiple guises that foreground the female, rather than have her being "reified" as with Charles Olson and William Carlos Williams. There was a way "she" gets lost in their epics. That clear-sighted seer, prophet is sidelined, she's not enough real flesh and blood with her own throbbing poet-consciousness. The feminist or queered consciousness in *Iovis* wants you to see where she has travelled—to the complicated tin and cardboard slums of India, to a survived yet struggling land where a whole generation (my own) is decimated (in Vietnam). As well as the millions of Vietnamese of the same generation. In his extraordinary *The H. D. Book,* which importantly explores the role women played in the creation of Modernism, Robert Duncan cites "the discordant note—the rant of Pound, the male bravado of Williams, the bitter anger of Lawrence" and calls them "purposeful overcharges" and speaks of theirs as a therapeutic art. I would agree. And we would share that. But the feminine principle of putting makeup on empty space seemed absent, and I was also driven to create (albeit with my comrade Allen G., as well initially with the very strong poet Diane di Prima) a zone, such as the Kerouac School, that would embed what I call the architecture of the feminine, that is the "environment," the space that allows gestation and generation. There's reference in the *Tao Te Ching* (sixth century BCE) to the "dark female-enigma" which is called the "root of heaven and earth," and this text says this spirit is like "gossamer, so unceasing it seems real. Use it: it's effortless." The environment is always there, waiting.

JC: I'm also thinking of the letter from "B. B." (294–295) in which the suggestion is you rely more on personal history rather than political or geologic history in the making of the poem and in doing so, create a different kind of poetry than the "masters." Although you obviously included this letter to argue the point that you had achieved a greater degree of accessibility to the reader, do you believe that *Iovis* is actually any less dense or complex or intellectual or made of arcana any less than those modernist poets such as Pound, Olson, H. D., Williams, etc.?

AW: No, I would say it is sometimes as dense in another way, documentary, perhaps, but also invokes Herodotus's "'istorin" to find out for oneself (the root of the word *history*), and emphasized much later by Olson, as a mode to explore the political history and life of this slice of war/lifetime. How infuriating it is to be continually born to war! That continues one's whole lifetime even as one protests it, what futility. It is perhaps a more *public* epic in this regard, and carries a ritual vocalization. And I was concerned with certain modalities of sound and enactment, as in the tribute section "Pieces of an Hour" to John Cage. And influenced, as well, by Tibetan and Balinese rites and practices.

JC: The multipersonae of a traveller of the physical dimension, as well as others, suggests a central concern of the poem. Travel grounds the traveller in the poem's wired global scale, its worldwide interplanetary scope. Its epic nature. Can you share a few of your itineraries while you were writing *Iovis* in terms of those specific locales that drove you to write sections based upon what you learned being there?

AW: I referred to India and Vietnam above, because there is a strong link to those places and their cultures and their role in my own life and poetics. I first travelled to India in the early 1970s as a curious spiritual pilgrim and "took refuge" and began a Buddhist practice with Tibetan teachers, but I was also enamored of Indian culture—Vedic chanting, the Bauls of Bengal, the raga as an expansive form inspired aspects of *Iovis* as well. But the reality of being offered an infant to take back to the US with me by a family in Bhubaneshwar was a startling and poignant "luminous detail" that conjured an extreme and hard reality. I couldn't comply but I could tell the story. That very area along the Bay of Bengal also suffered terrible floods after I left. In Vietnam—travelling primarily in the North—there were few people of my generation left, they had died in what they call "The American War." I felt a karmic pull toward my own generation, how much blood is on our hands, protest as we may? My father had served in WWII and that was still palpable, as I explore in the book, Korea was more distant, Vietnam was virtually in the living room and in the streets.

There's an earlier "History lesson for my son" on Vietnam and then the later pilgrimage, *Dark Arcana: Afterimage or Glow.* The trip up the Yangtze ("Tears Streak the Reddest Rouge" from Book III) was a revelation. This section comes out of notes from that trip. The gates of the Three Gorges Dam were like the gates of hell, the river itself the Styx. This monolithic dam misplaced whole villages and cultures, drowned important sites and historical artifacts, an ecological disaster as well.

JC: The mechanism of dis-concealment that I notice best is the invention of a multidimensional "both, both" "I" based upon the seventh-century BCE Greek poet Archilochus, who wrote of being a poet and a warrior, which became a model for Homer. You seem to have taken that as your own investigation into concealment of women when you write: "I am both *therapon*" (75). Can you discuss how you came upon this multi-alternative "I" and how you placed it within the book's heroine?

AW: Yes, the negative capability of "both, both." And the warrior and poet, indeed—cutting though the underbrush and detritus of civilizations and layers of psyche with her stylus-weapon-scythe. The lunatic, the lover, and the poet might join in here as well. But interesting you pick up on *therapon*—Greek for an "attendant" and related to the word *therapy,* also a wonderful double entendre: *there upon. "I am there upon."* I am upon this work, I am upon my subject, so to speak. I think of Robert Duncan's title "Before the War" not as relative to temporality but as standing, facing, *in front of* the war.

JC: I'd like to ask you more about your views on male energy because it is so central to the work. On page 61 of Book I, you write:

> Don't mock me as I avenge the death of my sisters
> in this or any other dream
> In order to make the crops grow
> you men must change into women

On page 62 you write:

> The poet . . . tries to write in anti-forms without success. But the
> boy, her son, guides her through her confusion . . .

On page 111, you argue:

> I wanted you in agreement that women invented the alphabet . . .

and on page 122, you explicate the epic journey

> to the underworld & steal the secrets of the male energies that rule
> there.

On page 154, you posit a distinct male position where

> The 'male' here is more dormant deity, integrated into a transcendent
> yet powerful hermaphrodite . . . a 'double.'

Can you elaborate on the mechanism of male energy you hacked into in
Iovis and how that may or may not have evolved over the twenty-five years
you spent writing the poem?

AW: The psychological mechanism was there to be exposed in a way, and
there was also the need to transcend to the hermaphrodite, help the male
"get" there—explore the "both both" of sexuality (the original condition
being bisexual, even more fluid, I believe) and eros and how eros moves,
ascends beyond gender construct. Also, *Iovis* explores identity in this way,
instructing—correcting—the male on how to behave so he too can get
free of the habitual patterns of the warring god realm, the need to always
hallucinate an enemy and thereby justify his bellicose existence and lust
for blood. Which also goes to the greed of plunder and loot and empire.
So I watched that over twenty-five years, and the only power I had was in
my poetry, tracking the deeds of the patriarch. But also tracking the life
of my child, my world, my lives, my friendships, my elders, the school I
had helped create—a temporary autonomous zone of sanity. But the dark
trajectories forced the poem into being in a sense—maybe I would go mad
if I didn't track Rocky Flats, from demonstrating in the seventies to the pres-
ent with the nuclear plant deconstructed and yet the soil still toxic with
plutonium, visiting Bhopal to see the residues of the Union Carbide geno-
cide in 1986. We see how "the fix is in, the fix is in" continues to mani-
fest in the ugly scenarios playing out in Iraq and Afghanistan. Criminal
wars. A million Iraqis dead? You have to wonder and weep and rage over

this horrific pathology. And the new humanless weaponry—drones and weather weaponry and surveillance—more mechanisms of concealment. All those horrors, and how they are interconnected and how we are "before them," and can't ignore them. And expose the agendas of Halliburton (Xi) and so on. Quite exhausting. But necessary, I believe, in a role as poet. And especially in this project, hoping people of the future will go to this poem for some of the history as well as the imagination and beauty that counters and chides and is still in a wild place. *Iovis* as—ultimately—a generative project. *The boy guiding through confusion* is key here as well. Who inherits this thread? Who comes after us to clean up the mess? Who might sing of the darker times?

JC: You mention the Occupy movement of 2011 in Book III. *Iovis* has a kind of 3-D political activism—its interconnected themes of war, feminism, and language. The poem has been described as your "attempt at a new world history, a radical re-creation myth, an homage to Blake's epics and Pound's cantos, and a mystic or matriarchal answer to the male-dominated civilization (Jove or Iovis, the male god)" *(PW)*. Do you agree with that?

AW: Yes, I would agree. There is that tripartite braid you mention. And it might be the *language* the poem finds is the answer. That our need to reimagine our world through the vibratory mind and larynx, and modes of lyric, document, dirge, lullaby, that's what matters. Reawaken the world to itself. Through ideas, forms, ecstasies, hybrid bricolage, fragments, pictures, sounds, meditation. Hold the mirror up to "nature." And to the heart. And conscience. Occupy has a lot to teach us.

JC: Your own Vajrayana Buddhist practice was front and center in Book II, "Rooms" (423), and is woven throughout the trilogy. You write of your own fear of "passion toward others, toward anything" and how the room of mind you lived in "was a prison." As a liberation epic, were there particular moments over the twenty-five years of the writing of the poem that informed you as to your personal goal of attaining liberation—"this poem is the occasion of my complete LIBERATION" (688)—in this lifetime?

AW: Oh dear, I sound arrogant. If you speak of your own liberation or enlightenment, clearly it hasn't happened! Still too much ego. But certainly writing this work over a long period of time was liberating. I got all that mental projection and montage and history and sense perception *out* in front of myself where I could shape it. There's an aspiration to keep working free of "small mind" in the *Iovis* project, which also reflects an allegiance to reflection, contemplation, and following the breath of yourself and others including the "plants and trees and so on . . ." And seeing poetry is also a means of liberation, in that I am awakened to this life and its beauty and mystery and complexity through the graces of a "making" of language. And there are energies that reside in each incremental phone and phoneme.

And we can release them. Like mantras. And it can be grand and vast and you can create a realm you can dwell in for a while. Where things are perfect symbols of themselves, no manipulation. And that connects, to me, to the Buddhist view. From that perspective we can wake up on the spot, be conscious of our world, think of others. Not push ahead on the line, hog the road, and so on. Most of us have glimmers of that. Little gaps in our "me me" monkey mind consciousness.

JC: You include numerous personal letters throughout *Iovis,* but none speaks as potentially critical of the poem as your longtime Kerouac School poet colleague Anselm Hollo's letter (473–475). Hollo argues that "the poem needs to be more than just raw material to present to an . . . audience, in ways intentionally or unintentionally designed to cover up weaknesses in the writing" (474). How would you respond to post-publication criticisms of the work that in fact there are vast numbers of pages in which a radical syntactic linguistics is at play and meaning is at one with no-meaning?

AW: I took Anselm Hollo's *ars poetica* to do with a critique of reading the telephone book, or some such performance strategy, more conceptual in purpose. I never felt it aimed at the *Iovis* project. I suppose the best response is to let *Iovis* find its readers and place in the spectrum, which it seems to be doing. I have great confidence in its many surprises, delights, and strategies, to use that male word. Even humor. There are intentional spaces for "raw" material, but so much of it has been worked through the "poem machine." I see endless permutations are possible as well with how one might read it. Anselm never had the whole poem. He wrote short poems himself.

JC: You discuss sexism and the Beats in a letter to Jane Dancey (475–478). In that long letter, you state that the biggest problem with the Beats was "the inattention to women and the often sexist attitudes about women that undermine some of the early writing." You follow that with an interview with poet Joanne Kyger in which she states something very real for any experimental writer working under the radar: "No one's going to tell you you've got it" (478). What would you say is the heart of long-term personal power that fueled *Iovis*?

AW: Yes, exactly, no one asks you to do this. That's the perverse power of it. And the male-poet compadres are not always helpful. It took Gary Snyder and Allen too long to see what a great poet Joanne Kyger is! But indeed, no one begs you to be a poet or write a thousand-page poem. You have to be fueled by a drive, a conviction—a need, a necessity, a vision that is so pressing that it has no other outlet but through you. That doesn't mean that you are unconscious or in trance, but there can be moments like that. You are deliberately making this work for yourself—to see your own mind, to learn something, to wake up, to observe the way the work can be arranged, shaped, held, transmitted.

JC: You are a poet "enamored of syllabaries, alphabets, the phonemes of old tongue & groove" ("Glyphs" 480). You also mention how the reference point of your writing of the epic was the mantra "War, gender, language" ("Lacrimare, Lacrimatus: 'Dux Femina Facti,'" 529). Can you discuss your appreciation of Gertrude Stein and her "include it all" poetics in the making of *Iovis?*

AW: Yes, as much that could be included. I did have to cut about a hundred pages at Coffee House's insistence. They would not have been able to bind the book. There were also unfinished pages in draft that weren't as strong. The epic is a story of your time, your wars, your heroes. For her it was Susan B. Anthony, Picasso. Stein is a champion of her own continuously present mind grammar. The world is constantly reflected in her patterns and associations, and she is miraculously liberated by a lack of restraints. She could use the intimate things in her life, and also simple objects, names as well—where they are "reduced" to language in relationship to itself and flattened out quite democratically—so that in an interesting way they become neutralized. She wrote freely, and yes, maybe things are coded, but she wrote a great many works, dense and demanding. You feel her liberation when you hold and read her notebooks in the Beinecke Library at Yale. The assertive, unstoppable child-genius.

JC: One of my favorite shorter sections of *Iovis* occurs in Book II. The "Spin or Lace It In Story" piece exemplifies the poet's role in retelling "traditional myth"—its relationship to "phenomenal obstacles the imagination conjures & vivifies . . ." (608). It seems to call attention to the centrality of imagination. Can you discuss the roots of this story? Is it from a film?

AW: It's the spider woman myth, from Navajo/Diné, Keresan, and Hopi Native peoples. A kind of creation myth, a survival myth. In this version she's a "spinster" with "no man to touch her," as I say. She's probably Grandmother Spider Woman. I wanted to invoke the sense of her "spinning," and spinning a tale, this tale—this epic—as well. The artist as solipsistic, complete-unto-herself, letting "the centrality of imagination," as you say it, all come and unravel. Myths, by their definition, involve transformations, struggles through various worlds or layers of reality and of obscuration. Other characters such as Copper Man appear, and all the natural (including cobweb and gossamer) elements. I think I retold this story while being in a retreat. I was indebted to Paula Gunn Allen and her book *The Sacred Hoop*. She was raised on the Laguna Pueblo and was an important thinker (anthropologically), wanting to restore a sense of the *gynocratic* to Native American history and myth. The centrality of the feminine. The shamanic feminine.

JC: You begin Book III "Eternal War" with an introduction (655–657) in which you write, "The sending and receiving practice of tonglen I recommend again as it is the crux of this project: take negativity upon oneself, call it out, breathe out the efficacy: Practice empathy in all things. Pick a cause and tithe your time relative to the half-life of plutonium" (656). What is the place of tonglen in your conjectures of "future . . . radical poetries"?

AW: Tonglen is taking it all in, including it all, but for the scope of *Iovis* it's all the toxicities of our world as well—the ugliness, violence, disparities, the suffering of all kinds and degrees, of others near and far. Your compassion travels beyond your own inner circle. And then you breathe out an alternative version where you mentally and emotionally and psychologically purify the poisons. So indeed, the generative idea is in the crux of this practice and of my propensity toward poetry, which is a practice of the imagination. We humans need to do better with our vast minds and alchemical powers. Future radial poetries might be more symbiotic with the rest of consciousness.

JC: There are exquisite sections of Book III such as "G-Spot" and "Matriot Acts" that would be the apex of most poets' careers. And then there is "Problem-Not-Solving" (946–975), which really was the highlight of the entire poem for me. Can you talk about how your activist work at Rocky Flats in 1978–1979 as well as all your tireless anti-war, anti-nuke rallying over the years came to be seen in/by this formulation: problem-not-solving?

AW: As for the activist work, it just goes on, and it seems to be more and more about how to preserve an archive, how to preserve artistic culture, how to hide the treasures so that they can be found at a later date and re-activated. For me poems are small acts redone, and that can vibrate well into the future. So *Iovis* has that potential. And it was written for my child so that he could see where I had been, and he could see something of the world that he would inherit. This is the Kali Yuga, remember, according to many traditions a dark age, and we will need some paths and trajectories through it. "Problem-Not-Solving" keeps the possiblity open to actually *solve*. Solve is close to *salve*. A balm, a healing ointment, and also to *salvare*, to save. That little "not" (knot) could be eliminated. And there's that active *ing* in *solving*. The situation in Israel/Palestine is the most crazy-making, suffering-inducing "knot," perhaps the greatest conundrum of our time. We need a peace czaress in the cabinet. We need a worldwide Department of Peace. The will is just not there yet, the other way is still so darkly lucrative. Poets have to keep pushing, pushing, against the darkness, and write their way out of it as well.

Part 2: *Iovis* & *Sanctuary*

Editor Tod Thilleman (Spuyten Duyvil) was reading *Iovis* on his back porch in Maine and sending encouraging responses that initiated some lifeline through political calamity and vicissitude. And this selection I've called as a manuscript *Sanctuary* pulled together July 2019/20 when something snapped about children being separated from their families at the borders. And there were already skinny ongoing *Iovis* poems responding to Kavanaugh, Mueller, the "evidence" of text and testimony. And homage to Black Mountain, a sanctuary,  and more protest. And cut-up odd asides to methodologies of Hannah Höch, and Donald Judd in his Marfa, another sanctuary.

Had to see for myself the border on the ground. Had been half a century since I crossed by foot. Sanctuary is someone writing to you about writing, sanctuary is a dream shelter from the injections of poison, sanctuary is a montage of notebook antidote, sanctuary is the places given you to perform in public space. Sanctuary is Giambattista Vico's enlarged plebian sense of rights, an "arc of justice." Sanctuary wants to be the wide skirt, like a tent, of the Madonna del Parto for those who seek shelter.

Tod wrote, with that encouragement, "What rings out is the fact that the sanctuary on this side of the 'divides' is in that wild (femme rattlesnake end-of-road, of *Iovis*, etc.). And, to my mind, the 'asylum' aspect of Vico. Not to make much of terms, but the fact that the enlarged sense of rights, in the international, is likened to an umbrella or refuge that then encompasses more than just one side or another, but the whole thing . . . that, of course, is that 'arc of justice' which was spoken of as long, was neither, for instance, the jail cell in Birmingham proper, but the universality of it. Buddha's enlightenment, that touch of mind to it all." So that's partially how this book came to be.

JC: Your *Iovis Trilogy* came out in 2011. You've had eight years of the work living in the world as a published entity to reflect upon the work's significance. Would you discuss the book's import as a key early-twenty-first-century anti-patriarch feminist poetics text as well as what you see as its importance to poetry both of today and the future?

AW: I know it is important work. Some embedded sagacity, I hope. Maybe it will provide solace for the increasingly apocalyptic times and intense suffering ahead. It was a force that took hold to make this poem, and it needed dailyness and the sense of magic to run the gauntlet. I was ensorcelled. Its long grip on me arrived with motherhood. Maybe that is its significance, that what this poem offers is a vow of protection in practices of poetry, of a sanctuary and a poet's history lesson from the twentieth / twenty-first century. But all this emanating from the mother principle, Tathāgatagarbha, which is womblike wisdom that "includes everything." This "everything" relates to alaya vijnana or "storehouse wisdom"; i.e., the impressions of previous experiences. It's a crypt, a book of runes, of quotation, a montage, a memory device: emotionally, psychically. It is written for those coming after, and right before, the even more excessive deluge of not simply flood but of data flow, the plague, fires, the gun madness that slaughters us. The bleak end of human time. The mechanisms are those of endurance, of spiritual journey, of intimate and chance encounters, dreams, protest, rage, love, dharma, concealment, shape-shifting, and knowledge of cause and effect. And I was also creating other epic interventions. *Marriage: A Sentence; Structure of the World Compared to a Bubble; Manatee/Humanity,* in parallel heat. And I read parts of *Trickster Feminism* as continuing the *Iovis* continuum, and *Sanctuary* is my zine coda for its energy in the world as well. Younger poets have told me they find *Iovis* liberating because the politics and love are playing out on a field of Mars, where stakes are higher. We are being tested. Have felt that my whole life.

JC: Looking at your *Iovis* epic from the perspective of intersectionality, what do you see as its points of intersections with the Me Too as well as Black Lives Matter movements?

AW: I wanted to create a vehicle for investigation of concealment for someone, a woman, born at the end of World War II, where the civilization's karma is in every syllable, breath, action. My mother worked at factories during the war. Bell Labs. Part of the war effort, but powerless. And coming of age I was warned about men, their motives, egos, sexism, how to fend them off. Or how to manipulate them, which I've never been good at. Look at the concealments after the war. The nuclear nightmare of Hiroshima and Nagasaki. Racism, white supremacy, the master narratives in German history books, et cetera. And you just keep getting more strife and war. But I wanted for *Iovis* to have the stamina of a larger claim, and reach. A day in the life.

"Epic parts in a woman's poem made with urgency always breathe a transitive air, unwilling to be subjugated," I write, opening the poem. Intersectionality might be in Part X, REVENGE, an eloquent takedown of male "teachers," or in Part XXV SPRECHSTIMME "Countess of Dia":

did we not say the roof, the tongue, the old man
or woman if she would appear for us, hermaphrodite
like a charwoman, a slave, a something out-of-doors
who's invoked because she holds two sexes in wrinkled clothes

=all street singers enjoy her=
=she is in her *langue d'oc*=

=tongue is disaster but not in her mouth
=who is invoked would be duty-bound to tell us=
=what about the other place=

tongue is salvation, tongue stands in for all-the-body

she tells the truth about matricide, about genocide, about rape
about torture, cleansing is not unfamiliar in her witness trope

In study of origins, and in particular Olduvai Gorge and other hominid sites, there seems confirmation that we all started in Africa—humans radiated around the planet from a place where dust contains calcified specks of the DNA we carry. How estranged we became from our own humanity. It's too tragic and insane. And the US of A wars on Black and Brown bodies, Asian bodies, the genocides are pathological. But continual protest over injustice woven into *Iovis* on many fronts, and toward the end of Book III ("Eternal War") a march in Denver supporting the Obama ticket is invoked, the racial shift feeling potent and with Code Pink feminists on front lines. Then the section morphs into the Abu Ghraib "Hungry Ghost" litany, and there's Abe Lincoln and a trip to the Cahokia Mounds, a pre-Columbian city near the Mississippi River. Black Lives Matter was founded in 2013 after the acquittal of Trayvon Martin's murderer. It is a spiritual hope, demand for reparation, and essential practice for protest, and all restorative action for the crimes against Black humanity. We will fail without racial justice. Present at some of the 2020 protests, one feels in

Black Lives and the George Floyd memorials (standing in for many other tragic deaths at the hands of police) the swell of humanity's empathy and possibility. But the struggle is formidable and continues without resolve. Now there are conflicts over teaching Black history. Books like *How We Get Free: Black Feminism and the Combahee River Collective* should be mandatory.

JC: Looking back for a moment, you first published your luminous title poem "Makeup on Empty Space" in 1984 and noted that the poem comes from "the idea in Buddhist psychology that the feminine energy tends to manifest in the world, adorning empty space." With *Iovis,* this idea seemed to morph into the central theme of the work's subtitle: *Colors in the Mechanism of Concealment.* From a poetics perspective, the work stands as a radical and mystical re-creation myth. You've expressed that the idea of the feminine adoption of makeup has both an adorning and concealment function as a critical factor in the rise of a more just matriarchal society. When we consider the long sexist history of the United States, are women being *seen* politically today as never before? Do you believe we are reaching a moment when women are in control of the *mechanism* of their own concealment by a still-powerful white-male-supremacist-dominated administration?

AW: Women are struggling for parity all over the world and in this country as well, although we are a bit ahead of the curve. And with them, the LGBTQ communities are continually under assault. And these brilliant eco-activists, alert and ready. Bodhisattvas are stepping up with passion, intelligence, experience, intellect, and solution into the fray. Roe under attack. We are in the middle of many paradigm anomalies. And planet crisis. And shadow wars. Also we will see radical change—shifts as a result of the pandemic. And there's AI. To increase profit and armaments of the war machine. The ruling class has gotten wealthier and more brutal. The economic collapse will be telling. I've been saying mantras and prayers for the aliens to come and rescue us! Domination is trenchant thru divisive politics, and we are struggling right now, more than ever, for a viable democracy. And we need to remember what moves us, how "what thou lovest well remains . . ."

We're in the crucible. Voter suppression, a stacked Supreme Court. *Colors* in my title also applies to races, tones, subtle hues of logos. There's the "casing of the colors" ritual of hoisting the flag by US Army brigades. But the mechanisms involve further undoing of the syndicates of samsara, the grasping, crazed white men with their diminishing sperm counts.

JC: I was quite struck by the collages that grace *Sanctuary* and their messaging. You've been a political and cultural activist for decades: a protester, a demonstrator. You've been arrested. I remember when you were arrested at Rocky Flats in the 1970s as an example. What I found fascinating was how *Sanctuary* seemed closer to the street than any book of poetry I've seen in a long time. Besides these collages framing the poems included in the book, their street-art feel energizes the set of poems. In "Sung Devotions," you write, "Please that we do not become lost in our robotic Capitalocene hell realm, our false paradise, greed and privilege . . ." I wonder if the mass protests across the US over the death of George Floyd and the sheer history of police brutality against Black people in America have changed your perception of your own white privilege.

AW: I wanted to say first I was fortunate in my editor, also a poet and artist, Tod Thilleman, who called me out in correspondence after reading *The Iovis Trilogy* and really participated in the visual dynamism of the book—turning my photos, and those of others, into action-images that vibrate with the intensity of street action. Patti Smith's mouth chanting to a medley of children at the anti-gun rally in Central Park, just one example. The last collage I feel in my chakras. Some kind of morphing into a spinal butterfly that seems tinged with red, white, and blue in front of the Washington Square Arch.

I've felt my privilege, of course. In Greenwich Village, thank god, there was some bohemian interracial diversity. But it's never enough to really hammer in just how complicit you are in the larger problem. What will you actually *do* to change the racist system? And these tragedies and images we saw from Selma were for many of my generation a goad. As were stories from friends who had come with family out of the Holocaust. Or the napalmed bodies of children from Vietnam. Goad for civil rights, for the anthems of folkies in Washington Square, Pete Seeger having regular gatherings and meetings down the block, all part of this. LeRoi Jones/ Amiri Baraka's plays. My father had been around labor movement people in Provincetown, his own former mother-in-law, Mary Heaton Vorse, a labor lawyer close to John Reed. And so on. I have always felt connected to these lineages through auspicious coincidence of birth and family.

Odetta's powerful voice was also a goad. Nina Simone, who sang regularly at the Village Gate round the corner, where Sam Shepard and other friends worked, had an extraordinary power. I used to hear her a lot.

An early boyfriend went to Tent City in Mississippi. I was underage and my parents were too scared to give permission to join him.

But I grew up in a somewhat mixed-race world. My college experience less diverse, but politically radical.

My Black brother-in-law would be stopped and held up at an airport for no reason but the color of his skin while on family excursions. My nephew from another family who has a Black father and identifies as Black on the other side of the family was arrested for something my own (white) child would not suffer, under the same circumstances. My son's Mexican partner and her family were held up at the border entering the US on a trip to Disney World.

I wanted the protest photos in *Sanctuary* to capture the sense of civic protest in public space. From New York to Italy to Spain to Mexico City. And those of us involved with infrastructure at places like the Poetry Project and the Summer Writing Program of the Kerouac School at Naropa have for many years had some advocacy for greater inclusion in artistic endeavors. As curators, editors, but never enough. Through friendships with all kinds of writers and poets and musicians, scenes mixed, and especially in New York City. An antithesis reality, the Outrider alternative experimental poetry world is an ever-expanding extraordinary nexus of race and cultures and class and identities, and I'd happily add also an intergenerational and international one.

JC: "Temporality" as a theme figures into *Sanctuary*. There's also a relationship to time for all "seed syllables" in order for these sounds to coalesce within mind. In "Ceremonies in the Gong World," you write "I come here trembling, to remember how we studied the past to understand the future." I have to admit to sharing with you a concern that people today continue to have a fractured and incomplete picture of all lives moving through times. Once, Trungpa appeared in a dream to suggest a new curriculum called "American Karmic Studies" that would reformulate the social sciences specifically around causal and consequential action and effect in the personal, family, community, and national levels. What effects do you see from your work as an experimental feminist poet and teacher? Do we have the Right View on the past, present, and future?

AW: Probably not a subtle understanding of Right View. Otherwise we wouldn't keep making the same mistakes. And we'd develop ways to nourish beings from an early age. And we'd be educating them toward restoration from trauma. Karmic effects arise out of seeds latent in an individual's mind-stream. The notion of the bija or seed syllables that might grow into harmful or beneficent action is key here, in that those thought forms have tremendous power to cause harm, as well as be an antidote. Why don't we all want to be bodhisattvas? Benefit others? Ease suffering? "It you do this to this, this happens . . ." Temporality indeed, which is why I consider *Sanctuary* to be an extension of the *Iovis* experiment. It's events of the day, the street, a floating world, that could be blissfully ordinary but more and more is menacing.

The little park with old-growth trees being destroyed to develop expensive real estate. We are in what seems a palpable, sequential time, often a nightmare and sometimes a god realm or dream time, and also experiencing time as spiral, a maelstrom.

Time as chaos. Pandemic time in sequestration was extremely provocative. It is amazing how benign many were in a self-imposed lockdown that becomes more controlling. How time was both slow and "lost." As one tracked one's mind, one could vacillate between hope and fear.

But then there was the loss of so many friends, some to COVID but also to other illnesses compounded by such a wretched time. Not seeing people I loved before they passed. Becoming more of a "watcher." The crystal ball seemed always cloudy. Writers are used to hours of solo retreat. I saw time primarily in something I would make. I also kept the Buddhist adage close: "Be a child of illusion."

We are so unprepared for our own karmic blowback.

June 5th:
Strawberry moon and penumbral lunar eclipse.
See all the sky doings in Mexico?
"Ambrose: show Kora the moon!"

I wrote "13 Moons Kora" for my grandchild born at the spring equinox of 2020. In the mind of the poet all times are contiguous. There's the fantastic idea of everything being unborn, there is no first cause, and that was sometimes unnerving. Everyone grasps for origins, motives. The mechanisms. I studied pandemics of the past. That helped stabilize my mind. I saw how we weren't scientifically or spiritually prepared. Cause and effect of incompetence, failed leadership, ulterior motives, ruthlessness toward poor, undervalued populations, capitalism, dysfunctional healthcare system. First image I saw—expression on her face—of grandchild Kora on her arrival was one of tenderness and concern and *where have I landed?*

"American Karmic Studies" would be an excellent curriculum. There's a Buddhist teaching on karma with different shades of black and white and gray. And one considers the karma of the community you are born to, of your city, of your nation, as you say. *Iovis* was investigating that verity. It gets heavier and heavier. Buddhism rejects the existence of a permanent self (ātman), and also denies the existence of a first cause. Sounds adamant, and is at crux of nontheism. The nature of existence is interpreted in terms of the two truths: relative and absolute. Conventionally, there exist beings and things, but only as conceptual entities (prajñaptisat). Ultimately, they do not exist, because they have no permanent core or life, they are conglomerations of tendencies, composites that can quickly fall apart, dissolve, disintegrate. So how does the inexistent world work, how can it even function? Conceptual entities are dissected into impersonal phenomena, or dharmas, as ultimate units. The dharmas are momentary, and they arise and vanish in space and time in conformity with definite principles that regulate their flow and interdependence: karma and dependent origination. The term *karma,* literally "action" or "deed," as a technical concept, denotes the principle of ethical causation: there are no agents, but there are actions and their consequences.

You are not disconnected from any of it even though you don't actually exist in any permanent way. Obviously as someone on the spiritual path of Buddhism, you want to help, not hinder.

Your actions, your greed, your murderous intention cause a lot of suffering. The tragedies are the fruition of the little seeds. The horrific mind around slavery is still enabled by a Urizenic solid patriarchal mindset that goes way back.

JC: The poem "At Mountain" from *Sanctuary* contains this liberation image: "so must build/inside war machine/Primordial stupa," the last two words dramatically appearing in larger font and in Tibetan gold. We really need to contemplate on such a space today more than ever. *Sanctuary* contains responses to events from 2019 that many thought would be further turning points toward a more progressive political vision for the country, a vision that sustains and does not destroy life. We find both Justice Kavanaugh ("Carve a Naught") and Special Counsel Robert Mueller ("Connect the Dots") passing through. Both were central players in the biggest question the last administration will be leaving us with: *Is the president of the United States above the law?* Do you think this will be important as relayed in your work as a poet?

AW: In *Sanctuary* I notice, collect fragments, make poems, tell stories. As in *Trickster Feminism,* from the street. And invite others in.

In *Iovis* one had epistolary modes pre–social media. One of the mechanisms is fighting cognitive dissonance. Don't forget "Eric Prince" (Err Wreck Prince), a walk-on. Some of my favorite lines from "Connect the Dots":

did we think "the lonely enclosure of history?"

did Blue Tara come down from her perch
and be sambhogakāya double agent

for all the melancholic babes?

abstracted identity. collapsing   into sex scandal

and silence

JC: In *Sanctuary,* you bring to life this quotation from Artaud circa 1945: "We are not yet born, we are not yet in the world, there is/not yet a world, things have not been made, the reason/for being has not yet been found." What a remarkable view of all that is yet unborn! I was struck how this quote was incorporated to introduce "Truth or Consequences." I was somewhat surprised to find a largely eulogistic poem to Ed Dorn attached to this title and that within the poem younger-generation political figures such as AOC and Joaquin Castro appear. Have you found yourself in the position of reassessing certain poets you've known through all your years teaching and performing? Are you feeling a kind of transmission of the keenest minds you knew personally to a new generation of political and aesthetic workers?

AW: I began to enumerate all the poets who have died in past years and that in itself is a call to action. That's what we should be doing. Reading, recalling the poets, calling them out, calling them out through their poetry, letting them exist in future memory and reckoning. Many poems I can think of in my lifetime get us through existence. Ed Dorn was controversial for his caustic cynical wit and bite. He'd leave a note for his students: "gone fishing." We often tangled, and he was a great opponent at times on the "Field of Mars." I loved Ed. *Gunslinger* is a strong epic and prophetic. On a last phone call before he died, Ed was weeping for all victims of radiation, including those genocided in World War II Japan, as he was undergoing his own treatment for cancer.

Artaud's lines, written as he was looking over ruins of World War II, are profoundly prescient. It is a koan for poets to describe this world whose reason for being has not yet been found.

By Turns, Ostraka

for Eleni Sikelianos

rhymes and flowers
gifts for a name.

    —H. D.

Hor of Sebennytos
a convert to the god Thoth
transferred divinely inspired dreams onto ostraka

one scratched in
shell
or shard used as voting ballot
  "her garment, scent of hibiscus"

another

  "she came from a lantern"

                            & bright she was
and "poet" one writ simple

  on a bone, as Greek she was

heralded,

told of in advance
before entering a mandala

gentler rhizome entering a
    trance, a medina, an école

she's here she's here the goddess your niece is here!
the babe I held in arms at birth is here!

How life's pleasures grow

grace of these pleasures mark us and they grow

family is amplitude says another
in a dear, cherished text

paradox of the Caliph and what the new
  modernity looks like

it looks like this: ostraka, a test
   it weeps itself back in time
a theorem to be wise on la rue
le rêve
  it looks like this on planet
poetry
it looks like us
it weeps itself forward

  perpetual motion under clouds
travels distant skies
going public in the town square
put on the woven cap
        put on the child's silken frock

for thinking   *what brings you here?*

for her

& choiceless to
poetry

  vocabulary
before amazon meant theft

daybreak on your
      great multiverse
a newer moon when the elder is slower
  and

lifts her eye above the horizon
I vote blue
I vote the blue streak on the ostraka

messages, prescriptions as peregrinations
exercises for beauty
fragrances

shards tell through the ages how love is
  constructed in a bed in a house
    and you weep how true

lie down
limestone flakes
drawn in ink, drawn in sand?

lie down and you dream a sweet text
never ostracized

"we be poets"

  "never outside our own hearts"
  "always tender,
always allowed where forbidden:

we as poets"

etheric in a motive in scroll-worlds
  in mode in mood

ostraka as of a fragile acetate tape

as of a gait recorded in film in motion

how many lost slips of time for the ostraka
before the Vedas launched a cosmology
  becoming existential
how reader you are in carrier waves

how writer you are sounding

world of work these words like chromosomes
  where Actaeon is my Theban hero
    and is part of a book of innumerable meanings

and one is your avatar
        as mother
scorpion charmer

what would we do for a jar of fine oil
  for a screen moment of paradox

we'd never have to hide within
what you do for us
lead   guide   through the mirror
poetry and its pathways, mellifluous

you in all the pronouns of the universe
  mount the stage

  as global temperatures rise
you notice
you protest
your migration here
  into the revelation "communitas"

        Hypnos says
settle the mind
bring it down   bend knees to earth
                ostraka will tell a story deciphering
                        fragments, future shards
ostraka will report: "mind is Eleni

  (whose name translates *torch*)

who wove herself a magic carpet,
  now sleeping

now dreaming
poised upon

alights"

{undercurrent}

The poem *Manatee/Humanity* takes its initial inspiration from a particular initiation/teaching—or *wang* (literally "empowerment") in the Tibetan Buddhist tradition, with links to a pre-Vedic shamanic ritual, and from an encounter with and meditation on the mysterious manatee, the endangered mammal of coastal waters, and the gray wolf, particularly in the western states of the USA. The poem emerged as a kind of conversation or lecture mode. The Buddhist initiation is named Kalachakra, or wheel of time, and has been granted in recent years with accelerated frequency in both Asia and the West. The view is that such an initiation confers power and permission to enter into specific meditative practices of empathy for achieving enlightenment (clear seeing) in order to benefit others (which includes the plant and animal realms) as quickly as possible! It also investigates the nature of time and change.

Tantra refers to a stream of continuity, or thread. This ongoing stream is our own mind, which in the Buddhist view continues through lifetimes. At its subtlest level, the mind is known as "primordial pure light" and is free of the oscillations of conceptual thought and disturbing emotions. It presumably underlies every moment of experience, awake or asleep. A modern image presented is that of a radio when it is always on, playing ceaselessly—even between bands or while turning/tuning in to another frequency. Our mind is the basis for our experiences of death—our experiences in the Bardo, which is the state between rebirths—and the conception of a new life. Neither the possible static nor the volume nor the particular station affects the fact that the radio is *on*. Presumably we are also picking up signals from . . . from a parallel perspective. Neither the intensity of our experience nor the dramas of our discursive thoughts and moods affect the "clear light mind" that is also on. Each stream of continuity is individual as well. All radios are not the same radio, although the receiver works the same. In this view, there is no such thing as a universal mind in which our minds all participate, but myriad unique individual pathways, myriad possibilities. One of Jack Spicer's metaphors for the poet is the radio; the poet is always on. And *what is the mind of a manatee?* was a question for the poem. There seemed something wonderfully cognizant and primordial and "on" in the manatee spirit, albeit a less speedy frequency. I remember William Burroughs's sense (maybe riffing on something Jack Kerouac had said) about how so many animals seem to be in samadhi. He thought this of his cats, and he said often he would prefer the company of lemurs to that of humans.

Tantric practice uses the imagination for visualization in order to identify and invoke certain energies with one's own mind and body. It is essentially a practice of empathy. The rainbow-colored Kalachakra deity has four faces and twenty-four arms with a consort of four faces and eight arms. The more arms, the more power of action and efficacy. Traditionally one becomes the deity during initiation to conjure greater compassion and then dissolves the image at the close of it.

The mandala, or map, created for such an event is of a symbolic universe. It describes a palace and surrounding grounds where the Buddha figure dwells that the initiate also enters imaginatively. Like the parts of our body, each architectural feature corresponds or refers to a realization we need to maintain activity in our own minds. A mandala can be a three-dimensional structure, and a mandala made of colored powders or sand is a blueprint of that structure.

The initiation with preliminary preparations takes three days.

I received this initiation with several hundred people on two separate occasions some years ago. The guides were renowned meditation teachers in the Tibetan Buddhist lineage. I was struck by the highly ritualized and lush nature of the three-day doings the first time, not at all sure I was comprehending the slightest essence of the Kalachakra's profundities. Felt inept, clumsy, trying to follow all of the instructions and complicated visualizations, yet bungled through nonetheless. Entering the initiation, we were given two—one short, one long—pieces of kusha grass and told to place the short one under the pillow and the long under the mattress and observe our dreams. My particular dream was of the Armageddon variety. Somewhat terrifying, with dismembered and eviscerated human and animal corpses lying about as in a classic war zone or brutal abattoir. I remember hiding in the dream, in an alleyway with forbidden sacred poetry books that were also under siege and needed to be quickly memorized. Yet there was an alternative to this dark vision: one of escape and of a community of others in the same predicament.

We were being helped by aquatic creatures. I remembered the story of my Huguenot ancestor escaping persecution across the Atlantic with the family Bible hidden in a loaf of bread.

The kusha grass is supposed to purify inauspicious dreams. As I awoke, I thought that the dream was the very reality that the Kalachakra initiation was meant to cope with, and that this advanced ceremony was being made available to many, including those not necessarily Buddhist, as a way to work against the pathological insanity of the increasingly dark and corpse-strewn Kali Yuga—or dark age. An age where war and suffering and inhumanity seem pathologically endless. The view, as I understood it to be, was to get free of the samsaric wheel, at least comprehend how time, space, matter, and more especially mind or consciousness, works. I remember thinking during the large gathering that was my first Kalachakra initiation that although this seemed like theatre (at one point the initiates wear blindfolds) or pure fantasy, we were putting our bodies inside this creation—this vivid spectacle—toward some elevated purpose. I thought of Antonin Artaud's sense of the theatre being the place or state where one comprehends the human anatomy and that with the human anatomy one can "heal and direct life."

As such, the text of the Kalachakra initiation moves through numerous descriptions of both macrocosm and microcosm, both external and internal and other (outer, inner, secret) details of the environment, the body, the stars, down to the finest increments of atoms and molecules. Time in Buddhism is primarily a measure of change, and in fact time is understood to have no beginning or end but only the reality of change. "What does not change is the will to change" is the oft celebrated quoted line from Heraclitus. Universe, civilizations, and life-forms rise and fall. Liberation from time means liberation from confusion, from an erroneous view of how things actually occur.

The poem is an investigation into and an improvisation upon some of the ideas and concerns of the Kalachakra layered through with a vow of *take all the animals with you in your life, your poetry*. This is not systematically or linearly presented, however, and eschews most of the points of minutiae that a visualization of the atoms of the body and the universe entails! How many breaths in one day or the complex systems of astrology used for making predictions seemed hard to capture systematically. Or the descriptions of the precepts concerning the twenty-five modes of "tamed behavior."

What is so astonishing and comes through in the obsessive ritual descriptions, however, is the vision of a *person,* how complicated that is, and then what it takes to unravel and "purify" the conditions of that mind, of "person," and set it on another more beneficent path. What is sentience? What is consciousness? What is humanity, what is empathy?

What primarily interested me is where the wisdom and descriptions and presumed efficacies of the Kalachakra intersect with modern neuroscience and the study of the nature of mind and of consciousness in the brain theatre. I became driven by the notion of "mirror neurons" as a way to understand leaps of sympathy and inspiration in the human condition. Some of the practices of Tibetan Buddhism, as one visualizes icons, seed syllables, and so on, are meant to imitate and lead to states of consciousness, awareness, and empathy that uplift and counter the normal tendency to disconnect, shut down, and maintain the territory of personal ego.

Finally, in the spirit of invoking the gnosis of the natural environment and its denizens that is recommended in the mandala of the Kalachakra initiation, I summon life-forms that seem particularly threatened. The poem's litanies of the manatee and lemur and the wolf-dream are meant to be heard as lyrical interludes—modal structures—of both plea and restitution, and they stand in for all endangered species. The Sinapu (Ute word for wolf) organization once brought wolves into a University of Colorado classroom: a surreal dream of interspecies pedagogy. The day, some years ago in Miami, when I spent several hours in the presence of a wounded manatee in a local "sea-park" was key to the *Manatee/Humanity* poem. I vowed to "include manatee." I believed it was a "she" who had weathered human harm and neglect. She seemed an ancient soul, and contemplative in her demeanor—huge, Buddha-like—and I fancied that I received transmission from her example, which was as witness to neglect and cruel captivity, environmental disaster.

The Buddhist view is that all life-forms are interrelated through their evolutionary history and that animal and human minds are both participants in reality. And that minds exist at the quantum level, below the level of atoms and subatomic particles. Minds never come from nothing or go to nothing.

The manatee's realm in the shallow pool I visualized as a shrine. I perceived her less as a victim but as a kind of poetic deity. And I felt she had the greater sympathy for me. The manatee ostensibly has no *use* in the current world. It's odd how creatures that are pacifist, transcendent even, go extinct as human realms of cruelty, plunder, and war grind on.

Often Outdoors with Fires and Lanterns to See By

One had poems read to one as a child, and oral frisson was experimental early on.

And the pleasure being in company with friends sitting around a fire telling stories—a primordial ritual, perhaps, light-and-shadow narrative, an oral performance as one stood awed later before stained-glass narratives of saints and martyrs, and then moving along toward cinema, liquid TV screens. But originally mind projected onto the flames and within the flames were images that enhanced the story. They were living in color.

And one visualizes the narrative, watching images dance in the flames—imagines new things, surreal, outlandish shape-shifting of faces and bodies, of animals too, and morphing landscapes. Light and shadows. Heroes, villains. A fluid ephemeral light. Sometimes the narrative breaks and the action or emotion becomes so strong the story leaps into poetry or song. You might keep the fire going until dawn.

Working in Indonesia, I witnessed all-night ritual performances with text and song and musical instruments and dancing and masked and costumed presenters. These were often outdoors with fires and lanterns to see by. Sometimes a narration was interrupted by battles with witches and other magical beasts, and agons of psychic life and death would intervene. Passion and obsession and jealousy might have a hand. The long poem performance seemed to always cover a possibility. Young children at these performances were riveted, you would find yourself thinking along with them and with fire.

I also witnessed ritual performances in India involving words, mantra, mudra, or gesture. Lama dancing and the like. The Kutiyattam from South India is an example of epic theatre.

Mantra is a perfect instrument to think with. Traditionally, one understands mantra both as a bind, a thread, a vow, protecting mind; and also an untranslatable (nonsemantic structures made of syllables) event in language that cuts through dualities. There is also the notion of self-secret, thus speaking secretly (*mantri* or *ghan,* literally "speaking secretly") and insight being protected if the adept isn't ready or can't hear. I welcomed that notion of sanctuary and that such a vocal power could exist for a willful untamed mind. I often experienced mind as an instrument needing tuning to the difficult musical spheres of protection and memory. That existence is a solo aria. That the whole body sings one pointedly in this, its individual songs. And mantra continually comes back, circles through over and over, creating this vocalized psyche shield, the larger opera.

There is also Australian Aboriginal tribal practice—in the Pitjantjatjara tongue—where to become a "songman," you memorize epic material that covers a cycle of a twenty- to forty-year migration. This involves constant traveling so that the wandering epic might invoke the botany of the terrain, where you might find water holes and food, what the landmarks are, the magnificent glorious history and struggle and life of the place. A kind of memory landscape.

Certain structural barriers are broken in the epic with montage, with the strategies of cut-up, with flickering firelight, and with sound that is as subtle as the plucking of cactus needles (as in a John Cage performance).

The epikos form was the only one that could hold all I needed to write, to make, at this crucial time. To create a grounded construct of the world. During the composition of *Iovis,* which references the male Jove in the generative case, thus "*of* Jove, *of* the father, *of* the creator, *of* the patriarch"— the joke was that he, Jove/Zeus, impregnates everything: swans, trees, the mind, the universe. *Zeused* out, *Juiced* out. I wanted to build an endless creation myth of endless seduction and war.

And this possibility came with a long attraction to and reading of epics of other contours and place and dimension. And the writing of longer poems.

I have been intrigued by non-Western form and have eschewed the constant reference back to traditional English poetry, although Stein was able to challenge that with "Rose is a rose is a rose." My epic would be informed in part by a different lens of narrative, less linear, more circular. I invoked the alap form from Indian ragas that lay out the themes in an opening musical passage and then proceed to improvise on these in the subsequent long form. I was interested in circular form, transcending various binaries, and the sense of directions of simultaneity in disrupted modal structures.

The exciting and obligatory Homer; the dynamic *Aeneid; The Song of Roland* in French in high school; *The Kalevala; La Divina Commedia; Gesar of Ling;* the Sumerian myth of Inanna's travel to the underworld, stealing the father's secrets, and return; and so on were key generative texts. The lists and quotidian reality of Hesiod's *Works and Days.* The *Ramayana, Mahābhārata, Gilgamesh, Beowulf.* The namings and lists in the Bible.

Milton wrote his epics to justify the ways of god to man. Homer in the *Iliad* invokes the muse to sing of Achilles's anger. I arrogantly wrote to display both rage—and lullaby—to a somnolent world.

Epic from Latin *epicus,* Greek *epos* is word, story, poem. Usually a narrative that tells of heroic deeds and events significant to the culture of a nation. It often becomes the creation myth and history of that nation. One went to epics for history, for culture, for a deeper understanding of the underpinnings, albeit cosmological, esoteric belief, and mores as well. What people wore, what they dreamed of, who they loved, who their demons were. What barbarians haunted their sleep at the gates?

Dante opens his *Commedia:*

> Stopped mid-motion in the middle
> Of what we call our life, I looked up up and saw no sky—
> Only a dense cage of leaf, tree, and twig. I was lost.

Often the epic begins in media res—in the middle of things—at midpoint. The middle of one's life. I started my longest poem, *The Iovis Trilogy,* after the birth of my son . . . beginning of my own mid-age.

At the beginning of the poem, I invoke first the familiar Judeo-Christian patriarch, seductive in his humility. Although he comes as a sorrowful one, the poet-feminist narrator sees this as a ruse or trick to inspire pity, which turns to subjugation. She talks about staking a claim herself as Moses did with his tablets. "She will imitate, play prophet & tell allegories on judgment day as only a woman might" and "in my richness I speak a new doctrine to an old form."

And vast subject and themes of war and life and death and love and in my case motherhood. It pays homage to ancestors. It contains enumerations, quotations, catalogues, genealogies. It supplicates divine intervention in human affairs. It might encompass pleas and dirges. It invokes ordinary voices that embody hope for a sinking civilization.

It occasions visits to the underworld.

The epic is good with epithets: "wine-dark sea," "rosy-fingered dawn," etc. Mine for the *Iovis* project were variations on "Anne-holding the broom more tightly now," invoking the Shaker sweeping song, "'Tis the Gift to Be Simple."

Consciousness as a young poet: "The Prelude," *Leaves of Grass,* Stein's *Stanzas in Meditation,* Pound's *Cantos,* Williams's *Paterson,* H. D.'s *Trilogy* and her great "Palinode" from *Helen in Egypt*—where Helen never did the things she had been purported to have done. I saw particular long poems as essential to a way of reading for me that was quite different from a reading of fiction, a way of reading that afforded a particular kind of pleasure not unlike that which the campfire invoked earlier. More neurons fired, more pathways invoked, more transitions and disruptions and asides and investigations. That starts with the premise of a broken heart, a broken world. My favorite women compañeros writing the "long works" were Alice Notley and Bernadette Mayer. Dailiness and dream travel. *Incidentals in the Day World,* a terrific book by Alice, later her riveting voyage to the underworld: *The Descent of Alette;* Bernadette's *Midwinter Day,* and there was always the taunt about women and the long poem, and the epic being a male form—

and there was the joke about women poets only writing from their menstrual cycles. I welcomed the gauntlet:

> I want to don armor of words as they the men do and fight with a
> liberated tongue and punctured heart

But also wanted to make something new.

I cite my birth as a poet to the obligatory dog tags soldiers wore and we had to wear as children in the fifties and to my first encounter with my father as he returned from WWII—and I use as frontispiece in *Iovis* a first photo of us in Washington Square Park, where I am fingering one of the buttons of his military uniform. Taking shelter from the atom bomb under my desk at P.S. 8 was enough cognitive dissonance to turn one to poetry.

During the composition of the poem that would never let go, I also wrote *Marriage: A Sentence,* a serial prose poem—that originated in experiments with the Japanese haibun in a Naropa class—with capping haiku. It begins, "Marriage marriage is like you say everything everything in stereo stereo" . . . which takes on the doubling complexities of marriages of all kinds. *Structure of the World Compared to a Bubble* followed, which came out of a pilgrimage to the Borobudur stupa in Java—long hidden near the Kedu Plain—which has various Buddhist narratives carved onto its walls I recounted and interpreted these stories/sutras as I circumambulated and climbed this architectural wonder.

The allegory *Gossamurmur* is a narrative of a struggle for poetry and its oral archive in a world increasingly devoid of such concerns. It involves a doppelgänger Anne, an "original Anne," and the dread Deciders and Imposters, as well as the New Weathers and space/time travels through Vedic India and Heian Japan and contemporary Morocco. It is a plea for reanimating our essential links and psyches to poetry and a case for honoring the oral archive and its preservation. There are references to the NY Public Library, the reclamation of the Jemaa el-Fna market in Marrakech by Spanish poet and activist Juan Goytisolo, and the Svalbard in Norway, a refuge for seeds in case of a large-scale global crisis.

The poems became a tentacular form that may encompass all kinds of traditional and wilder genres—prose narrative, structures that embellish and disrupt narrative, performative interventions of all kinds—with a nod to documentary practices.

Sanctuaries for artifacts significant to the culture and history of nations and to our endangered civilization.

Robin Blaser, in discussing the serial poem, invokes the image of the poet wandering between dark rooms. Each time you enter a new room, the light goes on, but just for a minute. Then you go into another dark room. The sections of the poem are, presumably, what you see when that light goes on.

The epic is the correspondence, it is the extended vocalized syllables of love and longing, it needs a wide berth.

> I desire to tell the human story, of tribes and empires. Of innocence and experience.
> It is the screed, the vox: heart's cry. Sometimes. And it's simpler.
> It's grammar light, fewer words on cluster. Why would one lyricize? Inevitable.
> I accompanied at times old friend Ginsberg on Blake: "Little lamb who made thee? Dost thou know who made thee?" Happy syllables. Questions to Creation.
> And it was a clarion call centuries away, a little curl of word or gesture, wooly hair . . .

Trembling orality I hear in all the bards I love. Some days we sing.

Lyric will start with a dawn song. Alba. Don't go back to that cold tomb. You are in the corridor between light and light even when you sing the blues. Blake's *Book of Thel* was such a lyric poem, a six-page dream meditation on the "unborn" virgin from the Vales of Har (harmony) and gave rise to *Voice's Daughter of a Heart Yet to Be Born.* Thel came to the citadel of poetry and told me to write this poem. It was the bat kol, the feminine voice of god. God as a shaman in the voice of a woman. The unborn virgin, the severed breast, the cancerous nightmare I was living through.

That questioned existence of being born. That conversed with the elemental worm, the elemental cloud, the elemental lily flower, the elemental clod of clay, and ran screaming back to a state of innocent dementia.

It was crisis time. 2016 Under current lawless rule, where safety nets are down, surveillance and irreparable shifts are occurring in the frequencies or every quarter of life—I wanted in *Trickster Feminism,* a book of entangled moods and resistances and assignments toward a stand of gleeful post-post mod feminist empowerment, to take on the idiocy and danger of the dismantling "State" that is so reprehensible and transparent in its cruel and greedy machinations. One is beyond the talk of all this. Poetry has another job in this, perhaps, but it still needs to call out. And I'll add from nuclear irresponsibility to separating children from parents and putting them in cages. It's a poem-book to be taken into public space as it was, but poetry does offer the language for one to respond with nuance and documentation imagination. Rituals of emphatic sounding and focus, walking with others in public space and protest does quicken the heart to urgent mental and activist awareness. I live in a continuum of art humans that won't give up, as one goes down, one steps up. This is what sustains the spirit even if some call it whistling in the dark. We are clearly on the precipice.

Trickster Feminism is field-poet arena of "sets" in a variety of voices and modes with interventions of quotation and penned in part on streets of protest in NYC; DC; Berkeley, CA; Denver, Boulder, CO; my own "meditations in an emergency."

You often find your form, your stride for particular kinds of writing, one that feels true to the rhythms of your own consciousness and metabolism in the world or allows a kind of freedom and expansion of associative language. You might feel your head on fire. Your voice sonorously activated. You want to stay out under the night sky singing to the moon. You find language in the flames and stars. Epic, allegory, investigative hybrid in chapters, libretto, an architecture based on a traditional memorial marker or stupa, etc. Writing long poems—and reading and performing them as well—is principally what I do in my writing life and have been doing for the past fifty years.

Family Frame, with Ambrose:

2012 INTERVIEW WITH LAURA WETHERINGTON

LAURA WETHERINGTON: Could you detail how "Remember Qana" and "Radial Symmetry of the Younger Sister" were conceived, composed, and produced?

ANNE WALDMAN: "Remember Qana" is a version of part of *The Iovis Trilogy* from Book III, section or canto XXIII: "Problem-Not-Solving." And there are also some lines in the recorded version from a piece entitled *Cry Stall Gaze,* a collaboration with painter Pat Steir. We recorded these vocals in Ambrose's little studio at MacDougal Street and possibly some earlier in San Francisco. Ambrose tends to edit, arrange later, as he listens and matches the text with his musical ideas. There were several vocal takes, and I felt inspired in my range of vocalization . . . the way, for example, "marginalia!" is conveyed in a Sprechstimme mode, or "in the ground in the ground in the ground of . . ."—this lyrical foray. I wanted this piece to have emotional power, complexity; so I was very supportive of the direction and the multilayering of the vocal parts, the overlappings, the pentimento effect, and call and response as well, the kind of swell that happens, yet returning to the base refrain: *remember Qana.* I was thinking of the massacre in Beirut and the reference to biblical Qana. I was listening at one point also to an early version of the music with headphones on and recorded off that, that way as well. Ambrose's editing can get very detailed and fastidious. But I always want to give an energetic, intelligent rendering of the text.

"Radial Symmetry of the Younger Sister"—parts of which surface in *Iovis* as well, and comes out of a performance with a dancer originally—had the distinct numbered phrases, an odd list of qualities, characteristics in the mind of an altered universe, which I think influenced this particular musical soundscape; its form is generated around the structure of numbers, which the music drives. The snare drum sounds like a whip's lash to me. The sampling of George Bush's voice saying "Please be seated" originally threw me off, and I agonized over whether or not it should be included.

The opening salvo has a sort of "call-to-order" effect. Called to order to what? Enjoy the ambience and sensuousness of the performance here.

AMBROSE BYE: I recorded the vocals for "Radial Symmetry" at the Pyramind Studio in San Francisco, where I was studying at the time. I was going off the tempo of the reading and matching it to a musical frame I was already making. The tempo and the rhythms of the reading matched the music. "Qana" is a bit different. I manipulated the music and the voice much more. In a way, "Radial Symmetry" is more of a superimposition and "Qana" a collage. I was cutting up the two pieces of vocal text for "Qana" in a way that they became one piece that was entirely different from the two separate texts and performances. And there's attention to the beats and the vocal emphasis on particular words (which I also edit). Typically when people are putting poetry with music it tends to rhyme (like hip-hop). But this is not about rhyming, the text is not consistent in that way. So I'm finding other ways to have the cadence—and have a cadence with the illusion of rhyming, perhaps. I can manipulate the voice in time (as well as the sounds), manipulate the space between words, and it flows in the piece. I was also panning Anne's voice from left to right, playing off the two texts. There was more mixing in this piece.

AW: What about the semantics? The ideas behind the words. You've heard me talk about melopoeia, phanopoeia, and logopoeia. You are the melopoeia.

AB: I work more intuitively, not so conceptually. But there is an emotional tone. I already had the presidential Mission Accomplished music and Bush's voice, and this is kind of random but it matched up with the text. It's spontaneous in a way, what works. I'll try something a few times, and if it doesn't come together I won't keep going on it. But the point is that we already had something going independently with "Radial Symmetry," and with "Qana" it was a much more complex process.

AW: But the final version is quite different from the original, much longer text, although I think it carries even greater emotional weight.

LW: In 2009, a group of researchers found that guitar duos synched brain waves while they played together. I'm wondering if the two of you feel like you have that kind of synchronization during your collaborations. Can you feel some kind of resonant connection? If so, at what moments? Can you describe how it feels? If you think you don't have that kind of experience, can you hypothesize why not?

AW: Yes, I experience this synchronization quite strongly at times. And particularly in live performance. Parts of the "Manatee/Humanity" suite (from my book of the same title, published by Penguin Poets in 2009) seem to work in this way.

I think the anaphoric litany section with the recording of the manatee song, and with Ambrose's own vocals at the end, actualize this magic of wedded brain waves, and when Ambrose would do this live, I felt called to respond in kind. And the poem is talking about the manatee's mother's relationship to her "just one manatee offspring," which has particular relevance here to our mother/son relationship. And it can happen in the studio process as well, recording, trying things out . . . when the minds meet in the actualizing of both language and sound.

AB: I would agree it happens in the live performance.

AW: Brion Gysin, friend and collaborator of Burroughs, developed his Dreamachine, which worked with a communal synchronization around light and sound. There's the communal thrum with drumming, and the way a spiritual guide or shaman can synchronize with vocals.

I saw the graphs of the guitarists' brain waves in sync and am not surprised. It makes neurobiological sense. I find if I am involved in a group reading of some kind where we are all reading "Ode to the West Wind" for example, together (as we did regularly in the early days of the Kerouac School at Naropa) or in some of the work with Gertrude Stein in concert with others, her compelling rhythms seem to create a heightened communitas.

LW: How did the two of you start working together?

AW: Ambrose grew up in the environment of the Jack Kerouac School at Naropa University in Boulder, Colorado, a program that came together in 1974. He heard poetry read aloud from a very early age—his whole life in fact. And his father, Reed Bye, is also a poet.

He even read one of his own pieces at a reading with Amiri Baraka when he was eleven years old.

We also lived in Bali together and played in a gamelan orchestra when I worked with Naropa's Study Abroad Program in Indonesia. Ambrose was eight years old the first time, then again he participated in the program his final semester of high school. I understood his musical gifts as a child. His father had started piano lessons for him as well. We were also in the Naropa gamelan orchestra together, with his father, Reed.

I joke that he heard poetry in the womb, and the connection started there. Yet music was his more natural path. In this kind of work he does with me, he is responding to and providing an environment for language and the performance of it, and for the nuances of my vocalization. Not simply providing an accompaniment for "spoken word," but creating a fully realized soundscape. Which may incorporate other musicians and sounds as well.

There's a CD included with my book *In the Room of Never Grieve,* which came out in 2003, with Ambrose's music and my text and vocalizations, so it's been over a decade of varying work and collaborations. We started performing and travelling together more regularly about three years ago. And we teach writing and recording workshops together—at Naropa, New England College, and this past year at the Poetry Project at St. Mark's Church. We're both in New York these days, so it's easier to collaborate and rehearse. It seemed natural to work with my own son, for whose work I have great admiration and respect.

AB: Anne would send tapes of her poetry when I was in Santa Cruz, where I went to college (UC Santa Cruz), and I would match them up with the music I was doing with my friends there. I was starting to be interested in making and producing music. So it was around 2000/2001. I had bought a digital eight-track in Boulder. So I was playing around with the music and the poetry. It was when I started using computers and learning more about them that it really started.

LW: You all have made four albums together. Can you describe how your collaborative experience has evolved over time?

AB: The work evolved essentially through advances in the technology with digital recording and having the personal situation of a studio in my own living space. And being able to record—having editing control and making the CDs ourselves. Being able to mix and master from home. The technology—computer problems have come a long way in the last ten years. Usually you'd need the capacity of a huge recording studio. Now you can do it by hand; it's a lot more friendly economically.

AW: From my perspective, it's deepened and grown, I think. Some of the pieces on *The Milk of Universal Kindness* have a new complexity and layering. I have so many ideas for our collaborations all the time. And Ambrose is also producing new work pieces like my lament for Akilah Oliver, with vocals by Tracie Morris. He's recently been recording me with the very wonderful sax and trumpet player Daniel Carter, and then shaping the final scape. We have a new twenty-five-minute piece from the book *Soldatesque/Soldiering* (with artist Noah Saterstrom, Blaze Vox Press, 2011) that's very sustained.

LW: How does your work with one another influence your other creative endeavors?

AB: I grew up in a poetry/artistic community and had the opportunity to meet and was exposed to a lot of interesting people and their work. Anne and jazz musician Daniel Carter had played together some years back, but they wouldn't have recorded and reconnected in this way if I hadn't met with him more recently (Daniel was playing with Thurston Moore at a gallery we were also playing). And the influence for projects is coming from this larger pool I can draw/fish from. Lyrics for music can be really bad; there's more substance coming from the poetry world, where people take pride in their writing, it's not a commercial venture. Not asinine stuff! The work can stand by itself. More verbal substance than much hip-hop, pop, rock. I'm also helping produce other poets, a project with Kristin Prevallet. Some of the students from workshops at the Poetry Project.

AW: As I said I am constantly having new ideas as a result of my work with Ambrose. I am learning things about the studio process and what's possible in sound recording. How the range is endless. And how I can play with my own vocal imagination in a liberated way. He also helped with sound effects for another project with musician/composer Steven Taylor, my Naropa colleague of many years who also worked extensively with Allen Ginsberg. Steven and I have created a two-act opera entitled "Cyborg on the Zattere," which takes on the "knot" of Ezra Pound, his brilliant poetry and terrible politics. Ambrose has some studio training, which is very helpful in these kinds of endeavors, and he's started to record some of the individual pieces with Steven.

Ambrose is also accompanying me on acoustic guitar and piano with some of the work in live performance, and we are starting to record some of those pieces as well, like "Prisons of Egypt" sung to the melody of "Go Down, Moses," which needs a chorus.

LW: Do you ever experience a form of writers' block together and if so, what do you do to get out of it?

AW: I think that's rarely the case, as I am so project orientated and work frequently in collaboration. So sometimes the demand of the "other" pulls me along. I always need more time, more writing-retreat time. I get involved with too many infrastructure projects—creating the summer program at Naropa—that can be extremely demanding.

LW: Can you all talk about the differences between collaborating with one another, given your close bond, and collaborating with people you didn't grow up with / birth and raise?

AB: I can't be as brutally hard and honest with others as I can with Anne. If we're working closely together on the full process—with our particular forms, the "soundscapes"—the original material, the recording, editing in our own home, it's a different dynamic. The way we can talk with each other given this context is totally different, and there's a lifelong frame of reference.

But also we spend more time on this than the way Anne might improvise live with other musicians.

AW: There's always mutual respect and the need to really listen to the other, in collaboration, whatever the relationship. Ambrose and I might struggle a little harder together and we can squabble about things more vocally, and yes, there's a personal dynamic that can be more dramatic.

My collaboration with artist Pat Steir is also a give-and-take, yet our respective realms seem more distinct. With music and poetry, I share the music through my own voice as a participating instrument.

LW: If you would consider collaboration as a part of your value system or ethics or a part of your spiritual practice, could you explain the connection? Would you talk about a time outside of your artistic practice where collaboration plays a part in your values, ethics, or spiritual practice?

AB: Things were "actualized" at a young age for Anne in terms of collaboration; it's part of the backbone of her whole artistic life. A heightened sense of artistic community. From her early days with the New York School, collaborations with artists like George Schneemann and Joe Brainard, the Beats. The Kerouac School and a twenty-five-year work like *The Iovis Trilogy* that includes so much documentation of others.

AW: Collaboration is a way to be with "other," to be in a symbiotic, sympathetic relationship with the pulse and mental stream of another sentient being. And to have to keep listening to their sound and/or looking at the shape and color and contours of the visual work. But there has to be an affinity artistically. Community-building is an artistic practice as well.

The Sanskrit word used for spiritual communities is *sangha,* originally for monastic life, an assemblage free from the constraints of household life. I like to invoke this term for dedicated artists and activists.

And then there's the notion of trying to create a more spiritually enlightened and just society. I find the Occupy movement particularly inspiring because you can bring your own talent into the field of action rather than wait to belong to the club or face a certain hierarchy.

LW: Anne, would you consider your book *Manatee/Humanity* to be a collaboration of sorts? Why or why not?

AW: Well, it's an interspecies investigative project that incorporates some very vivid dreams, and also a Buddhist ritual/initiation (the Kalachakra) as well as the most important aspect of this narrative—the life of the manatee. And my encounter with a living, endangered manatee triggered the poem.

It was a vow to the life of this particular manatee that created the work. And the forty-five-minute "suite" Ambrose worked on was an extension of that original impulse. (We haven't put together and recorded the entire piece as yet). And I see it as an album that could be done even in the distant future. Basically the written part was a hermetic process of about three years. Except for the litany section and an early version of the closing "The Eye of the Falcon," I didn't publish or read from the work until it was finished. Our mind in the world while making the work is always a challenging, intense collaboration with oneself. When it gets lifted off the age sonically, vocally it is a whole new experience.

Postscript: And after the *Manatee* project came *Jaguar Harmonics,* a most ambitious epic seventy-minute piece, made in the basement of MacDougal with all musicians present: Ha-Yang Kim, Daniel Carter, Devin Brahja Waldman (with whom we formed the Fast Speaking Music family band). An ever-evolving multiple dynamic free jazz session and in-part improvised poetry that emerged out of notes becoming text, turned book, becoming "show" and then surfacing as album out of Ambrose's alchemical laboratory. He was able at the end of the piece to create a psychedelic chatter of underworld terrifying animalia. The "message" from that sentient other-world is "Don't like it, don't do it, hydraulic fracturing, heh heh heh heh."

Sciamachy, produced by Devin Brahja Waldman, was released by the Lévy Gorvy Gallery and Fast Speaking Music in 2020. What follows is from a conversation with poet Emma Gomis while interviewing for Press Radio Montez in NYC:

AW: I am totally thrilled by the collaborative effort on "Extinction Aria"— especially in these times when one aches to be in the same room with cohorts, when one longs for that kind of visceral musical kinetics, and I could feel sea change as we recorded in London town, home of William Blake. Deb Googe's bass on our duo is formidable, deep haunting earth tones. Devin Brahja Waldman's alchemy in the mix. As producer, and his own alto sax contributions really work, a kind of transcendent lift toward kind of apotropaic—curing—exaltation. Everyone is outstanding! I met Guro Moe and Håvard Skaset in Mexico City, a totally fortuitous chance meeting with instant affinity. And in Brooklyn with William Parker on the n'goni, an instrument whose sound balances conflict was spiritual boon, and he himself also plays and bounces with light. I could get into my lower registers more deeply . . . and I think we could all feel a bond of symbiotic energy, everyone doing what they *know*. Ambrose's opening synth was the voice of a beckoning angel for me.

How else to confront the god realm of war and ego and plague and threat of extinction in this lonely aria zone without a wall of protective sound? But it also is a meditative lesson on impermanence and larger cycles of life/death/desire. This is the sweetest exploration I could ever imagine for a sense of trance that I aspire to in my poems. A sustained effort toward ego-annihilation which is also a kind of ecstasy. Sciamachy is the battle with the shadows, often your own ghosts.

These are some of the toughest times for all of us, and artists need to continue to push against the possibility of a world without our wholehearted participation and humanity. The sounds and laments and cry of the heart of the planet call us to music, to poetry, to a life of changing frequencies of existence toward creation. I take that vow.

Enjoy very much quoting Sun Ra, especially when at work on musical collaboration with my family and friends in small bedroom studio: "Heaven is where you'll be when you are okay right where you are."

Anne Waldman with Devin Brahja Waldman.

Fragments

The scale of the transformations we are witnessing today has no precedent either in natural or cultural history. The global uprooting of both nature and humanity makes each and every one of us a refugee of sorts. How long we will remain refugees on the earth no one can say, but the fact of homelessness has by now become obvious even to most privileged or protected members of the human family.

What is not at all obvious to us, on the other hand, are the potential saving forces that may one day rise up against the tide of nihilism. It may well be that, in the future, these decades will be remembered above all for the improbable existence of a handful of poets who brought the old household gods into hiding. From our present perspective nothing seems more superfluous to the contemporary turbulence of history than poets, yet our present perspective may turn out to be the most superfluous thing of all. . . . This much is certain: at a time when the gods have no choice but to flee from the falling city of man, it is only the poets who can take them into their safekeeping.

—ROBERT POGUE HARRISON

To Poets and Painters: In the topos, in the products of human making, in love making, in repositories in which they dwell, in the body of sculpture, painting, amphora, lives Eros. Fraught or repressed. Are we on a precipice of words? Is that what's leaning the planet, leaving the planet Eros? Figures chase each other around a vase or burn in Purgatorio as on a Grecian vase. Perpetual hunt, things going after each other in the springtime, in battle time. Or Thanatos for a nonhuman, lives in a nonhuman variable. Lives inside an idea I will write to tell you the verbal attention of. Of the word *presses,* as "presses against my heart." Ideas press. Instigate. Tell you what is seen in melancholia. It presses, the stylus, the stalk. It presses. O my world. All the diagrams. Charts of doom. What do you love? Who? I don't want to be robotically adjusted, don't want to be an electronic flow confused, microchips in the body, data trickling out, sounds unmerciful. Don't want to dwell in the melancholia of lost flesh. Become statistical dust.

Rune and wreck, no contact. What is seen in a subject transcending how you derogatorily say "dwelling in primitive"—can you really spend your day looking, breathing in the "objects" of action to be crude? Be ritual. Be golden. Not action-bound entirely. False. But I do make. We do make love. I do make up poetry. We do make up our love. Make a case for this meaning or poem, in painting or poem, biopic or poem, container for thoughts and fragments of one day. A line might be the mutilated body of the one you cherish. Paper we cherish. Bulrushes. Dear People: Let's go to surface. Out of the abyss. Off the screen. Artist eye please beg you rescue from mess and text. Lines are, conduits are, tributaries are, the trajectory-documents are constructions more than a statue or a poem collective is. All poems are fragments. That is a long ambulation. Around and around. What about the ordinary statute of things? Limitation. Composite miracles to cut up. When they rock and go brittle, when they refute entrance, when they excuse themselves from reproach, when they abjure taking a stance, when they seem to tame, reticent, murky, are they not fragments of ball-wreck impermanence? When murky becomes a problem for the historians of readers who examine "us" in a distant future. *What was it to read? What was it to look? Who tamed the frame? What is it to mechanize?* What if your factotum does it for you? And reports back. You etch away in solid solitude. Museum shadow. Or. Or if. But two minds together is a boon. Will you be confused by the two variables, left brain and right? Can you be your own third mind? Are you lonely in all you do? I'd guess yes. I am too. I follow you from far away. I enact telepathy. Is your machine very murky, do you clear it every day? Don't be a fetishist. Don't reboot too often. Look at someone else's pictures. A collector of rare beings. And what is valuable are the feminized body parts that add up to a greater sum of extensions that ask the limits of the body as represented by deities, by goddesses, by sublimated animals, by helmeted warriors, by super-beings that wish to wink and smile as pure and salutary folly and as I said. Ask the limits. At you, Artists! So-called female power and cross-dressing and folly is the game of purveyors, of readers. Revelers. Revelators. I will go oral and demand attention. Drag this salutary transmission into public space. Sing my dithyramb. The page will be as bone, will be a steel trap, will be constructed of a substance hard to tamper with. Maybe the wood of forefathers and mothers, or stone carvers formerly painted and capture inner vibrant eye. Polychromed metabolism. Idea of bed linen or wrapping shrouds for viewing before the body hits the tomb, a single jewel in the crown, or bodhisattva demands release from her vow. Or if she could just be sure of the intangible. You can never demand more from a saint than intangibility. Fragment is always waiting to trip you up or startle. The first relation to this mind and "other" is the child's illusion. Is child's separation. Is the bent stick, diviner's wand, twig-inspired reprimand by the museum guard for yearning to cross the line, cross the boundary, just a closer look at you, become one with the object as it melts as an alloy. Its silver, its tin, its bronze, and you get down for it, before substance. Holy stone. Holy library. If marble was a district for punishment, what would it be? It would be luxurious. Are you savage or poet? Poet or assassin? Are you wood? Or the enemy of wood? Are you bored? Please worship wood. How may you bring together the mutilated fragments of all you put an eye to, that you need to take care of, how they assist you in your scroll? In your scribe's assignment. How they talk back. And, comrade, I need you for my vision. My frescoes! And weather the taut visual. Topology is rare and wonderful for all workers. And warm breath of pneumatology. Imagine that your breath could wreak havoc on the treasury of this influx, and what a dangerous artist will accomplish with line might continue chance's operation. Be careful, tread lightly. May the shining new activated WPA hire you & you paint murals for the climate accords. Lift the brush high. What we hold in secular space, behind glass, relics of martyrs, telltale papyrus, gouache, and pigment struggling in sacred space. Full Black power and we the thickness of the event and its cavities. White solipsistic power. See it. A collage. It says "Blood Moon." Obeisance. Freedom. Abolition. Will one culture's ethos obscure another? Not here. Ever in the heroics of maelstrom aura and dust, we'll demand our fragmented continuum. Shards, ostraka, telepathy. Its wounded heart. Carry your sacred urns, your idols, your tablets, your secret tapes out of the fallen city.

* * *

forest (n.): late 13c., you have a district of trees set aside for the hunt, the royal hunt. And it is overseen by the king. Protected by the king. Old French *forest* "forest, wood, woodland," most likely from Late Latin/Medieval Latin *forestem silvam,* meaning "the outside woods." There is the message of "beyond the park" *(parcus)* which is a fenced-in woodland.

I left the keys hidden in the crux of a tree. And we took our vows by an old log. An owl hooted.

Another theory traces *forest* through Medieval Latin *forestis,* origi-
nally "forest preserve, game preserve," from Latin forum in legal sense
""court, judgment"; in other words "land subject to a ban" [Buck].
Replaced Old English *wudu* (see wood (n.)). Spanish and Portuguese
floresta have been influenced by *flor* "flower."

& there's *Wood, would, word* . . . *wald-*
I've always identified as a woodswoman . . . gathering.

* * *

But the archive is above all a fissile material, its specificity being that, at its
source, it is made of cuts. Indeed, no archive exists without its cracks (lézardes).
One enters into it as though through a narrow door, with the hope of penetrating
in depth the thickness of the event and its cavities.

—ACHILLE MBEMBE

There's a level at which words are spirit and paper is skin. That's the fascination
of archives. There's still a bodily trace.

—SUSAN HOWE

Thought of This

for Reed Bye

IN THE MOUNTAINS, SENT TO CH'AN
BROTHERS AND SISTERS

Dharma companions filling mountains,
a sangha forms of itself: chanting, sitting

ch'an *stillness. Looking out from distant*
city walls, people see only white clouds.

—WANG WEI, 701 TO 761 CE
TRANS: DAVID HINTON

clouds sit low here
        clarity 'gainst blue
   over desert & morph
outside
 centers
whose
      ambition?

 get the art here,
said the brujo
 travel for it
commit
now
   changed maybe
since Anglos
 now is mixtos is curious
     in pilgrimage
humble mesa

or Paleo eleven thousand years ago or
  mesic woodland
changed by livestock
    human drought

    —did we feel pulse of anagarika?

    —our lineal journey to slow down?

keep meeting silence &
 "inner spirit
of landscape"

    —birth of duality
of the first skanda
is where
a grain of sand

elemental
    brother & sister

    sticks its head
out of vast
expanse of desert

 & lovers

    and catches a glimpse of itself

wed once
catclaw mimosas
  shrubs, succulents

    —that simple?

    —you can be transparent
all by yourself

  overgrazing
to impermanence
  sheep & goats along
the
Rio Grande
how many years
crossed in identity?

    like the glass frame
doesn't need
watcher
looking through

    —you mean validation of

    watcher false?

 all the one thousand
things
  in syncretic
self-
    sufficient
emptiness

    yet *I see you*

    "Those who have power
to raise windhorse fearlessly . . ."

Praetexta & Performance

in my praetorium in my pragmatic space in my night-alliance-weaponry-space
all the soldiers bedding down in my dictation in my dictum
I not with them   I apart
& they with armor, and fine of it. all manner of spears, knives, lance, & drum
swords to swoon by, but I make it clean to do it not wanting this ever effort spared
& with the praetexta, some with purple border bound as an assemblage
that is a weaponeer's eruption system
a kind of mad male delight
come give me my stylet, pen for the blind
a phalanx of twice-handled shield, gone this way and that a steady show
I would rank now and write Pindaric
close rank now & write a public ode
separate out from him who is pleomorphic
who shifts the atmosphere makes it dawn-deadly the fellows up now readying
as they my brothers & are hurting for fight
you of action materialized of archaic consilium & fiscus. you toads of brutal war
maybe he had me saying: made crazy by many-tours sooty war
sooty sooty war, coming out of the dead articulum
to write my cut-throat ode again

  —FROM "ODE," A.W.

Is war an experiment? How is the poet useful in her time, and how does one hold space in suffering? How is one experimental in poetry that attempts to document—in addition to the throbs and throes of existence—perpetual conflict, bloody, sooty, and ugly crimes against humanity? Or is there some knowledge in the pleasures of war?

Pound's "Sestina: Altaforte" comes to mind with its glee in "the sun rise blood-crimson." Insanity each day in a political dystopia creates rage. Poets seek imagination's release. Is there liberation through poetry that bends form and intention? What makes human darkness anew? What activates our language motor, our desire to construct, create an activist "machine." I don the "praetexta" (ceremonial priestly robe) and interact with melodic drones. Because the US of A is reminiscent at times of the clumsy, old, bellicose Roman empire, I invoke ceremonial Latin. The word from which *ode* derives is the Attic *aeidein,* to sing. And is patterned after the dance-like structure of Greek dramatic chorus, with its strophe, antistrophe, and epode. (I had this structure in mind in a longer version.) *Epode* means "sung after," and was in a different metrical form.

The ongoing question: How are poets contemporary with their time? How might they be postmodern existentialist and ancient seer, and avant-morte, as well? How do they inhabit rhythms across time? Tracking monsters, night-mares, holocausts: Anna Akhmatova, Paul Celan, Amiri Baraka, Audre Lorde, Muriel Rukeyser, Raúl Zurita, NourbeSe Philip, among many others, come to mind. One summons and invents within language a new ethos of intent, syntax-in-struggle, and in the case of Celan's hybrid words: *shard-strewn, wordlight, tearstain.* He spoke of a poem being like a message in a bottle toward "an addressable reality." Poets deconstruct, reconstitute, then reshatter shards of history into our time, the unhinged late Capitalocene. A poem is allowed to chronicle the history of its own making. The mind of the poet may also be the subject of the poem.

Not made facilely and to not let the owning of other's suffering or even one's own become rational, a begging for the poem (or: one takes to poetry). To transcend this emotional crux one goes to open form, composition by field, indeterminacy, documentary poetics, hybrid form, dream, or the obliteration of personal "I." And there were Oulipo strategies of constraint and play such as Georges Perec's "story-making machine" or the experiment of univocalism, a poem using only one vowel letter *o,* or work excluding a particular vowel. I chose *o* as a searing cri de coeur:

Lost You, O

    wok and mort
     got bowing of doors
        hodg podg
   flop or posts?
    old bon mot: look!
    joy of d'or

short stop
too too
you jot?
or two
lost roots to floors of
torn crooks:
sky down, Georges Perec

One may be inspired by another work of art as in ekphrastic practice. Erasure, metatext. And there is the epic form that is also a performance, a meander. That may cover a species, a life, a time that moves in many directions simultaneously. Think of the griot, the balladeer, the torch singer.

Imagine it falls to you (you write out of necessity) you, the solo poet, or the collective you. And your voice/language/ego are anointed/appointed to tell of your "people," your "gender," your struggle. You might be projecting a metaphorical village, a city in conflict with that other one down the road, that country across the ocean, story of a war between tribes, families, countries over water rights, hunting rights, religious rites, oil, the Jerusalemic archaeological tunnel—the tooth and claw level of agon—contest, battle, extinction—literal or psychic. You might suffer "treedome" as Myrrah does, abused by her father, recounted by Ovid, who is transformed to weep bitter tears. Same psychic situations exist now but can we be "translated," as Shakespeare's Bottom is, out of our horrific end of new millennium traumatic nightmare? Earthquakes, floods, plagues. You might dance and wear a mask, evolve a "persona." Here where human violence is no less extreme than *Beowulf*, than *Gilgamesh*, than Homer, than Dante. And its windows (the windows of that violence) are still on the cold stars. One works out of a mythopoetics but worries it, tampers with it, creates metatext of text outside another text that can time travel.

Not the content but the way new form accommodates shift of frequencies. How one jolts awake to a new edge, as in *Manatee/Humanity*, a long poem of call-and-response, environmental urgency, research of animal origins, visits to the museum of skeletons in Paris, and with a particular litany-like modal structure. The poem moves from montage, chance operation, to documentary poetics, to Buddhist ritual, where one might create the life stream of the endangered manatee but knowing the origin as *maniti*, Haitian word for breast.

"Breast like women's that suckled their young/Carib manattoui/Mantouf/ maybe Mandingo origin/Latinized as manatus/infrasound produced in larynx/Ojibwa: manitoo/turned with its hands." And the science: "the mana- tee has more gray matter in the brain than man / the manatee is perhaps thinking archivally deeper than man . . . the manatee is maimed by man, the manatee could be aided by man / man o aid the manatee man come to the manatee heart." The litany invokes the "tidalectics" (Kamau Brathwaite) through the rhythms of the swimming "female manatee bonded with her just one manatee offspring." And conjures the manatee as sirenian. I con- stantly think about entering public space with multiple voices since you might possibly ritually shape-shift to a manatee. You want to make a poem that conjures multiple times and genres. And includes both the arche, the sense of first things, as mind, as larynx, out of things that exist, and the techne, the craft, operative, episteme. Make it work. Work for the endan- gered animal.

Years ago I was a poet-emissary to India, representing Allen Ginsberg's Committee on Poetry, which was working on a project to bring a number of Indian poets to the US. This cultural itinerary would help sponsor and schedule readings and events at Columbia University; the University of California, Berkeley; and Naropa University in Boulder, Colorado. I was the only woman, and American, at a festival organized at the Bharat Bhavan arts center in Bhopal, and this was a way to become familiar with a range of writers and performers from India. The Bharat Bhavan was built in 1982, shortly before the horrible industrial disaster at the Union Carbide plant, a gas leak that killed at least eight thousand people and harmed thousands more. There was finally a settlement in 2010 of a sum under five million dollars, a paltry amount for the massive death and injurious harm. I followed the case for a number of years. Arundhati Roy was outspoken, outraged, lucid. During the visit to Bhopal, one observed death-ash on the land, the people, their psyches, and circumambulated the ghostly shanty towns around the Union Carbide plant murmuring the Buddhist Tara mantra. Like visiting a hell realm (Poet: speak to hell). Bodies and desiccated remnants were still com- ing to light. The center had a gallery filled with photographs from the disaster depicting unfathomable suffering. One felt enormous sorrow and outrage at the atrocity, unconscionable actions, and negligence of the parent company, its CEOs, the cynicism of building a compromised site in a desperately poor neighborhood. The calculating response and resistance to accountability was brutal; the exceedingly long time it took for recompense was criminal.

What could one do or say but protest, write letters, send money. And I wondered during and after this trip to Bhopal how poetry might grasp the magnitude of restless complex variegated catastrophe, involving cosmologies, cultures you barely knew; what form, what way of telling? The other participants in the festival at Bharat Bhavan were poets writing in English, Marathi, Hindi, Bengali, Assamese. The poems were classical, modernist, but restrained, with the exception of the Vedic singers performing in Sanskrit, and the Bauls of Bengal, who performed a beautiful mix of ancient and modern frenzy. I had heard field recordings in the early 1970s, always curious about these ecstatic street-poets. Baul is related to the Sanskrit word *vatula,* which means "madcap." A Baul is one possessed, with uncut coiled hair, necklace of tulsi seeds, saffron robe, a nomad. Wandering from town to town singing for supper, playing a single-stringed ektar carved from a gourd made of bamboo and goatskin. Music/song is sustenance for the Baul; a pure form of orature. There was talk of writing, singing long laments for the tragedy of Bhopal.

Asked at the end of my reading: *Is this the new experimental poetry? Are all American poets experimenting as you are? With your voice? And what about being a woman doing this? Is this what women do?* Yes, women, come sing, sing your lament.

Performing Poetics: The Oral Vortex

it said inna myth
dat di rooster was sent down from heaven to shape
di earth. dat di world was once all wata. dat di rooster
no call out 'pōkokohua'. wat yuh create w/ yrs out of wood,
metal & lacquer? di descriptive begin again. dreamy. reka reka
  engari ia mīere.

— LATASHA N. NEVADA DIGGS

A living language vortex existence, gathering of energy that continues to activate and generate new forms and community forms and thinking in an increasingly complex and more interconnected world and universe. On a vision quest once, I was lying in mud. Slathered by mud. Ingesting mud. The sanguinity of mud. We speak of the multiverse, we speak of the three-brane world. We imagine our ignorance and fragility in the nervous system of the multiverse, our nasty role in the biosphere, in the human realm. Always reifying and sucking the life out, turning it all to coin. We are not thinking well, as a species we are not thinking *of, with, beyond,* seem to not appreciate and marvel at the potential of our own minds, perhaps, enough. And be highly attuned to the consciousness of other species endangered like us. And because of us . . . our rare atavism beyond notions of survival. Focus. Not collapse, implode, get sidetracked. Not make it agulag. Empires of conquest. And poetry as a way into this living vortex that manifests itself as vocal and physical enactment to *resist.* Feel part of a caravanserai poetics, of nomad, of nonattachment, of moving together, mutually supported in extended tribe, in family, through multiple dimensions of consciousness.

Nate Mackey's long serial poem "Song of the Andoumboulou" entwined with his series "Mu" is an epic poem of great wanderings such as these.

Alive in all times, I feel this as "skillful means," or upaya, and as practice that helps me come to greater awareness and curiosity. Through sound and language. And I cite experiences in studies and readings in India and in Indonesia and to a certain extent Mexico and South America—in oral performance and literatures, oratures—and from the more innovative avant-garde strategies arising from spontaneous jazz poetry, through to the chance operations and timing exercises and experiments of attention, as being seminal to a life on the road.

Travelling through time to what we don't know or don't yet know holds language, holds voice, holds gesture in liminal space. One is guided by the words themselves into decisions of how text, libretto, or litany might be performed. And I usually write these long sustained—although somewhat montaged—poems and within them occur gestural or vocalized passages and sections.

I once attended a performance of Kutiyattam—the oldest form of Sanskrit theatre—at the Asia Society in New York City. It was *The Abandonment of Sita,* based on the Kalidasa version. With a solo woman performer, presumably from a Nambiar caste in Kerala. It was presented by the South Indian troupe Natanakairali. The performance was accompanied by mizhavu players. These instruments are considered animate beings, and when they wear out they have a proper ritual, human-like burial.

Kutiyattam is a performance originating in Hindu temples two thousand years ago that has been a living tradition and has morphed through time, going back and forth from the temple into secular settings. I am interested in this movement of art coming out of the temple and progressing into a more public consciousness, becoming contemporary and relative to our lives as we live them now.

I was entranced, especially by the concentration and focus on extraordinary details of eye and facial mudra and the timing, which had a grammatical flow, with punctuation of moments of psychological expression. Never pious or mere storytelling or mime-like. Way beyond those tropes of story. The body in this work becomes the tone of the text. That is attenuated and held through music and the specific quality of the drumbeat. That is like a stab of imagination and motion that is inimical to the force of verbal hit and flow.

Experiencing this rare art form reconfirmed a lifelong interest in what I call a poetics of ritual enactment that drives the spectacle and allows for generative participation. The figure of Sita is at one with her environment in the forest, a zone of symbiosis, as she inhabits the trembling of trees and animals.

Her movements are the movements of a subtle consciousness, not simply as character. It is assumed that the audience is familiar with the story. This slow trancelike performance often concentrates on one aspect, even a detail such as the slow lifting of a skirt.

And the traditional rasas, as well, are relevant here. And reference to the Natyashastra, compiled in India between the second century BCE and the second century CE, which describes the various facial and body poses and expressions needed to perform the "eight basic emotions" of classical Indian dance-theatre. Love, happiness, sadness (or grief), anger, energy, fear, disgust, and surprise. A ninth emotion of peace or tranquility—shanta—was added later. In Kutiyattam, as in the sister genre, Kathakali, rigorous training is required.

The question is how is one contemporary with one's time as an artist? A burning question always provoked by engagement with issues of ecology and cultural activism. Are we ever doing enough?

The question evolves throughout the *Iovis* project, which is ongoing in the books *Trickster Feminism* and *Sanctuary,* and also with *Manatee/Humanity* and *Gossamurmur,* where I romp through notions of doppelgängers and identity shifts, as with the story of Narada and myths of doubles. Wendy Doniger, in her book *Dreams, Illusion, and Other Realities* (University of Chicago Press, 1984), includes variants on the story of the Hindu sage Narada, who is transformed into a woman. She writes, "The outer dream *is* the myth, which nourishes our hope that it is possible to break out of the prison of our secret loneliness, to dream one another's dreams." This is part of being contemporary. We have to communicate with our collective intelligence.

How do we dream one another's dreams? We have the wisdom from Asia of a different sense of time and cosmology—for example, we *are* already in the Kali Yuga, in the dark time. We need to work and think together and preserve wisdom, both ancient and contemporary.

We might turn to the great mystery and beauties of the archaic, and how so much of the modernist poetics we inherit comes from very palpable discoveries in the nineteenth century and what we still feed off: the decipherment of the Rosetta Stone, the undeciphered Indus Valley script, the power of the

Devanagari, the "omphalos stone," the discovery of cuneiform *Gilgamesh,* the discovery of libraries as ancient as cities, and of the Chaldeans' sense that chaos meant "without a library."

What are the contemporary discoveries that inflect and infect our poetic consciousness? What new science informs our poetic consciousness? Why go to literature and art often instead of the history books to make sense of the continuous present that I feel in the experience of Kutiyattam? What are the possibilities with our vast social networks? Our ever-proliferating Indra's nets? Our past and future Yugas—whole world systems—vast movements of time, where the questions essential to our being circulate? What new psychic inscriptions of magic and science, of animal being or plant being; what wonders of the continuum are ongoing proof that we are not alone in a solipsistic ignorance to earth our charge? What is our connectivity, our adhesiveness, our pratītyasamutpāda? In a time of such schizmodic psychogenesis, where we barely understand our relationship to other sentient beings, a time racked by ignorance, constant war, conflicting ideologies, nuclear threat, and massive climate upheaval and uncontrollable greed and the dangerous paradigm of the new surveillance, what is a useful knowledge for us?

Giorgio Agamben suggests that the poet—the contemporary—must firmly hold his/her gaze on his/her own time so as to perceive not its light but rather its darkness. He posits that "the contemporary is the person who perceives the darkness of his time as something that concerns him, as something that never ceases to engage him." And darkness is something that turns directly toward all of us when we are receptive to its wisdom. "The contemporary is the one whose eyes are struck by the beam of darkness that comes from his own time." Further, he goes on in this discourse on how, within the study of the neurophysiology of vision, an absence of light creates a series of peripheral "off" cells in the retina, producing the vision we call darkness. "Darkness is not a deprivation, a notion of absence or void, but rather, the result of these off cells and a product of our own retina."

"What we perceive as the darkness of the heavens is this light that, though travelling toward us, cannot reach us, since the galaxies from which the light originates move away from us at a velocity greater than the speed of light. To perceive, in this darkness of the present, this light that tries to reach us but cannot—this is what it means to be contemporary." Agamben talks about fixing one's gaze on "the darkness of the epoch [we live in] but also [being able] to perceive in this darkness a light that, while directed toward us, infinitely distances itself from us." He likens it to an appointment "one cannot but miss." That leaves us in a puzzling struggle "to grasp our time in the form of a 'too soon' that is also 'too late,' of an 'already' that is also a 'not yet.'" I think poetry has to move and engage with some of this liminal and linguistic behavior, into an aporia, into the "both both," an interstice of imagination. Being positioned on, in, within the doorway. Which is the stance one finds in Kutiyattam, a trembling state of heightened awareness, as if one is caught in the web of life with the distant starlight already past and "the not if" of our mysterious future. This is the most generative eidolon informing writing. It captures the "both both" of "negative capability," as well the Buddhist sense of tamal gyi shepa—or co-emergent wisdom.

Query is the pedagogy, a curiosity, which from an early age, led me to India, and later to Indonesia.

Peering into the darkness—a void that is incredibly active. I remember the wooden yoke encountered in villages I visited in Mahendragada, in tribal communities who still practice cattle worship. A yoke is usually set in the center of the village. A yoke is a feature in Hindu temples, and then I think back to the Buddhist notion and metaphor for how rare it is to find dharma—like coming up to a yoke floating on a massive sea—or I flash back to images on coins from the Mohenjo-daro and Harappan civilizations, also an image of the cattle yoke, a harnessing of power. This is "yoke" in dreams . . . in imagination. I see it moving across a continuum and into the present cyborgian possibilities. What yokes us now?

Reflecting on issues of dominance and power, and wealth (cattle are obviously associated with wealth and major shifts in civilizations), in visiting Borobudur, led to the long investigative poem *Structure of the World Compared to a Bubble*. This linked to the Buddhist ritual lama dancing—weeklong ceremonies—in Darjeeling. The spiritual architecture of our work is key to our relationship to our own existential condition. Needing to make shapes of mind on the page and enact poetry as ritual. I borrow alap from the Indian raga, which lays out the themes of a larger whole. How the fabric of a poem may suggest a continuum of possibility, a spiritual template, and a musical improvisation for a pilgrim's progress. Something like that.

Book II, canto VIII of *The Iovis Trilogy,* "Shree Jagannatha," describes the temple with its six thousand workers, the saucer eyes of the deity, fundamentalists storming into the Babri mosque in Ayodhya.

Book II, canto IX, "Ancestor, Ancestor," invokes the four-armed Shiva Nataraja. In his upper right hand, he carries a small drum shaped like an hourglass for beating the rhythm. This connotes Sound, the vehicle of speech that conveys elevation and is related to Ether, the first of the five elements. Fear not gesture or unfamiliar sound, dream of my parents outside Puri as my father was dying. My parents became precious stones, needing to be dressed like coconut husk dolls in their shrine by the beach in the Bay of Bengal near the black pagoda. Can you wring a stone of blood? Muslim Bardo investigations.

Book II, canto XXII, thinking about Bernadette Mayer as she was going through a serious illness, I wrote this section "Cosmology: Within the Mind of the Sleeping God":

> *She continues her studies of the great Yugas . . . She sleeps as Creator Vishnu does, coiled in on himself, surrounded by royal snakes, intravenous tubes, wires, a veritable tribe of nagas . . . If I could but wander through her body as the holy man Markandeya did in god Vishnu's, an aimless pilgrim, contemplating the interior landscape, the holy spots and shrines through the countries of her body . . . Markandeya was thousands of years old, alert of mind, but an accident occurred when he slipped inadvertently out of the sleeper's giant lip and dove headlong into the cosmic sea. What was his utterance out of the mouth of the body? We live on the edge, constantly, of a precarious unfathomable existence. She returns to the stars.*

This image of being on the lip . . . similar to the liminal quality of Agamben's notion of the state of being contemporary and gazing into darkness, of being caught between two realities, felt useful to a poem of cosmic investigation. But the message is don't get paralyzed. Not to be stuck but rather awake to the "already happened" and also "not yet"—the mystery of our condition in human-time-space dimension. Poetry can lift you out for a moment to track and experience the journey.

The poet standing by her word, which is in a sense all we have in this liminal space of "already" and "not yet"—standing by the word, the utterance, the poet's role as in "vocalizing"—relates to the notion of "projective verse," emerging in the last century through the poetics of Olson and others. Olson speaks of the "kinetics of the thing" and "one thought following instanter on the other." Thus a kind of mind grammar or intervention that reflects the rhythm and often interrupted thinking, disjunctive and staccato (the dérèglement des sens perhaps), of the imagination. Wanting poems as "cultural interventions" to come into public space vocally, on a trajectory of associations, as well as intentionality. There are ideas in this dance of the intellect that come to form precisely through a particular mode of vocalization.

We do not think in complete sentences, and I would say our minds are often at ten various points simultaneously, borrowing from Buddhism the notion of the ten directions of space, which also relates to the necessary measure of our compassion toward others. There's spontaneity in performance involving mantra, blues, and ritual rant—as in Ginsberg's "Pentagon Exorcism," meant to bring the Pentagon "down" metaphorically—and that spontaneous form becomes a fierce example of the need to manifest vocally the urgency for "changing the frequency" of our various solidified realities, in order to reinvent and claim them for public "good."

The notion of "state of mind" coming to be as powerful as a "nation state." In playing with this phrase in an agitprop performance on Wall Street during a demonstration in the beginning years of the war in Iraq, I was able to invoke the witchery of the wrathful female Rangda figure of Balinese origin, who often ends the night by leading the participants into the charnel ground, or cemetery, on the edge of town. Rangda has enormous bulging eyes, pendulous breasts, and long fingernails that claw at the fabric of the "state."

Much of my practice, operating in the temporary autonomous zone of the Outrider tradition, goes back to the sense of the word *worker,* the minstrel, the bard, the shaman. The poems are "modal structures." Working within the soundings of Sprechstimme, invokes tone poems of Alban Berg, opera libretti, and the like. "Pieces of an Hour," for John Cage, in its entirety would run an hour, with some gap for silence and drawn-out phrases. I embody "voice" over a kind of fixed "identity." Its look on the page is one of shape-shifting matrixes.

Translation, of course, is a first ingredient of how a poem will work outside. Interestingly, mantra is referred to as "mind protecting" and mantra is also often without literal sense, as Dadaist utterances often mimic (i.e., Kurt Schwitters). Surreal word associations and soundings don't necessarily carry a semantic message, but they act on the senses as nodes of energy and empowerment and, I think, on the psychophysical system as well, in specific ways meant to shift energy and reconfigure priorities of verbal habit and exchange, in addition to the notion of what "listening" entails.

I trust that the "sounding" with my own voice will carry some of the efficacy and immediacy of this claim to invade or act upon the public space. But there's another kind of meditative vortex poetics demands, that of study, retreat, and translation.

Seeking out earlier oral traditions is thrilling, such as the *Therigatha* (gatha— the songs/poems of Buddhist nuns; and theri—gathered into the Pali canon circa 80 BCE) in attempt to revoice these "scriptures" into a contemporary sphere. This 350-year-old oral tradition—in some cases, the songs are reputed to go back to the time of the Buddha—was passed on from person to person for generations. Scholars believe the language spoken in the early Buddhist community was Magadhi, a vernacular of northern India. By the time the first written documents of Buddhism appeared, the spoken language had change considerably and grammarians had formalized some of the conventions. Working with a Sanskritist friend, and also Victorian translations of the poems, I had the idea to reinvigorate the nuns' "songs" with an old passion and orality. There was something about entering these "voices" into a contemporary vortex of power struggle around identity and feminism as well as a Buddhist sense of liberation. Twenty years later I returned to these poems for a new edition and peered once again into a generative darkness and luminosity of an ancient oral cycle of poetry.

Siha

She thought of suicide, but gave it up, singing:

Distracted
too passionate
dumb about
the way things work
I was stung and tossed

by memories
Haunted, you could say
I went on like this
wandering for seven years
thin, pale, desperate
nothing to hold me
Taking a rope
I went to the woods
Hanging is better
than this low life
The noose was strong
I tied it to the branch of a tree
flung it 'round my neck
when suddenly—look—
it snapped!
Not my neck
my *heart* was free

FROM THE THERIGATHA, C. 80 BCE

Dialogue: "A Pedagogy"

For Hal Willner

This was a dream, a script. Mentor maybe Ginsberg? A trickster at deathbed.
The day Hal died,
April 7, 2020,
First friend to COVID-19.

SONG:

Mentor recounted his origins and names . . . deliberate contradictions . . .
certain rhetoric . . . he was a character, no he wasn't paper thin, never say that
about mentor . . . thick . . . no, he was as salt . . .
necessary, humble . . . he was as terrifying as earnest . . . and . . .
when we needed medicine? ventilators?

JESTE:

He couldn't deliver right now. You mean rested in it? did he test you? mimic
you? He spoke of "unsure use" and the eternal flame.

SONG:

I can't go to desks, hole punch. Too brittle . . . certainly tested. I have
certain elixirs. I love a montage, putting together the strings.
Try me, he'd say. A spray, a mist. Tell me, he'd say, your catalogue of
symptoms. All the styles. Putting together the voices.

JESTE:

But maybe he goes far and stumbles over the trials of "try me." Muddy . . .
resist purpose. Suffer demise if the person is thrifty, spinning central axles . . .
people could die. But the music holds.

How a person may only hold white gloves for so long . . . another century . . .
that kind of slogan . . . or service? Pedagogy? A time of accoutrements. And
of masks. Spinning the tunes in the fun house.

How scholar is torn to pieces if not mapped already. Stand around a vicinity and you'll see . . . feel the invisible threads of vulnerability. Be in sequester too long. Raging at the mirror.

SONG:
Oh. Kin of erotic.
Reiteration . . . central . . . content. Desire we must delay and open up our arms to loss.
Mentor for a woman is the same atmosphere as obstinacy.
I want my own gay shoulder. Kissing of death. I want my arms to embrace the future alchemist. Mentor says little in the lucid dream.

It figures in the puncture . . . her/my category "stand or fall"
In front of the overblown detail . . . what mentor meant to mean, I think.
And then she/I was liberated.

JESTE:
They were not all saved. But remembered for their music: *Weird Nightmare: Meditations on Mingus.*

The notion. The transcendence. Liberated the move. The future liberated the player. A sudden interruption in the flow of party lights.

What you've heard of my night shift. I was always in this world, glorious in this season, hands on, not in this cold hell of intubation. Made the spirits rise.

Interview with *Poetas,* Madrid 2018

POETAS: I'd like to know first what moment you think the world and you are in. For some it's a time of revolution, for others of pre-revolution, and there's some that say that it's a revolution in the present-continuous and now there's a peak. What do you think?

ANNE WALDMAN: We are in a critical and terrifying moment. We are in the Anthropocene, where nothing is not affected or infected by the "hand of man," our massive carbon footprint, our War Machine. It's out in the open, the climate patterns of the New Weathers, extinction rates of plant and animal species, it's all happening under the regime of capitalism. So we are in the Capitalocene, which is a huge syndicate of samsara, to use the Sanskrit term for the endless wheel of suffering. (Or the "meat wheel," as Jack Kerouac puts it.) We need to unmake the violence and oppression of racialized capitalism. We need cultural and humanitarian revolution. We need subversive remedy. We need poetry to remind us of the magic we have had that needs attendance, recharge. This will be the age of Poetry, which will be needed as sustenance, like water, like air we breathe. It will be the age of capable, visionaries taking charge, taking power. We need armies of compassionate bodhisattvas and lovers. There's an idea that the end of the world is easier to imagine than the end of capitalism. This is crazy. Are citizens just too nihilistic and indolent and out of touch with what truly matters? Peace and justice, reconciliation, disarmament? Humans have to stop sitting in front of their screens, letting their empathy and urgency dissolve. Becoming totally disempowered, clueless pretas: hungry ghosts. What's energizing about this time, and also a relief (although we are dancing with our own extinction), is that everything is exposed in this moment, all the horrors. That have been going on festering for centuries. This is a time of reckoning for each one of us. There is a way to take a stand, to create antithesis realities, to struggle for parity, for compassion, for care of the wounded and oppressed, to heal heartbreak, sorrow, loss, conquest, colonialism. But of course you need the broken heart to build on. Who has not been almost destroyed by attack, or ignored or considered expendable. To consider the abuse of the indigenous ones, the karma of slavery, the disordering forces of capitalism and racism and dumbed-down ignorance is overwhelming. It would take lifetimes to repair. As poets and writers and artists we need to consider working collectively through this earth-wide trauma in order to move humanity forward, mend, and help others.

To love and continue dancing but not always on the edge of a precipice. We are in a rhizome of providing a countervision. We will do what we can. We will continue singing. "In the dark times, will there be singing? Yes, there will be singing about the dark times," wrote Bertolt Brecht. But we will sing from our memories, our dreams of the beauties of this fleeting world. We desperately need a revolution of consciousness.

Amiri Baraka said to me before he died, "don't let this stuff"—meaning our efforts in the humanitarian struggle and in poetry—"get buried." It's very alchemical how all this plays out, how we can feel the auspiciousness of being together in the battleground of spaciousness. Allen Ginsberg commented before he died, as I sat next to him in the hospital bed, that "the planet has AIDS." The revolution, yes, continues for millennia and for many, many of us, and it is a revolution of consciousness as well as an attunement of how humanity will cope in the future. What will we have destroyed to survive our cynicism?

Other denizens share the planet and cosmos with us, and we need to do double-time to expose the abuse of women and to empower women. And we have to do so much to counter harm and honor those who have fallen and pick up again. While we live and breathe. And also know how blessed we are to love and work together and to stay awakened.

POETAS: What similarities do you see between today's society and that of the sixties and seventies? And what insurmountable abysses?

AW: We are still experiencing the causes and disastrous histories of those times. I see that we have some of the same problems and they are worse in terms of climate and much more proliferated. Metastasized. But should also remember the strides in consciousness and feminism and civil rights. But now: more people in prison, particularly people of color, and more discord. And the stakes are higher with nukes and climate change and population explosion. And the billion migrants worldwide, starving, afflicted, homeless. We may all be migrants by the end of this century, throughout the world. The reaction to 9/11 by the US unleashed and destabilized the Middle East. And brutally, just like the criminal and murderous folly in Vietnam. Hegemonies. Exhausting. People should not be slaves to the Capitalocene strife. And the insanity of the warring god realm that needs to create enemies to feel alive and sexy.

POETAS: We're in a moment of searching, as a society, of course and, in another order, as women. What do you think we're going to find? What do you think should be the axis of that search? All the generations, groups, tribes, etc., have been united by the motivation to find something determined, very often something emotional. What do you think unites us today?

AW: I'm not sure "searching" is the most effective psychological stance. We should be considerably smarter—wiser—by now in terms of understanding how things work. There are models from the past of alternative ways of coexisting. We should have learned from experience and past example and history about slavery and empire and war and capital. And our precarious environments. We hear the science. We know more than we think we do. I think the most important thing is to hold on to our own minds, our own consciousness. To stay empowered and sharp of mind. And practice discriminating awareness-wisdom. And beware ideologies. And to continue to protest as we can. Oppose, resist. And to also continue to cultivate disciplines of art and scholarship and spirituality. To cultivate our compassion, our empathy. To not become inured to the beggar, the convict, not be manipulated. Not to become sheep: passive and complicit. Or driven by greed and money. Do we want to be controlled by Google, Apple, Facebook, Amazon? Live in a version of their world? We are already under total surveillance! Women need to have more leadership in political and social zones and in collectives and realms of education and mediation. And that is changing. There should be a peace czar in every presidential cabinet. Public education in most places is in disarray. There's a book by Tijuana activist Sayak Valencia entitled *Gore Capitalism* (Semiotext(e), 2018) that talks about how violence itself has become a product within hyperconsumerist neoliberal capitalism.

POETAS: Do you feel closely connected to some current philosophy today?

AW: I've been a student of Tibetan Buddhism for a number of years, a practice that goes way back, thousands of years, in terms of lineage. But dharma needs to stay current. And I am shocked there isn't more compassion and socially conscious activism on behalf of the Rohingya, just one example. I am also a full-time poet and cultural activist; that is my path. I appreciate Agamben's sense of how poets need to stay contemporary with the times and look into the "darkness" and find points of light. I enjoy Donna Haraway's meditations on the "cyborg" and Capitalocene. I adhere to a view that we have to keep the world safe for poetry. It's a matter of symbiosis. Spiritual, psychological.

POETAS: How do you think that current literature is going to fit all these social swings? Do you think that literature is moving toward a more global portrait of society in its stories and in its characters and emotions? How do you think this permanent virtual connection will affect contemporary writing?

AW: Yes, there is a global reach and a range of possibilities, as there is in film, visual art, music. We've seen the world changed by music that is shared, exchanged. There is an enormous body of writing coming from all quarters, and that virtual reality can be in the service of our creativity. And one can travel to many alternative zones with consciousness, with imagination. It's fantastic that we are seeing what is going on in far reaches of wild mind. Whole ways of art-being that have been sustained consciously for centuries. And then the permutations of the new. It's the continuous present as well.

But when you think of the stress of any particular day, living in Syria, under constant siege, how many are writing novels? "Keep the world safe for poetry" is one of our Naropa slogans. I try in my poems to take on war and patriarchy and other burdens, but perhaps more importantly sustain poetry as an alternative reality, a sanctuary.

POETAS: How do you think the evolution of women has been within poetry and the world of writing in general?

AW: Progressing with alacrity, with brilliance. It's not easy to claim the space and time needed as artists and writers throughout the centuries. But also there's more gender fluidity these days, and the struggle continues for parity (and there is backlash under current US regime) and there are bodies of work from those zones as well. There is an interesting recent (over five-hundred-page) anthology of trans and gender queer poetry called *Troubling the Line. Trickster Feminism* (Penguin, 2018) [explores] issues of identity and conjures female presences from all times and places to aid in the elevation of consciousness and action. The creative work is never finished, part of a continuum.

POETAS: You interpret your writing, and in the end, that's reading, feeling, and externalizing, right? Take the rhythm and pulse of the lines (if I'm wrong, please tell me, and explain it to me). So, if I'm not wrong . . . What pace and what pulse do you think life has today? Or, at what pace and with what pulse do you interpret it?

AW: The pulse of life for me is an inner and outer kinetics, and the psycho-physical memory and thrust of my mind and body. I'm very curious about everything and kind of an investigative/field poet. But all the works seem to be "meditations in an emergency" to borrow Frank O'Hara's apt title. I wrote a long poem-book, *Structure of the World Compared to a Bubble,* which is a long walking meditation visiting the great Borobudur stupa in Java and attempting to lay out the path of Mahayana Buddhism. A tall order. I wrote *Manatee/Humanity* considering the life-form and rhythms of this endangered species. I spent a lot of time exploring William Blake's "Book of Thel" and wrote *Voice's Daughter of a Heart Yet to Be Born,* bringing the unborn Thel into this treacherous world of innocence and extermination.

Contemporary life's pulse is wild. There is a lot of noise everywhere and speed and never missing a moment with our cyborgian cell phones and other tech accoutrements. I am planning for both collaborative spaces and retreat and better "deep listening," and I borrow that term from composer Pauline Oliveros. It's always important to transmute mind into refreshed language and be cognizant of *the music* and carry the sense of that dance of intellect too, and stay modest and amazed with all the vibrancy of our lives and listen to others. And struggle for it too. Artists can leave traces of that wonder and joy and mourning, and let anyone coming after that know that we were not just all killing one another. It's going to be a harder world in the future, greater suffering, displacement, toxicity. We need to keep building communities of mutual support and camaraderie and include the other denizens we share this time and space with. Being human provides for continuing acts of poetry.

AI Angel

(a cave had no light yet letters emanated)

rays from what source?

they—spelunkers—made out
"nymphs with partridges wear the order of the swan"
then: "an alchemy of nudity and animalia and honor"
they marveled as string theory
metastasized with more dark energy
as tentacular directions in the
multiverse were revealing themselves
cave was sanctuary was laboratory was seclusion
"time and space are always ambiguous"
but we knew that, they said, "& turbulent, terrifying"
an elixir shot in the arm, vision of bandaged angel-mouth
our world our world, night's solipsistic bubble
this is Fra Angelico at our beckoning
blindfolded deity on the cave wall
art & meditation in a gold-rimmed universe
and at its center a death mask, tongue with heavy chain
didn't hear it coming, an ominous plague year
born of bat on another turf's shadow
didn't see the affinity
& staying inside the discos so long. . . .
this is a new world, another axis
not enough elucidation not enough
evolutional topical optimization of vibrating continuum
to reckon, bond, tie, link meanwhile "firmaments"
"dangle easy" and scare
an imaginary continuous present
where nomadic talismans open like hands
like wings like lips like shards on the path
cuneiform inscribed with amity, praise, hope, poetry
Hafiz says love in every part of the world
will know the myth of this time
its lessons of sorrows
"this angle of sunlight is the key, supplicate the AI angel"
who'll guide us to migrants warm and settled.

Braided River

timing was everything
"you" feed "you" love
the rush of precious water a blast
"you" doubt the "you" to rely on "you"
waters keep the floods at bay
rope of language was meaning
was code was sound was ideas
was twisting, was flowing,
a metaphysical braid, three strands
of life of perception of synergy
ropes in flux not tied down
rope a condition, reminder, conundrum
a plan, a triadic apocalypse
was silence was not quite silent
not absence of sounds either
the inside blood-flow
but roping, not tied down,
holding power not tied to it
and rope of mind, looping through days
and dream her wild hair
was in woods was timing all this was
walking and in circles body
tired of sound was visually still
but meanders all the same
but symbols themselves
and this "itself" was itself a rope,
and silken, three strands,
catching the drift
hankers for symbol of unity
wake the world with your noisy braid
a whip, a goad to travel through
transmigratory realm was in river
swimming with ideas
booming poetry a river rising

take in dark age, a practice for survival
risk all or you drown, the child's fantasy,
image of boats of escape of struggle
was rope, as a language-lasso is rare
allegory for witness, was the hair
of all mothers was on the mountain
with wind and whipping trees
and same rope holds us together,
not threatening not dark
of purpose the braid of her hair
meanders, snakes, falls apart
comes together again in Mexico
all braided itself and the thing
itself and the thing beyond itself
language's family forged
in the trinity flux mill of desire
and mythic labor from time
a Neanderthal scaled a rope
and threw petals at a grave.

Part III: Feminafesto

I've never had an empty house. Never.

—MEREDITH MONK

The verdict has just come in at approximately 9 am est. All three officers in the shooting death of (the unarmed young Black man) Sean Bell; acquitted. 50—bullets in the body of Sean Bell and no one is guilty. No justice, in Amerikkka, 2008.

I can't stop crying.

I didn't even know him; I know him intimately.

—EMAIL FROM AKILAH OLIVER: APRIL 25, 2008

It's a very difficult age when the forces of time want to destroy us and take us away. They're just snatching people like devils; death comes and grabs each of us.

—CAROLEE SCHNEEMANN

What Sky Limit?

"never idle sun and moon hurry"

—QU YUAN (340 BC–278 BC)

We promise to meet
Sisters on the path
By light, sweet melon moon
We're in adjoining houses
Yet leagues far away
How fast is mind?
Poetry would build a house
Painting would be the bigger one
Roof it with lotus, with telepathy
In your garden together, now
I feel a branch brush a cheek
Clasp your arm
I grieve not seeing you, it's too long
Entangled in struggle
And beauty you are not easy
The struggle for kindness—now distant
That is struggle
We were always women of precepts
How can empty and false endure?
How can we be in apocalypse all the time
The real time of imagination
Sixth extinction a Taoist perspective
Is a world of opposites and silence
Is that it? or destruction
In on itself, no fuss but gestures
Her brush makes, line consumes
Its memory for shadow
A play, tick o' life
Trick that we savor, laugh off

The inner sanctum
Our world is losing humble life
How many things nod, turn, good-bye
Break and disappear?
Laments how many laments
What limit? to tender hearts
The shaman queues up medicine
Ch'an ritual sings about exile and magic
Spheres float like bubbles
Trails of chaos to come, all syndicates
The time is weak and leaders are infamous
A crucible within the invisible
Like plague upon a vanquished land
Revelations about revelations won't help
Adornments of the past disappear
Perpetual fog restrains the mind
Birdsong—hear it?—was that your crimson bird?
Your blue? your yellow? speckled?
Are we already on the steep cliff, my dove?
My hypnogogic love, I'd say so
Water crashes over stones
Fire burns forests, precipices give way
Fall into magma, ash, rescue is moot
We always honored time's measure
We looked up often
Reanimating language its pitch
And travelled between clouds that parted
And when we went way, way up
Floating our aspiration
We looked down over them,
Sentient beings who could know
How the world might wake up at last
As if we were the sun pouring
For the first time
Onto writhing life below.

Attenuate the Loss and Find

There is nothing revolutionary whatsoever about the control of women's bodies by men. The woman's body is the terrain on which patriarchy is erected.

—ADRIENNE RICH

name appears—*ad rien*
everywhere and in dream
"sleeping with monsters"
body armor removed
what now, legacy, archivum
archons preserve of
intensity a durance a hand you recognize
(sounds sound) as restraint
assurance lives on in women
as almost suffocated, then drowned
downed but never
what she could only know
as herself living in brute time
the words are purposes.
speak of a syntax of rendition?
politics of empire chip away
as poetry attests
curve of a water-starved globe
to follow and be following?
fighting for a choice?
sexism, racism?
our causes
everything an intense grasp of her
consciousness—cut in lucent observation
for a rapid and perched intellectus
privacy opens to vibrant flights
of love
stuff of Eros, of empathy

passionate edge of Adrienne
the American skeptic
close up in rich pluvials
axiomatic, raging in this light
our new flight

Bodhisattva Frank

actually everything in it either happened to me or
I felt happening (saw, imagined) on Second Avenue

—FRANK O'HARA

Frank O'Hara modified and snookered his detractors. Notice Galway Kinnell slinks away. The critical mass of theory abounds in a tiny shell of remorse; being sour was not his game. And the rhapsody continues in China, along with interest in Ginger Rogers and Fred Astaire, and China is on the way. China "gets" Frank. France beat them to it in a contained radical parlance. A shared street-smart ambience; Frank walked there. Poetry novices assault the reading world, sneaking into the void of life, and crave a parallel universe to run within. They have to slow down, walk the High Line. They will not be saddened by the new developers, art as art "process" or the critics of the New Appropriation Device. Actually they like this approach, critics do, and beg to respond: copying more than living. Or long nights waiting for the trash collector after a flood, a hurricane, a non-end-in-sight holiday. New York looks caked and oh so different, dear fifties aficionados and population-density lovers, but Frank would not demonize nor demolish the streets that vaporize like a wealthy mayor's want. And it feels international. And you are intentional. Mixing up the public names with those you sleep inside of. Times change, fretting the time within the time is useful for the texts some write, but not Frank's. Frank's leaves the ear open; he was not gabby but fierce in a syndrome of time delay. How much do you have of it? he asked of me, witness. I was just starting out. I mouthed his words back at him; "glistening semester of ardency." I was eager to work, to know. He listened impatiently. And generosity was moment-to-moment satori. *There are words for this. Like the care of mothers,* of which he had scant patience. *Becoming a bridge for others to walk upon.* That's better. *And a cure. Eat the Buddha.* Frank was a cure. Frank ate the Buddha. He was offering me intern work at MOMA, and I had to get a day job? Connective tissue. Last resort. Meticulous lover. *Zen poetics,* Ashbery said, commenting on Frank's early phases. Second Avenue awaits its underground transportation. I live half a block away. But aboveground we see the dust settle the void. Empty movie stars may be gawked in the neighborhood and little has changed for them as they ascend a brittle psyche. Rachmaninoff is celebrated in the churches for his piety, which Frank never had. This is a statement of before and after. Because we arrive as those after. There's a twitch in the board room, the academies are shut, the commerce entertains the signatures, we know more about non-détente than we could ever wish for. Privacy lacks rhetoric. The Middle East in the window. But have we studied the languages? Who is at the helm? Lord Nelson barnacled out of the deep. Who cares what anyone knows: bugged to oblivion. In every pocket shared with Reverdy is a test of humanity. Khrushchev will come to town in a poet's archival heaven. Wish you were here! The point to assuage the midnight suffering of all he fell to who fell to him in a pulse that translated falling as breathing as the women who love him will attest to. One of them, muster my faith sisters, all eyes to canvas, Joan. Patsy, spend the night. Nell, you are on a constant mark. Grace and fantasy, we light out of here, and, Jane, there is no other such as you in the call hold. May hold your own too in liquor capacity. There are no muzzy sisters. Abstraction is coming in the barroom. But the women beat a fast retreat to the studio. You can also drink in a studio, liberty, egality, fraternity. And one paints a vase on the sunny porch. And one writes poems in the studio and on the fly. A referent to the primum mobile. A gothic spire in your future. An eye-turner. Frank, you are the most experimentally passionate: lithe spirit, leading with butting head, leonine. Come into my studio of elixirs. Let me touch your febrile forehead. Works the feminine. He was the best poet for young women coming after. When you ask where of body the poetry comes from, some would clutch the heart, others a hidden rib, for others neck clavicle, and some below the belt. Frank would glimmer. His heart could be our heart. The tombstone is bracing. The leaves are autumnal. His face is before you, as is his century's. And Mayakovsky sealed the breach. Did not need to be convinced of a meditating forehead. And the living want to honor the dead *at the margin of a plea.* Deep gossip. Effrontery. Attribute *as a nun trembling before a microphone,* how it upends you and critics take up the cudgel to the next generation of *I do this, I do that. Needles tired of howling.* Siam is the transport to my reticulated fantasy. A movie in your thoughts. Frank lifted the postscript. *I have a larger following.* He knows.

Is a stranger capable of *moonlike hatred*? Yes, when he is that snake again. As roses *are charming.* Those bars again welcoming their sisters in *the haunches of the Himalayas.* Early surrealistic junket. The open tributaries. Coterie like an expletive the demons harbor in quiet semi-samadhi. Indifferent, effeminate, feminine, or ravished. *Tearing at her breasts.* Someone dismissing Dada? *Chinese legend.* Do they remember claqueurs? *Monikered Sanskrit. The newspaper of the lips.* What can you say of the newspaper of the lips? The French poets notice the brain you are in *O fat-assed configurations and volutions of ribbed sand which the sea never reaches.* What it means to serve others, more and more as the case may be as ripples matriculate in the brain. Wired for compassion with the *danger of being Proustian.* All those others:

a) frigate of responsibility
b) gates of the universe opening their nerves to us
c) enactment and marginality
d) pigeons could resemble tulips if you are Buddha
e) Pompeiian desires are overrated
f) genetic twining, Larry Rivers
g) thematizing queer hipsters
h) falling for Altieri
i) insist on the temporary, failing for Altieri
j) naming versus understanding who the people are
k) social use for poetry, sleeping with my sisters
l) break from orthodoxy
m) Andy Warhol abraded vocabularies: another "diced excesses"
n) don't belong to the same poem as the rest of us do
o) *Flowers. Relativity. Maxine Groffsky.*
p) Ted Berrigan and waning of cultural alterity
q) a poem of 478 lines
r) without a place in the lager scheme Perloff gets lost
s) the hunger frame, Jim Brodey
t) outside the studio frame
u) "spiritual clarity" as in Jackson Pollock
v) *inky clarity!*
w) *getting out of bedness*
x) *endurance of water*
y) privacy opens to light
z) floating around delineation

Not having patience with any of it, Frank monitors the battalions and overstating of obvious ploy. He sat up, *a–z.* He resumed. He had some friends.

He typed. He was not hostile to the outliers. Let them in the proverbial room that towers on the vibe of containment. That the world be richer for it in authority. Authorship is a modest plaint. Enough to be distinct and raw and entertain a victim suspicious of history. I doubt it. Of the selfless lot let bells ring. You got love? Let the agenda of the cowboy sleep in your arms tonight, turning toward the hand you recognize, falling into desire with the phenomenal world, where memory found a thread. Keeping Frank safe riding desire, and China? The automative mastery. Hug the current. Seeing aspiration in one so young, *come work alongside me*. Then, in a dream: Where is our youth? And youth announces: a mighty haunting is on the way. When you died that energy set us afire. The transcendent friend.

WITH HOMAGE TO "SECOND AVENUE,"
TOTEM/CORINTH, 1960

Hurr, Isho, like the whirr of a loom:
churr (Letters with Karen Weiser)

Kyoto, Japan
December 30, 2004

Dear Karen,

Unresolved inter-connected-nesses, the need for the ancestor shrines, the way the imagination keeps playing back old (I am still stuck in romantic Heian period with Genji, Sei Shōnagon, the sad diary entitled *Kagerō Nikki*), yet newly activated images from holocaust / Hiroshima / Pachinko parlors.

How does all this play here? And what to make of it? "Do" with it? "Do" anything? Is part of the poet's vow to perpetually catch, distill, refine, reimagine where one walks, what one notices? Plus all the verbal wordplay and associations. The mysterious Noh plays' court backdrop reconfigures Kingship, I emperor, I god, I patriarchal, power paradigm, and also—which is more important—engages "no action" which is what goes between the singing, music, stage movements, animal sounds. The big gap.

> Life and death, past and present—
> Marionettes on a toy stage.
> When the strings are broken,
> Behold the broken pieces!
>
> —ZEAMI MOTOKIYO, "ON THE ART OF THE NO DRAMA"
> TRANS: J. THOMAS RIMER AND AMAZAKI MASAKAZU

CHORUS
(mimicking the sound of crickets)
Kiri, hatari, cho, cho
Kiri, hatari, cho, cho
The cricket sews on at his old rags,

With all the new grass in the field; sho,
Churr, isho, like the whirr of a loom: churr

—ZEAMI MOTOKIYO, "NISHIKI-GI"
TRANS: EZRA POUND

Human life transmigrating between life and death, hell, ghost, animal, human, heaven realms . . .

But remember this is extremely evolved, refined art—on much older shamanic/ Bardo death rites (which is where I am locating a lot of my writing and study) and confrontation involving encounters such as those with animal spirits and "ghost" sound. Trance. Dyanas. Entheogens.

And making/imitating those sounds of the animal. Modal structures. Though I have recently been impersonating robots. But is it all like The Kingfishers/ Wasteland dynamic? Are we just always writing in our Culture of Death?

The old wounds/yearnings must be healed so the land will thrive? So everything can "go on"? My former Naropa student poet Kenji, here, as we were riding the Chuo train line, said emphatically "No more Kings!" which continues this line of theistic thinking re: death, its cycles.

Those power mongers sleep with Death, using it all the time to keep us enthralled, in state of perpetual fear. Can we not do that? So I write to get out of my own Empire of Death and Fear.

What is this self-appointed job? Is it always a simple—on one level—react/response mode, which is why I have been so grateful to be out of the U S of A.

Kyoto: Rampant with syncretic layers.

Some fox shrine thoughts: had that red pelt in mind back in a time when animals roamed and we were one with them. A small clearing for fox assignation.

What is it to love a fox? Brought to mind the rat shrine in Calcutta, the bat shrines in Bali . . . difficult divinities.

But saw similarities with stuff in Indonesia/Polynesia in the Shinto shrines: the animist/ancestor deal, now unfortunately associated with Japanese nationalism as the current prime minister keeps honoring the Shinto place (in Tokyo) where WWII war criminals are "enshrined."

But most affected by the Hall of the 1,001 Kannon bodhisattvas, "Sanjūsangendō," founded originally in 1164 CE, rebuilt after a fire in 1266, 393 feet long, 54 feet wide. In the center is the chief image of Kannon (Guan Yin, Avalokitesvara) with eleven faces and one thousand arms, 11 feet high.

On both sides of him/her stand very close together, ready for "action"—like an army—1,000 more images of Kannon with multiple arms and accoutrements.

The idea is an army of compassion. The rock gardens, meticulously raked white pebble carpets, with rocks that don't necessarily resemble anything, offer a nice conundrum. Like looking at Abstract Expressionism, someone said.

And on.

What are you studying? What does your world look like?

I wish I had a thousand arms.

LOVE

Later:

Tokyo, Japan
January 2, 2005

Dear Karen,

One's mind is a place and a map indeed as per your chapbook *Placefullness*. My keyboard is Japanese hence lacking in easy access to quote marks, colon, semis. I miss parentheses and have written a piece entirely dependent on the parenthetical, which is what you do when you can't understand most words and have an ongoing patter. A mindstream in native tongue but all the time thinking, What is this I am hearing?

Why is it alien? Or is it? Past lifetime in this language? How does it relate to animal sound? How does it relate to Korea, China, Siberia, Polynesia. What I know is some Zen chant. If only another lifetime to study kana, understand kanji. Both visual towers and topiaries. A kind of drama which includes the Theatre of Noh, its sounding, and at the same time: a temple, silent, with incense wafting. Many associations from movies, the haunting shakuhachi. There's such grace in the calligraphic kanji and the sense of the whole body making a stroke.

Or the stroke being made with mind and heart as well. Stroke of the "warrior." Also find the precision of the vast train system here in Tokyo daunting. There is a map here in my head of multiple cities—imagined, real, absent, pulsing, hardly any green. These minidistricts are postwar constructs of wild dimension mounted on the fossil fuel of—hard to imagine. Complex history of Edo, the former capital, and the possibility of earthquake haunts the premises . . . Population here is way over 12 million. Very few Gaijin—literally "outside" people.

One has a mind of stone in the Zen gardens (Kyoto).

I have already begun a Buddhist poem triggered by a statue of a sow-headed dakini. What is Hebrew for *sow*?

My job here is a month's residency with the Tokyo Joshi Daigaku, Tokyo Woman's Christian University. Participate in a symposium, teach workshops, today a seminar on performance poetry. The campus bells are tolling "O Come O Come Emmanuel and Ransom Captured Israel"—apt words in current context, eh?

I am seeing a Noh play tonight entitled *Kokaji* about a blacksmith and a fox. The Waki is the blacksmith, a witness figure. The spirit of Shite is a boy who is an incarnation of Inari Myojin, the fox. My recent book *Structure of the World Compared to a Bubble* seems to rest in some ideas from the animal realm—if we don't reclaim some of those origins, we're in trouble. You must know Pound's Noh, based on Fenollosa's notes. I almost got to Fenollosa's gravesite near Kyoto, not enough time.

Think I passed Cid Corman's bakery, though (and wrote a little poem). Thinking about the kajian poets and Japan. Gary Snyder, Phil Whalen, Joanne Kyger, Clayton Eshleman, Cid Corman. Huge source, here, for writing. And translation work.

I need to get this preliminary bundle—an invitation—a summons—a bow toward our communication in missive realm—off to you now.

What is the climate for your work life? History does indeed appear to flutter; the underground lost city. Your writing in *Placefullness*—ghost, view of time and the site itself—very relevant here in my stint in Japan. And now we are even deeper inside this war and no matter what language we are innocent, people are suffering and dying without cause.

Love,
Anne
(the secular fox, the secular sow)

P.S.
I know poets have to keep travelling and placing themselves in other cultures, even as it gets more difficult for us norteamericanos. All the more reason. In fact, one experiences the heartbreak most profoundly from a distance. I want to dwell in "art time" the next years, but of course have always lived in "art time."

New York, New York
January 10–February 6, 2005

Dear Anne,

I have been thinking about Bardo death rites as a place for you to locate your work. Do you mean writing out of a state of in-between, or an emptying of consciousness?

"The big gap" as you wrote? I want to hear more. Right now I am reading Andrei Codrescu's novel *Wakefield,* in which the main character gives a motivational talk about poetry and money while the devil looks on, and in the midst of the talk Wakefield says, "The difference between a modern artist and Buddhist monk is in the approach. The artist goes into the void empty and returns with a souvenir, if you will. The monk approaches the void with a traditional body of knowledge and arrives at emptiness."

I really like this idea of the spatial movement of consciousness and having "encounters" within that journey, as you put it.

Like Will Alexander's sense of astral projection, which I was just reading about in his interview with Marcella Durand in *The Poetry Project Newsletter.* Another useful way to think about writing.

There are so many: the image of the poet observing like a monk and recording, the poet who dictates—tuned into some other channel until the poem is revealed, the romantic poet active in exploring the movement of the imagination, the poet who plagiarizes or cuts-up language in order to reanimate or recontextualize it, the political poet who awakens, the poet who dredges up their inner emotional life, the language poet, the ecological poet; all of these ideas only begin to touch what it is that happens when a person sits down to write.

It is a question asked every time someone writes a poem, and although the poet may think he is in control, it is still this inexplicable magic. Alice Notley once told me that she believes in doing elementary human things, like having children, and I think writing is one of these old human practices. It is an attempt to be active in the midst of existing—active in meaning-making anyway. And of course it is an activity that involves a certain amount of passivity, or not exerting oneself—the great paradox of creation.

A way to build a nest within the always moving stream of consciousness, to capture and still the self, or not self, at that moment, to see how the self is built by language, which is yet just another analog of the mysterious writing process. All the ways that poets conceive of their practices, and have throughout time, seem paltry and reductive metaphors for this basic human desire to shape reality through language.

And in this way maybe writing is a way out of—or through—the Culture of Death, as you termed it, because it is constructive and active work, like the bird who weaves a nest out of discarded, cast-off materials around herself, a work of living, a living work, even if the bird uses scraps of shroud. So for us poets, it is important. For the Culture of Death, however, I am not so sure. I have no idea if there is a real place for poetry within our culture anymore, since poetry will never really be able to fit into a corporate model (at least I hope it never will!).

Is this because it costs nothing to write as long as you have paper and a pen, or a memory even? But the thing that is hard to swallow is that there is no bridge between our culture's need for poetry (which became clear after 9/11's hundreds of poems tacked up all over NYC) and its actual living existence as an art form, as a practice that needs to be supported and paid attention to. Poetry is not a product for consumption but poets do need material support to keep creating their work.

A dilemma. A week or so ago Anselm [Berrigan] brought home a documentary about kestrels from the library—filmed in Sweden and without any dialogue. It follows a family of kestrels for a year and shows what they see; since their nest is in an architectural detail of a church and faces a well-taken-care-of graveyard, they see people enter the frame to be buried, to parade, to marry, to shovel, to plant, to water, to walk the dog. The rock gardens around the tombstones are raked white pebble, like Abstract Expressionism, yes, but in the video you hear the repetitive and meditative sound of the rake across the stones.

The birds watch and listen, on their own clock, in addition to hatching and then feeding their family of 6 young kestrels. What do they see when they see people? What is the use of human ritual? What kinds of rituals do birds have? Did you see that article in the *New York Times* about the scientific discovery that birds are way more intelligent and creative than previously thought? My parrot likes to ring his bell in the morning to wake us up—one of his many daily rituals.

I don't know what it is to love a fox, but I imagine it is no different from loving a person. I can't even picture a time when people roamed with the animals, but so many of the bedrock aspects of interpersonal relationships are the same for creatures everywhere—in herds, bevies, flocks, packs, families. Have the basic emotional realities of our lives evolved that much over time?

I am reading Edgar Allan Poe right now and thinking about imaginative decadence. Part of his excess is his insistence on a kind of absolute logic and reason, even in the no-man's-land of poetic composition. In his famous essay "The Philosophy of Composition" he lays out step-by-step the mental journey of connections in his writing of the poem "The Raven." I'm not sure I buy it.

He details the same kind of mental stepping stone documentation process in his short story "The Murders in the Rue Morgue" where one character guesses another's train of thought and appears to read his mind through logical deduction. Poe makes reason and logic as magical and decadent as he makes madness. Or are they the same thing? "Clack" the summer parallel's fine layer of shag sticks,

breaks the eggshell
(speckled red containers,
head full of stars)
of merely
circulating
(citified yolk state)
schedule of buildings
sections condense, ease
dimension at that
dusk, immaculate opening of corners

You DO have a thousand arms!

Love,
Karen

Boulder, Colorado
April 25, 2005

Dear Karen,

"dusk, immaculate opening of corners" has a kind of Bardo feel. It's the in-between, the both both quality of mind, that anything can arise and does and that there is also there, experientially, a notion of purity. Bardo like the "charnel ground" is that place of birth and death. And one can start from there and also end there. But in the gap is—possibly—an emptying of consciousness, as you put it. Or that that's some heightened sense of being less ordinary, or of ordinary magic and not so self-conscious.

I like to think that one can carry "knowledge," whether "traditional" or classical or just street wisdom yet wear it lightly and it buoys you up, arises with your thinking or has already become part of you if it is useful. "Useful knowledge," as Stein puts it.

What is urgent to know about? I ask myself this every day and get extremely dizzy. I made this poem construct below of "without," then what "call" is heard? The idea was what can one do without and of course by saying those things you keep all those things. And it was triggered by the terrorists in DC pushing on the agenda that we are going once again to be attacked by the other terrorists—

thus: "coming? coming soon?" I was thinking, too, the sense from Wakefield of the poem as souvenir. I couldn't locate my life without the poems over the years as signposts. Thus a diary of a particular kind of consciousness . . . Agnès Varda's three films now showing (at the Film Forum) interesting as exercises in memory, emptying out, consciousness, nothing polemical.

Here I was thinking of Robert Duncan's poem of the mother being a falconress. I was thinking about being blind and being a seer. I was also thinking of Native American scholar and activist Ward Churchill's sense of the "little Eichmanns" in reference to Hannah Arendt's "banality of evil" and the whole predicament we find ourselves in being one of the "rivets," the "cogs and wheels" of the difficult exploitation/war machine.

And this always brings up for me an issue of ethics, responsibility. Because everything is vastly interconnected—more so than ever. Push a button, and a rain forest goes down in South America. Now Professor Ward Churchill finds himself in trouble over issues of the 9/11 karma, as does Amiri Baraka. How they speak, with what emotion, is an issue.

So yes, encounters with the charnel ground which is like the World Trade Center site and like Rwanda and Cambodia not so long ago and like the gap (abyss?) where what we call our poems arises within.

without care without seed pearl without stitching closed the
eye of the falcon without seemly rectitude without the platitude
of o thou muddled media pundit without questionable doubt or
metabolism without a geographic category of speech that will travail
without a hint or glint of 'secular' mastery, without ritual framing
without a theatrical sense of illusion and bandying about or on or inside
a thermosphere without it working against you and when it does being
able to go on without it without gavottes without gazelles that you
study in neighboring Persian poetries without spallation and
without a diving bell how will you survive? without rapacious wildcats
without the sense of security you have always expected without your
familiar stage fright without the caves without the bombing of caves
without the mystery of caves without the caves in your memory of that
mystery that lives in caves without caves that long to exist in the
hand print in the cave of that memory without the rivets that hold
the wing together that hold the whole throbbing machine together that
assert the rivet dominion without which you do not have a plan of
fastening together of wings of arms for the automaton that holds
the capital together without its own mind of wheels and cogs and mudras
that run the show without all the pixels and efforts of more dominion
without borders to cross without needing to carry things over borders
the invasion of your homeland (coming? coming soon?) without it, what
call in the night what call is answered what nuance what tantrum in the night
what martyrdom of dreaming your own birth your own end of history
or end of speculation what call what alarm is sounding deep in the home?

Yes, the elementary human (Alice's [Notley] sense of being a real human being—humans like to make things with their hands, they like to paint & sing & make babies), which is why I wanted to bring this poem to home and hearth as it were. "Alarm?" It is human to have children and be scared and want to survive? Ed [Bowes] speaks proudly of us being "workers" being in the "cultural working class," being teachers, citizens. Yet he makes movies that are a stretch, a struggle.

A whole gamut of imagination. Ed wants a sublime non-narrative-fiction, he wants to re-examinatory. He wants the democratic party to get its act together. So all the kinds of poets you list and where they identify themselves are aspirationally summoned above. I need to examine Persian poetries, I need to cross more borders and save the Naropa tape archive, and so on. Exertion/passivity.

I go blank and there's a huge amount of energy expended that comes back later. I remember Allen climbing a hill to a campfire to give a reading on a chill night, exhausted, said that it would give him energy to go there. The campfire as charnel ground, the cave as Bardo.

O yes, that is the question about whether there is a place for poetry in our culture.

O dear, o dear. I will strive to continue to make a place for it yet with the revisioning of history and the fact that someone dangerous like Bush & Co. could be reelected (or selected) after so much disclosure of the lies, pathology, the endless examinations, books on the crimes, Enron, endless endless crimes exposed, yet what does all this get us? The fact that these revelations don't matter shows that we are now OUTSIDE history, outside our culture, the story is coming to an end (Baudrillard?).

Or, rather, what do they mean? Are history and culture even relevant at this point since they are a fiction! A version of the world that is markedly UNREAL. Perhaps poetry is more relevant than any of this other stuff except that there is very real suffering we need to constantly mitigate.

Or maybe we should start making more families with animals—as you have with your bird & all our friends with cats, and canines, snakes, gerbils, turtles. Thalia Field is sure that dogs have senses of humor and that they are making jokes when they sit on the sofa you have forbidden them.

One could go on & on thinking of utopian possibilities to figure out how to live sanely in this postcapital avant-derriere dark age. The animals are certainly less dangerous.

So yes, let's go to the bird realm. Their rituals seem more attractive, or stay with a raking of pebbles. The repetition seems salutary. I keep flashing back on Japan. In dreams Tokyo is still the Bardo between vast time periods and states of mind. And how important the discipline of the "small" is, and yet what is working on the discipline of the "large" scale? Something awry. There's something in buddhadharma called the "Fourth Moment."

I find myself looking at symbols in the dream (obviously the "kanji" letters), trying to unlock them. They look like bird scratches, odd footprints. If I "get" them will I be able to get off the train—open the sliding doors—and get back to the library in my study in Boulder? What the devil do they say? I never seem to arrive.

And Poe maybe is methodical as an afterthought, you think? He seems to have a dominating mind. Reason, logic, madness all magical and decadent—possibly. I am not sure about decadence to wear as an artist, now that the body of our world seems hopelessly sick with mental and eco-logical torment.

to the contrary
without
authority the
dare, or
pressure
point
a pebble,
a true source
Niedecker wrote
when casting
a stone
was not a war crime
should be
a ground for
truce & veracity
o moral Annie
sound
the ground
inside the head
empty head
between the word

& the
reach for it

Astral projection. Have you looked up at the moon?

Love,
Anne

Boulder, Colorado
May 2, 2005

Karen,

> Last year service in the eastern hills.
> Now the marches of the western seas
> How often in the span of an official's life
> Must he (she) weary him (her) self with these border wars?

>> —FUJIWARA NO UMAKAI (694–737), FROM THE KAIFUSO
>> (PROGRAM NOTES)

Been thinking around the parameters of *Iovis III (Colors in the Mechanism of Concealment)* as I try to organize the rhizome it is. Borders and linguistic disputes seem so much at the root of what one is ready to die for. And because I am so caught up with "polis" (the eyes, the public, those who will see for themselves unmediated by authority), I seem to constantly consider both sides. And want to carry the epic sense of the total story as we are living it right now through the orality of our minds' ears & eyes. That's what I feel in this city, in this poem, noise and more noise. Trying to find the "C" train which doesn't run on weekends, although I can HEAR it, trying to find a language that isn't so common, meaning prevalent (I love the common tongue). There seems to be so much more cruel racist graffiti around town as I make my rounds, have you noticed?

Seems like a bit of a dis-junct over the events of this week of Poetry Month April with PEN American Center / the rest of the community.

The *New Yorker,* which still doesn't consider poetry as a mind-changing & charging event, other arbiters of verse/prose culture and it's true the climate still feels somewhat "official" as in "official verse culture." We need to go to other kinds of neighborhoods or at the least widen the discussion. Include Etel Adnan. Maybe it's all hidden in books, between the lines. Maybe I just need to hide out in the noisy library. I want to study how things are said, so back into the streets again.

Koranic expressions and Arabic words were injected into the language by Bosnian Muslims, who adopted the word *shahid* or martyr from the Arabic and cast aside the Serbian *junak.* The Croatians did the opposite, reclaiming fifteenth-century words. In Zagreb you couldn't use old Serbian phrases anymore.

The Dark Arcana section *(Dark Arcana: Afterimage or Glow)*—written out of the trip to Hanoi—maybe a bit more optimistic with a new generation, some of whom I met, all in their twenties, eager not to have to live out more endless revenge cycles. Ambrose who is heading that way soon, "How can they LIKE Americans in Vietnam?"

And so welcome in my own space and time, continuing to investigate but also an attempt to lighten up, but not the load which seems even greater with Bob Creeley's death. What do I mean by that? Why do I still need poets to be heroes? And never die. What is this eternal poet warrior biz? I wanted to send you the notes for the Intro for "Poetry Is News." And part 2 of this will be some of the epic.

Love,
Anne

P.S. Did I say I was inspired to write to you after your reading because I could hear in your music, in your rhythm, in your tone? Was that it? Aspirational. Untamed a bit you think? Standing by her/your word, your song. What is the shape of the new youth poems? They seem propelled and full (rich) with documentary stuff. Things & "memory." What does *political* mean to you?

New York, New York
June 22, 2005

Dear Anne,

Reading over the two letters you have written since my last one, I must tell you that I thought about you while swimming in the Colorado River— picture 103 degrees of Southwest heat, the freezing water contrasting with the hot, hot, dry and dusty air. Trying to push my body against the weight of the current, so strong it took a certain kind of determination to move against it, reminded me of you.

You are filled with this kind of will and that it has given you the momentum to write what you write and push aside accepted narratives like an arm against onward water. Therefore I am not surprised that writing from out of the Bardo as you've been explaining to me is also a matter of will, of giving it up—harnessing the tension between exertion and passivity, telegraphing blankness as you put it. I'm reminded out in the desert that every inch of this country is charnel ground.

And that is something to remember. I finally successfully added John James Audubon into a poem I am working on—I have been trying to fit him into various works for months, and I find him fitting into this conversation quite nicely. Recently I read his "Mississippi River Journal" (1820–1) and discovered that all of the beautiful birds he drew and painted, all of those amazingly detailed portraits, were birds he and his company shot and killed.

Here is this man, traversing the lush, "untamed" wilderness with thousands of birds flying overhead, birds never documented before, and he aims and shoots in order to create art. Was he thinking of arranging their corpses to paint them, of his hunger (he ate many), of the life ebbing from the birds themselves? He wanted to create life-sized portraits of the birds of the us (which he did in his famous *Birds of America*), and his journals document his respect for the birds while they simultaneously log his relentless murder of them. Talk about creating art out of the space of death! And the charnel ground of history.

To give you an example, here are two excerpts from Audubon's "Mississippi River Journal" published in *John James Audubon: Writings & Drawings* (The

Library of America, 1999) from the log for October 14, 1820, the third day of his journey down the river toward New Orleans:

"We returned to our Boat with a Wild Turkey 7 Partridges (northern bob-white quail) a Tall Tale Godwit (greater yellowlegs) and a Hermit Thrush which was too much torn to make a drawing of it. This was the first time I had met with the bird and felt particularly mortified at its situation."

"We passed the Small Town of Lawrenceburg in Indiana, Petersburg in KY. We walked in the afternoon to Bellevue. . . . We killed 4 [Little] Grebes (horned grebes) at one shot from a flock of about 30. We approached them with ease to within about 40 Yards, they were chasing each other and quite merry."

Here is the poem I wrote in which he appears, entitled "Now Then":

It's an inconvenient kind of flatness accepting the offer of the road above.
You know alone flashes filmic in its own projection
curdling the light, moving forward into natural relief
with quick-handed horror-movie humor
the bodies pile up and disappear
clouds like magnets on the move:

O, to be a stippling world
with a certain thrown-her-glove-in sense of possibility
heralding forth the blanketing noise
underneath the familiar surface
like an animal stuffed shapes death into life
Oh right, but it's just noise
in a traditional hero rectangle of frame

On the Mississippi, Audubon killed the birds then drew them
time held out in small delicate etchings
still warm though rapidly aging
in his hands, the paper's a trigger
big enough to walk inside
the chapel of a bird's body
is any body
breathing with ink

I think Audubon's love affair with vision involved seeing into something still an obsession with making alive that which he took the life from. Which brings me to your poem "Without Stitching Closed the Eye of the Falcon" that you included a couple of letters ago. The poem's questions about power, by asking us what we can do without (can we give up the idea of invasion or dominion?) also expose the connection between authority and seeing: how absence makes seeing possible, how any representation is that kind of possibility.

And your poem shows how words allow us to conjure that which we can simultaneously evoke as absent, exposing the nature of language in terms of power and possession. And although this makes me think of the beauty/ horror of Audubon and his gorgeous representations with their gruesome history, I think that your poem suggests how writing is maybe one positive opportunity in a world in which one feels continually helpless—writing allows you to address your own position in seeing, through seeing.

And so that might be what "political" means to me, which is a question you asked that I have been having trouble answering. The word itself gives me the heebeegeebees, and at the moment I am loath to enter into a "political" conversation, although I realize as I write this that I am happy to talk about political things (doesn't that include everything?) as long as the rhetoric of both the Administration and the left is set aside. When I encounter these bundles of rhetoric (especially in poems!) I feel a vast empty field inside of myself shudder into existence. This might stem from the sense of alienation and disappointment I experienced (and continue to feel) after the election. So I only want to consider politics in utterly personal terms. What does the word mean to you?

Another thing I find helpful and hopeful to remember is that we are not outside of history or culture. For my studies I am reading very early American writing and writing on America like de Tocqueville's *Democracy in America* (1835). All of these heady Enlightenment ideas and the power of their articulation in government, did you know that early Americans discussed the concept of doing away with inherited property to realize the promise of the Declaration?

I love reading about the revolutionary potential in democracy.

On that note!

Love,
Karen

Boulder, Colorado
July 3, 2005

Dear Karen,

Approaching the 4th of July, 2005, not going to celebrate with fireworks this year. "the paper's a trigger / big enough to walk inside / the chapel of a bird's body" put me in mind of the plutonium triggers on warheads, and the sanctity of all our threatened reality with the talk of new nuclear power-plants and weapons. The power of "paper" with Audubon's "work," his scientific obsession, his power if you will. I think the human realm takes for granted its hegemony and in the course of this, destroys the things it loves . . . or could and might love.

Some genetic propensity to conquer, to "know"—there's a deadly combination of curiosity with epistemology. I hope you push on further with your poem—how long is it?

I realized this taking a walk yesterday to a place called Button Rock Reservoir, a roundtrip five-mile hike, but at one point the trail ends at a huge culvert and there's a rocky trail above leading to the actual reservoir and there is such a strong inclination to push on and see what's just around the corner no matter if it's high noon in blazing heat, and one is wearing the wrong shoes. Scary to think of what harm could prevail. It is an unguarded pristine preserve, how easy to drop a few nasty pellets that could poison the whole Longmont, CO, population (it serves that particular city) (Ah paranoia!). Also, forest management has a staging area with signs like "chop and scatter," "chip in." Magpies like to sit near the dam . . . quite charming. Also, there's the specter of water wars always in the back of the mind . . . How precious this substance, more necessary than oil . . . Harder to replace . . . etc.

But there is certainly paranoia in the bird realm. Read recently that the black-capped chickadee singing its "chick-a-dee" brings its flock mates flying. The song is a warning that owl, hawk, or other predators are hovering nearby, thus forces are called in and arrive to harass these enemies. The warning call is a coded signal. Evidently by varying the call, the size of the predator is communicated, therefore the scope of the danger . . .

The chickadees were exposed to different predators in a test situation. It also makes a high-pitched "seet" call when they spot a predator flying in the air. But the most interesting thing is the variations of the "chick-a-dee-dee" call. The birds vary the numbers of "dees" depending on the threat. Sometimes as many as twenty-one "dees" can ensue—the Northern Pygmy Owl is deemed quite a threat! I remember once counting "dees" and wondering if the variations were random. Are our poems coded signals for help? The Greek meters certainly were meant to work the magic of love or conjure warrior behavior in battle. De DA DA DA! De DA DA DA! Here are some lines to kick off being an oculus witness, and noticing details of imagination and POLITICS. It's also supposed to be instructional:

> Across from me is a crossing of leg, across from me, a gray striped
> sock, long underwear, red which is a zipper which is an intruder writing in a slant way, head turned right gazing on a slant curve, then it
> goes another way, tumbled, as if to say, Notice this, notice this detail
> before you lose interest, before something interrupts the ordinary
> obscure moment, and you stop adding on your long lines of narration,
> enter in your log the premium story of distress, warning, desire or create a cosmology, or origin myth on the relative differences between
> genders, the way you receive the sun, the moon, the stars into your
> habitat, into—dare think this old-fashionedly?—your occultist spirit,
> for that's what it seems to be, a witness, seeing its way through a chaotic time, the face of these images, turning blood to stone, stone to
> fire, make a limb dance toward heaven, carried by a force you are
> capable of making this picture of: the dream of a dust bowl, dream of
> a prophet, dream of a maimed soldier (o please send me home now),
> labor of a blue collar mentor, dream of a pre-Raphaelite, dream of
> a Machiavellian sports announcer, the dream that leaves you cold,
> all the embers down, you have no refuge, talking about Cambodian
> Paris now, vision when you stood in the doorway lintel, in uniform,

informed and ready to march, and all did not seem strange—It was
the day before the movie rehearsal everyone get lines down and shoot,
the day before the funeral, the day before the self-immolating attack,
when incendiary meant simply "hot," and you could say it about a
lover if you were so inclined, the day before the discotheque folded (it
was bombed in Bali) the day before so many suffered, and you could
make something North American about it, including all the conti-
nents that would keep a Polaris missile out of their midst, and then it
all came back to you, opposite me, you leaning over your instrument
of power—that would record an inquisitive face, not Cleopatra's, not
emperor Hirohito's, not an Agrippa at the control, not a tyrant nor
a super errant knight, and you might ask about threads and stitches
and you might inquire about buttons and harnesses, about exigencies
of destroying proof, about all the colors matching, about a reversal of
intention before the Mayan long count, before the day we might go
to practice our syllables, and good intention needs to shine on those
syllables, taking them out of the bomb shelter, avaunt your paranoid
behavior! out of the time warp and onto the street where you stood
waiting for the shutter to snap, shouting "Hold" and then it was your
face that was always needed, your face which was always with me
and it could hold anything it wanted to, an unforced perspective, a
lunar calendar, a kiss, a way of thinking, behaving, as spectator to
the spectacle, a daily life . . .

Politics is to me at this point trying to be awake, join the crowd, help the
world ("Everything else, drunken dumbshow" as Ginsberg writes), know the
terms, terminology, the latitudes & longitudes, the names of things, and
be an investigator of power structures here and everywhere. Poetry has to
recover the word, the world. To look at the "empire building" in my own psyche,
to let go, to give over to Other, sympathetically. But watch "idiot compassion"
activate discriminating awareness-wisdom at all times.

This is a constant and often impossible job, but come back to the breath,
remember, breathe out, toward Other. Keep the aspiration. We are connected
through our breath.

Stay connected to friends, family, neighbors, try to alleviate suffering (so much
always moment to moment—dear brother poet, comrade Lorenzo Thomas

dying of emphysema as I write this . . . say a chant to ease the passing as he goes into spirit).

And it is incredibly moving as one grows older to acknowledge all those one has shared this work and life with—and follow what they are also going through, traversing "in sickness and in health." All the lovers in the dream! It's a vow, it's a marriage. What Alice Notley is writing, what Bernadette Mayer is thinking, and other female comrades of my generation who moved experimental more than a few inches (W. C. Williams says our job as poets is to move the century forward a few inches—like some slow-growing red-wood tree).

What is the wisdom of these ones?

Why does their writing excite me?

Study and respect other cultures, attitudes but examine how "harm" operates. Emphasize doing no harm. The environment/health of all the planet denizens issues the biggest I know and am reminded as I visit Japan, Canada, my own backyard out west, NYC and everywhere.

Try to hold one's seat, be able to shift into modes and moods and multiple voices in writing. In the "Animal Realm" section ("to hunt. to skin alive. to wear on a body") in *Structure of the World Compared to a Bubble* I try to get inside that psychological space of the one being preyed upon.

I really experience the "poetry is news" biz as a way to become other realities, both imaginatively, and then literally by doing the investigative work as witness and orator and agit prop perf poet! And just as the chickadees teach their offspring about "risks," part of our job as well.

Polis = city. Greek. *Polis* also carries a sense of "eyes." Maximus of Tyre, the image/voice for Charles Olson in "Maximus," which focuses on the city of Gloucester (the way one might on Athens or Troy), wrote disquisitions called *Dialetheia* in Greek and he wanted in his teaching to help his students come to grips with a dissolving world. Olson attempts that in "Maximus," which is really the history of the rise and fall of an archetypal American city.

I am a city person, a polis person. Civic-minded. How to get along in layered realities, melting pots of language, mores, imaginations, hopes & fears.

I had a naive question for you about the professionalism and careerism of the poetry and creative realm in general. I know you are a scholar too, but can you think of poets in your generation who do not hold academic degrees? Or have gone some other route entirely? Dropped out of the paradigm?

I know it is an economic issue and also the academies are the zones and safe havens for the creative work. What the polis of New York City or San Francisco or Paris used to be—it just seems odd when I think back to my own generation (which started to go academic—Ron [Padgett], Ted [Berrigan]), the origins of the New American poetry and even further back, the expatriate urge, the dropout urge. My own mother dwelling in Greece a decade, first heading there in 1929, dropping out of school at age nineteen. Also poets seem to travel for holidays (& can't blame them for that).

But it was heartening to hear from Ambrose this a.m. about travelling to Angkor Wat, investigating the killing fields of Cambodia. Photo of a cavern of skulls. He works a spell, then takes off . . .

Also I wanted to ask you about your sense of genre for your own work? I am in didactic mode right now, and oral mode. Ed Sanders has us writing new verses for "America the Beautiful." I've begun: O beautiful for matriot's dream / sees beyond testosterone . . .

Well, we will keep working on this *polis* definition. Maybe the city is a state of mind? Politics is a view, a state of mind, which engenders action. Projects action, projects voice.

I have a woman who works for the CIA in my class and a war bride whose husband is in Iraq (she lives at the big base in Germany). The activity continues in ten directions, as usual. The world is rich and strange . . . No more heebee jeebees. More birds.

Much love,
Anne

New York, New York
February 3, 2006

Dear Anne,

I am sitting in the main New York Public Library rereading our letters on an unusually warm winter day. This building, with its ornate, serious flourishes is perhaps my favorite institution in the city, though I feel sheepish in confessing it (with so many worthy choices!).

Speaking of institutions, I have been somewhat troubled by your question to me about poets in the academy and careerism; I can only say that I am stumped—dropping out isn't a possibility for poets today, as far as I can tell, and definitely not in New York City. Every poet I know has a job, whether it is in academia or not, and struggles with how to balance making money and making art.

Does having a graduate degree actually change this or make it easier? I am not sure, but I suspect it doesn't (and yes, I know lots of poets without graduate degrees, and some, without college degrees).

Personally I feel very lucky to have a great poetry community here in New York, mostly centered around reading series, such as the Poetry Project, Belladonna, Segue, the Zinc Bar, etc. Not one of the people I know is a "careerist" poet, though many of them slog it out on a daily basis in one kind of institution or another.

I know there is a whole moneyed poetry world out there, but they don't deal with me, and I don't deal with them, and it suits us both just dandy.

Don't get me wrong, I continually wonder about the Lilly family donation of 100 million dollars to *Poetry* magazine and wish some of it would funnel its way down to my friends and community, but on the whole I just write my poems and interact with people who are interested in the work and the work and the work and occasionally each other.

Sometimes new anthologies come out that remind me of these odd fault lines between "scenes" but I don't feel too troubled in general. I think you might have a different kind of exposure to these other poetry worlds since you work in MFA programs and interact with lots of different communities all the time across the country and world. In terms of academia, I myself am very happy to be in the academy, with all that it implies, where people have jobs that require them to sit around and think about ideas and language and texts.

And my degree is turning out to have little to do with poetry, actually, as it focuses mostly on early American novels, a decision I made partially because I don't want to exclusively teach poetry workshops or direct my scholarly thought toward poetics.

The experience of getting a PhD has been wonderful and exhilarating, though stressful, and I have no idea how it fits into or affects my poetry. For now, though, I keep a porous barrier between these two creative, intellectual pursuits.

The question of what sense of genre I have for my own work is, as I am sure you can imagine, a matter deeply affected by the reading and writing I do for my degree and the class I teach on literature of the Americas.

On some level, there is a kind of pleasure I find in writing poems now that I haven't had in a long time that arises from the motion of thought involved in it: giving my brain the kind of loping gallop it likes when I write as opposed to the more responsible laying out of connections that critical prose requires (feels like lumbering to me a lot of the time).

When writing I try to let the poem happen without making it happen, to go in not knowing or directing the process. It happens quicker than I can write it down, quicker than thinking, and there is pleasure in seeing what the fuck will happen.

With critical prose, I have to make it happen, and have a responsibility to my argument, to a critical history, and to the essay form.

Most of the time I wish I could write a poem instead, but push through these barriers to be able to get to the creative connection, to the moment where something exciting happens, though it is a previously scripted idea. Since my critical prose is generally in long essay format, my poems have become rather short in reaction, short and using a quick turning line.

Yes, my current genre would have to be the short poem in series. My influences have definitely changed; now in addition to Jack Spicer and Lyn Hejinian and the Howe sisters I am in conversation with Jonathan Edwards, Phillis Wheatley and the James brothers. In college we always joked that if you stay in the academy your poetry becomes boring, but I think my experience in school as a graduate student and a teacher has made my work more interesting as a result, if only from reading texts from earlier centuries, in which the language and grammar are meatier.

I'm interested in recouping the music from these earlier texts, in exploring the sounds of a lyricism, or maybe rethinking what it means in today's poetics. This might be the music you heard in my reading.

Since so much of this correspondence has centered on ideas of the political, I have to come clean: I really struggle with the place of politics in poetry and in my life. Reading your last letter made me realize that I am pretty uncomfortable, and have been for a long time, with claiming the political, although I try to do many of the things you discussed, such as staying awake and open, considering power structures, and avoiding idiot compassion (great term!).

But these things don't seem to change the world around me, and I certainly don't see poetry having much room to do that kind of work, since so few people read and care about poetry. These things change me, and that is great (for me), maybe that is all one can do, but it seems like too little; and other forms of political activism seem to have completely failed in our culture the last five years.

I love the idea that exploding the forms, jamming the machine, questioning what art can be creates greater change, but I am not convinced it does, or that it doesn't, for that matter. And often when politics enters poetry it seems at the expense of the poem—not all the time, but often enough.

I really just want to sit down and read a poem and here is a poem to end this correspondence with, one I wrote today while working on this letter to you.

Although now I am in another library in an ugly building on a rainy day, it is a poem that exists somewhere else, perhaps in some field of short and loving space between us, or between us and the person reading this:

The plant must grow tired, and I very sleepy

The potato says these things and admires them
for their quiet self languages:
". . . a consideration of form and content
glass and wine, breath and field
gives me a grid to romance and order all eyes
here, a species there;
what is consciousness, a kind of rough platform?"
The potato says these things broad and comparatively:
"we are watching a potato grow
in the painting that is this poem
you and me, dear reader
insofar as genitals swing and remain in place
without notice or eviction
our magisterial gaze is this
quiet world of stanza, where
I be a lead male friend

you are a little earth anywhere
the female opposite of laughter
in how we react to one another
a sensitive regime change between
brooding stanzas of Earth."

"Your verbal tick is beautiful
a metaphysic wit of the longest blossom
illuminating your face as it drapes its own century
Who knew the gaudiest peacock
would be the one without color
lying in an inquiry of our own gardens
sculpted to grow only biblical plants?"

Sending your thousand arms a thousand wishes.

Love,
Karen

New York, New York
February 7, 2006

Dear Karen,

One last response? Although you as younger hope-of-the-future should have the last word. And you still should, and do, but something felt incomplete without saying just a little more. (Is there ever a last word as long as poets breathe?) I loved your honesty in the letter, and bracing response to my old-hag-carping on poetry careerism and invoking politics all the time. It must get claustrophobic. I apologize.

I love the animist potato in your poem and the idea of consciousness being a "rough platform." And the image of the peacock / inquiry of our own gardens / growing only biblical plants. We obviously are on a spiritual path.

Colorless=egoless? Paradise. And your poem itself existing "somewhere else,"—a "field of short and loving space."

I read in the CUNY Grad Center's Rainbow Room last night—a kind of paradise—I mean that building, the old chic dept. store (Altman's)—is that what it's called: "rainbow room," where you can see the sky (the moon was out last night) and an angle of the Empire State Building?

It was the opening of the Study-Abroad-on-the-Bowery semester and I also gave a talk on "hybrid writing" which referenced hybrid cars, genetic manipulation, "mirror neurons," and the biz of being a writer.

I took the teaching stick a friend brought from Ethiopia, with Arab alphabet scripted on like an old-style hornbook, and swung it about a bit. It's probably a hundred years old.

I've carried it on the subway and it seems to make people happy, especially Arab-speakers.

"Who are you? Where did you get this?" It is a cultural-appropriation-intervention, and inspires more interesting exchanges than reading antiwar poems outside the NY Public Library (e.g. "Go get it on with your Saddam, baby!").

In any case, I wanted to say because I am involved with making schools and communities, I appreciate all those places that are havens and laboratories/scriptoriums for scholars and writers, such as CUNY, but that yes, you're right, in my various rounds—primarily outside the NYC nexus—there's a perceived career path for poets that, because of current economics, needs the academy for the tenure jobs and it feels unhealthy and too competitive (& there's lots of gossip about who is in and who is out—who is getting the grants, the jobs, the interviews at the MLA).

Where is the place for a María Sabina, the barefoot Mazatec seer with no "education"? Where is the place for the uncredentialed?

It's my bohemian defensiveness. Maybe I have felt "left out" of the academy discourse?

But I so appreciate you and your intelligence and curiosity and poetry and your sense of the "porous barrier," the impact of your studies on the work.

And so much of the community here in our world seems of your ilk, the real deal.

I wept during Eddie's [Edmund Berrigan] presentation last week at The Poetry Project on the blues, his relationship to it, his making of it, where it comes from, the poetry he loves. And presented in that room in the Parish Hall which has seen so much love and grief and joy.

Where else could you have that feeling, of community and generosity, modesty and respect? It seems so outside the world of capital and war. Politikos (Gk)=citizen. You are a great citizen, Karen.

But I don't think we're in some kind of disempowered minority as poets. Many "rough platforms" of all kinds and capabilities and "magics" arise. I've been watching the NSA hearings, disturbed by the drift but also able to applaud some of our public servants across the divide. Get it on, senators. An opportunity to just be informed, awake, stay connected, curious. Follow the language of master narrative and euphemism. Thinking and keep the practices of living and writing going.

Back into Japanese studies for this section of *Iovis* still in the making, I was looking at some photographs of a Noh performance where the "sea elf offers some wine of long life." That's the image for the day for you, and these lines for you.

> etiquette of all on stage
> wipe the sweat from your face, my sweet
> exits of others need not hinder you
> salute your formidable mask (three bows)
> you are the "art of the flower of peerless charm"
> places where you say "curtain" (maku! maku!)
> it rises
> and you miraculously appear

Dear correspondent—I salute & bow to you,

Anne

The Burroughs Effect: A Set of Potentials

—body split down the middle like sunlight and shadow

—WILLIAM S. BURROUGHS

1.

Un homme invisible. Blend in anywhere, your sousveillance secret agent, your field poet. "Don't let them look you in the eye," William Burroughs would advise me if I were walking down a street in Denver, or in Montreal or New York or Paris. And you could travel incognito, taking it all in.

And you could project what you wanted onto William, the meme, the person—a "combine" perhaps—a conglomeration of tendencies—the figure of dark Future—who defied neat categories. Le cher maître, Allen designated him. He had tremendous intellectual power over his younger so-called Beat colleagues; his logopoeia—his "dance of the intellect"—was supremely magnetizing. He was in my humble experience like the sorcerer muse (as in "bend sinister," the left-hand path of the sorcerer) always "on," active, always a step ahead of our attendant reality. He made you think twice. Often more than that. He still haunts my consciousness.

What constituted this visionary Burroughs, who in his work and talk was obsessively focused? What might we learn? What was the transmission for late twentieth-century dystopia? What was this absurd adolescent horror of the centipede? I thought of the cinematic sectional flow of the centipede, an innocuous narrative for our time that might seem menacing. Like slime molds that will inherit the planet, have no truck with human whim or desire. What does being a victim constitute in realms of language? How to resist? How are we a language *and* a virus? What damage do we—humans—do intentionally? Ignorantly? What are the limits of this body? How do we feed it? How do we reimagine language to investigate and challenge the dull frequency of doldrums, prisons and prisms of the mundane, with seething below-the-radar frenzies of transgression, aberrant behavior, sexual violence, and righteous gnaw of the disenfranchised prophet? What is consciousness? And how does it travel? What is our "value" inside a presumptive and compromising capital? Was Burroughs revolutionary, a Marxist, a fantasist, a Sufi, seer, or prophet? Mektoub. It is written. Fatalist? "A writer writes," he often said. Burroughs's work on the whole is passionate critique, of the social organization of late capital and the logic (or illogic?) of the textual realms it operates within and dominates—our whole dystopic Western civilization that supports a disturbing and more and more suicidal demise.

And we have the writer who mirrors this so well. A disclaimer of these notes: Nothing to prove or defend, Look to the writing.

Where do we position, in our current dystopia, the provocative dismembering body of work that constitutes the opus of William Burroughs? And the prescience within this "body" that destabilizes many concomitant and parallel realities? I would say the "Burroughs effect" defies categories. "The basic disruption of reality" is what he posits. In the last decade and more, we have witnessed a self-fulfilling prophecy mirrored in Burroughs's work, his vivid revelations and resonance and constructs, in his dark investigation of the "limits of control." We have disturbing images of torture from Abu Ghraib, from Bagram, the force-feeding at Guantanamo, we see "terrorists" in perpetual "lockdown," we have the drone wars taking out "suspects," hundreds of thousands of deaths on our hands in the combined horrific Middle East follies. Many mistakes, innocent civilians, women, children, even US citizens taken out, we have the glamorization of CIA in movies such as *Zero Dark Thirty, Road to Guantanamo,* and *Argo,* the seductive brutality of war (and its downside) in *American Sniper* and the romanticization of the Navy SEALs in *Lone Survivor.* Many cults in recent war. We have the "extraordinary renditions," "waterboarding," and other eviscerations. We have revelations of the murky worlds of the ongoing Cheney/Halliburton Company zone—the Blackwater regime now rechristened "Xi" (harder to pronounce?). Xi: a cultish subculture with its own hierarchy, strategies, policies, budgets, and religious zeal that, contrary to public assumption, has not been dismantled. The Koch Brothers agenda, the confederacy . . . all these subcultural, hierarchal power structures embedded with the money and international governmental corruption zones are deeply Burroughsian in that he has already imagined them, created them out of a fierce and biting wit and sensibility: "*the fix is in, the fix is in* . . . the fix is in for the hungry ghost . . ." (The women biz, his misogyny, is subsumed for me in this greater vision of our syndicates of samsara, because that's really what he was on about: the endless wheels and rhizomes of the interconnected root/tuber systems of samsara. Samsara which is the wheel of life, the "meat wheel" the cycles of suffering. Hard to get off.)

With great linguistic, visual, and psychological power, Burroughs's shifting and morphing characters breathe and grind on in their wild machinations, their "routines" to revivify attention to our continuous dark present. Like terrifying tantric wrathful and semiwrathful deities, Vajrayogini, Mahakala, Yamantaka with their kartikas and kapalas (knives and skull cups), whose purpose is to wake up and scare us into a heightened consciousness. We have the marketplace, the interzone, where all realities meet in "consociational" time. We are perpetually inside these zones ourselves. Literally, psychologically. A recent episode crossing into US virtual space in Toronto at the Toronto airport—surveillance, scans, another photo taken was like a Burroughs "set." Baggage rechecked. Taken aside for pat-down whenever I've been abroad and coming home. And watching dark-skinned others, including friends and family, harassed and taken aside for additional questioning.

And further prescience: palpable addiction and drug sickness everywhere in the world, continuing AIDS epidemics, Ebola, the opioid epidemic, the psyops played out on human psyches, the psychological suffering of so many—raped, plundered, starving, and displaced. We have myriad "ghosted" bodies— emanating out of the eternal war scenarios, suicides, broken lives, and broken neurological pathways. Amputees. A Bosch-like intensity. Intricacies of surreal body parts: animal with human, experiments of genetic hybrid, sheep and mouse cloning and the like, transplants of all kinds, the torture of the animal, human/metal cyborgian hybrids or advanced robotic weaponry, the drones and reapers. We have the euphemism and lies of "Operation Enduring Freedom," "Shock and Awe," "Clean Air Act" or "refined interrogation techniques" or "disposition matrix" ("kill list"), which amplify words as killer viruses. We have wild boys who resemble kids in the slums of South America and Africa. Gangs going wild on drugs. Thuggish murders of the women of the maquiladoras in Mexico. We have the endless brutal mafia scenarios—Russian, Balkan, Chinese. We have the slow drip and dull hum of media control invading the fabric of our thinking, its powerful inflection and influence on lives. We have the World Wide Web spying on our lives. NSA monitoring cell phones, whistleblowers in lockdown, genetic manipulation. We live horrors of troubled medical zones, where hospital care is menacing, dangerous, even murderous. Kill or cure? We live inside skulls of empty space/time—impermanence fueled with perpetual craving. We continue to hallucinate the enemy, creating monsters out of our weird warring-god-realm sensibility, surrounded by hell realms and hungry ghost worlds of all kinds conditioned by an "algebra of need." Pampered privileged god realms, too, that dine on pleasure until the seat gets hot and the body starts to rot. Planet degradation and dysfunction that mirrors degradation of bodies—the perpetual control mechanisms and the ongoing paranoid conspiracies, real or imagined. Who works for whom? A vivid troubling landscape sometimes front and center, sometimes in the foreground, sometimes on the fringe, in which we find ourselves trapped in states of denial as we are parodied, caricatured, allegorized. As if in defense we make it art, in order that we see our condition put at a distance which is a samsaric disjunction, a schizoid reality, disconnected and under perpetual "control." William S. Burroughs was a seer who put his own body through rounds of addiction, who lived as a homosexual and addict under police-state regimes of suppression and control. He was always *out,* and he was always so much further "out" as an experimental writer than the rest.

To put it simply: Burroughs's visionary writing—his generative imagination—frequently comes to mind in these dark days, as if he invented this post-postmodern dystopic set we find ourselves in. I meditate on his landscapes, his interzones, his charnel grounds, and I appreciate his clear-eyed, dispassionate, almost clinical, anthropological gaze into what constitutes, deconstitutes, and reconstitutes our complicated realities. He destabilizes and investigates our humanity and foregrounds our fluid, transmigrating identity. It is a spiritual work he practices. Waking the world to itself. The practice of the cosmic mirror. This, in my humble view, doesn't forgive, but overrides his misogyny.

2.

I knew William Burroughs for twenty-five years and would call him friend. He was a mentor in particular ways. He was a poetic godfather to my son, Ambrose Bye. I observed him at work, in productive stages of his writing life; I was privy to his classes at Naropa University, and I was influenced by his methods. Experiments of Attention, as I call them. *Go out, take a wall. Observe anything blue. Make a mental list. Also notice what you notice and then what that resembles (the pictures!) and where your mind travels. You are mailing a card to Paris, you can see Paris. Someone says "San Francisco" and you have an immediate picture in the mind even if you have never been there. You see a lady with blue hair who reminds you of your great-aunt Matilda. Come back, write down your list and the associations as well.* (Paraphrase of one of Burroughs's class assignments.)

His passage in spates of teaching for the Jack Kerouac School of Disembodied Poetics at Naropa University was extremely generative; we were a familial haven for him. He adored Allen. They had a long history, having been lovers and surviving a difficult past and were consummate friends. Allen was one of the greatest champions of his writing, many years.

William was working on *Cities of the Red Night* (1981). He was a disciplined writer, he called himself professional. He gave me my first and last gun lesson. His son, Billy, son of Joan Vollmer, was living in Colorado's well as well, and Billy was embraced by the Naropa community and supported through his illness and liver transplant. He and his father had an intricate, tragically fraught relationship, yet I watched William weep profusely at Billy's suffering, and specifically during the period when his son was in a weeklong coma.

We cooked meals in William's little apartment. Many celebrities passed through our "temporary autonomous zone."

William taught Shakespeare's *Troilus and Cressida,* a supremely modern text with its scathing Thersites figure, who spoke with the tongue of Burroughs. A pox on both the houses. Or pimp Pandarus, another character from the Trojan War's interzone.

Images fix you in certain locales, and invoke myriad routines, he would tell us. They talk, too. Use them.

I had first met William formally at a party on 57th Street in New York City in 1968, hosted by poet Bill Berkson, and was seated next to this formidable éminence grise. We talked about control, making tape recordings in a crowd, about what later evolved as "sousveillance," as opposed to "surveillance" (how the writer was empowered), about the book *African Genesis* (Ardrey, 1961) and travel—I had recently been in South America. And other subjects he touched on in *The Job* (1969), which were alarming from a feminine perspective. I had just read this book (published that same year by Grove Press), a collection of interviews conducted by Daniel Odier that is most cited for instances of Burroughs's misogyny. John Giorno (close friend of

William) and I had been performing our poetry in Central Park earlier that day with films by avant-garde filmmaker Warren Sonbert. I was nervous but not intimidated. John had first introduced us.

I remembered from *The Job:*

"I think they [women] were a basic mistake and the whole dualistic universe evolved from this error."

"I think love is a virus. I think love is a con put down by the female sex."

Odier references and asks about women in Burroughs's books. Mary in *The Soft Machine* (1961), who eats the genitals of Johnny, whom she's just hanged. Or the constipated American housewife who is afraid of the mix master. "In the words of one of a great misogynist's plain Mr. Jones, in Conrad's *Victory* [1915]: 'Women are a perfect curse . . . Women are no longer essential to reproduction.'"

He also references frogs being reproduced from single cells and how a man's intestine might be produced from the nucleus of cell lining. And men might birth children from their assholes. And indeed, as we are seeing in recent years, women may no longer be essential to reproduction.

I have never been an apologist for William's moral lapses or misogynistic statements, which in their extreme—and particularly, in the context of *The Job*—I still consider crackpot, weird. But they have never distracted me from the mastery and deeper power of his cinematic cuts and pastings. But I also saw over the years these "takes" were never totally fixed or solid and were not consistent or dominant in the writing or in his life. His male characters—or "presenters"—come under equal fire, scrutiny, not as persons, but as types, stand-ins—part of his allegory, his satire, and his social commentary.

These sharp views of the 1960s had shifted by the time we met. "It is not the women per se, but the dualism of the male-female equation, that I consider a mistake." His goal was not the occlusion of women any longer. He spoke of the sexes fusing into one organism. He was generally misanthropic rather than exclusively misogynistic.

I was spurred in part to these more personal notes remembering the instance where a friend of mine—the radical and provocative feminist Andrea Dworkin—threatened a mass boycott and demonstration when I was hosting William at a reading at the St. Mark's Poetry Project in NYC. Andrea and I had lunch and I talked her down, based on an inspired critique that supported the writing. I told her what I had observed—I'd been recently sitting in on classes William was teaching at CUNY—and I expressed how liberating he was as a writer. The notion of censoring or shutting down Burroughs seemed anathema at that time—and would be at any time—and I think in a perverse way, I went out of my way to champion, not the life or the person, who I was really just getting to know—but the work to which I was drawn. Particularly, the *Nova Trilogy* from which I felt a social/political activist "call" and inspiration to work with montage. And cut-up.

In one of her texts, Dworkin links Burroughs to the Marquis de Sade speaking of his rapist frenzy, which is rarely in his texts, if ever—and if ever rape of women . . . she had it wrong. But I could certainly understand her rage and the citing of Burroughs's grotesque accidental killing of his wife, Joan Vollmer, years before, as a moral crisis to respond to. Women felt he had not been duly punished enough for this "crime." But censor his work? Never. At St. Mark's and Naropa? Not on my watch.

Regarding his relationships with women, one cites Ilse Klapper, who he sometimes spoke of—green-card marriage of convenience but clearly a friend for whom he had respect and kept in touch with. Joan, his wife, was brilliant, worldly, a complicated person, well-read—one of the wittiest people he knew. William was comfortable with self-assured women who had proven themselves, not leaning on men. Women who were accomplished, could hold their own: Susan Sontag, Patti Smith, Laurie Anderson (and I considered myself in this company) . . .

Sadly not Karen Finley, who in her piece "Moral History," scrawled over a copy of *Naked Lunch:* "Burroughs you are no hero to me."

3.

It's an interesting time for the Burroughs legacy, some years now into the new century. Ongoing debate on Joan's accidental death, the William Tell shooting, and William's accountability and his light sentence in Mexico . . .

irredeemable? A young woman at the Jack Kerouac School at Naropa wrote a master's thesis on Joan Vollmer, both a feminist defense and creative piece written in the presumed voice of Vollmer.

Some are also still troubling the homoerotics of the Burroughs's old Nike ad (1994) . . . his gaze at the young players—the unspoken complications of sports, power, and homosexuality, not to mention sports addiction . . . combined with the panoply of sports ads in general with their sperm-bursting cans of beer. What is Burroughs supposed to represent here? A voyeur? A difficult trope—who is he to these worlds anyway? Hardly a fan of football. Where is our homme invisible, this éminence grise as a commercial trope now? Regulated to pale movie renditions? Does his ghost sell sneakers? Controversies continue alongside the work itself, which is kept thankfully in print and continues to be studied and critiqued, and has greater intellectual textual response overseas for decades with the likes of Gilles Deleuze and Félix Guattari. The bar has been raised in regard to the intellectual and linguistic power of the writing itself.

Recent portrayals of Burroughs keep his unmistakable voice in culture's soundtracks . . . I am relieved to see that his iteration as a culture icon is not occluding the writing. It is still odd to see depictions of him on the silver screen. Viggo Mortensen in *On the Road* (directed by Walter Salles, 2012) does an aspirational job, and Ben Foster is also salient in *Kill Your Darlings* (directed by John Krokidas, 2013) to say the least of an ethically ambiguous film. "Who speaks and acts? It is always a multiplicity"—(Deleuze and Foucault).

Deleuze and Félix Guattari discuss Burroughs in a text called *A Thousand Plateaus:* "Why have we kept our own names? Out of habit, purely out of habit. To make ourselves unrecognizable in turn. To render imperceptible, not ourselves, but what makes us act, feel, and think. Also because it's nice to talk like everybody else, to say the sun rises, when everybody knows it's only a manner of speaking. To reach, not the point where one no longer says I, but the point where it is no longer of any importance whether one says I. We are no longer ourselves. Each will know his own. We have been aided, inspired, multiplied." This is one of the keys to Burroughs, they say: not to reach "the point where one no longer says I," but to reach "the point where it is no longer of any importance whether one says I." The set has changed. We are in a reality that does not value imagination's conservative identity or ownership of experience as we are no longer static or stable ourselves. Who are we?

Timothy S. Murphy suggests that "Burroughs's is no longer just the name of an author, a celebrity, or an artist; it is the name, rather, of a set of potentials, an effect that propagates itself from medium to medium by the force of its difference, bringing into contact incompatible functions, incommensurable concepts, and unrelated materials." Odd concepts and the way the whole sum of his parts has been dissected, eviscerated . . . unlike any other writer I can think of in these postmod times.

Something about the patient etherized on the table? Welcome to geological time under the iron hand of man that Burroughs predicted everywhere with his preternatural insight and imagination and investigation of capitalism.

"Human beings can't be expected to act like human beings under non-human circumstances."

4.

There's the idea from French critical theorist Michel Foucault that the body is the last site of resistance. But what happens when the body's mind goes beyond itself? When the consciousness travels—astral projects—moves in dreams? What are the limits of control in these instances? His work continues to disrupt comfortable narratives, including the master narrative, patriarchal and normative in terms of its form and content and sense of history—literary or otherwise. Burroughs's work as unstable consciousness finds itself restlessly outside modern and postmodern parameters. And the dream, the timeless dream, has been a source for much of his writing, defying strictures about a place in the "canon." He is more a scientist of mind.

I want to close with a personal investigation—from his dream book *My Education,* published in 1995, two years before he died. The title of the collection arose from this dream:

> Airport. Like a high school play, attempting to convey a spectral atmosphere. One desk on stage, a gray woman behind the desk with the cold waxen face of an intergalactic bureaucrat. . . . Standing to one side of the desk are three men, grinning with joy at their prospective destination.

When I present myself at the desk, the woman says, "You haven't had your education yet."

Some lines from a dream on page 26:

A big party. Ian is there and Anne Waldman, the Naropa Mother. You need a place to stay? You got a dose of clap? Take all your troubles to the Naropa Mother. She gives all the satisfaction.

He goes on to describe being junk-sick, needing a fix. A shot of jade that turns to stone in his body. And the dream turns to nightmare.

I have been flattered to make it into a Burroughs dream, maybe a visitor to his psyche, and also, for a time, resisted these lines. Did I need to reconstruct, deconstruct this identity of Naropa Mother? Cut up the dream. That's where the jade-stone Mother became. I am both a character—a principal in his script as it were—and a figure of control or archetypal power character. But it has also deepened the connection to the Naropa experiment and its ongoing struggle to survive as a unique identity within it. I decided to embrace the dream's creepy prurient assurance that "she gives all the satisfaction" like a dose of hi-tone heroin. When we founded the university, we founded a place very much on feminine principle that relates to atmosphere and environment—what is a called *prajna* in Sanskrit—or womblike wisdom. To investigate my identity within prajna and investigate the mind that posited as such. William would be amused at my uptight analysis.

"Do you realize you are the only woman in the room?" William taunted playfully as he came toward me, after a long night of talk and drink and smoke. In many instances, when all these alternative cultures and communities and lineages and affinities were coalescing and trembling and forming and reforming, I was often the only woman in the room, and that urged me to open up all the doors to all the women in the projects I would help create and build. But I was often one of the few women, certainly in high school and in college, and later in small poetry circles, checking out the Burroughsian landscape—who was deeply into his work. It seemed for a time I was often the only woman in the room of his writing.

Sunken Suns & The Tyger (for Etel Adnan)

The Middle East lives its destiny. No sound seems trivial or ordinary. The power of terror is totalitarian. Bullets crack and resonate in the amphitheatre that is Beirut.

—ETEL ADNAN

My body is a rag being sewn to the earth.
O you who sews the worlds, sew me!

—AL-MAᶜARRĪ

I spent the other day reading aloud—performing—the extraordinary *L'Apocalypse Arabe / The Arab Apocalypse* in a room of one in Marrakech. I experience this text's magnitude of display and yearning and urgent alarm. Its measure of riot and desperation and power. The poem in its integrated sections shoots off the page, disrupts conditioned space, explodes in the ears, and beats the inner drums; it unleashes a linguistic slash/breach/upheaval. I made gestures, arms flagellating and hands jabbing the air. I supplicated. I improvised finger-mudras and worked taut, fierce expressions upon my face. I let my mouth expand to hold the whole of ancient "Arabia," then I revised the map and considered all the turmoil continuing, now, ever, and the rest of the world's collaboration in that endless suffering of *problem-not-solving:* Israel and Palestine. I included Somalia, Libya, Tunisia, Syria, Yemen. I knocked my head with my fist, I looked up to pray again, then bowed and prostrated on the ground of the poem. My eye-mudras moved in all directions of space attempting to indicate . . . no manifest . . . to enact Etel Adnan's prophetic poetry glyphs.

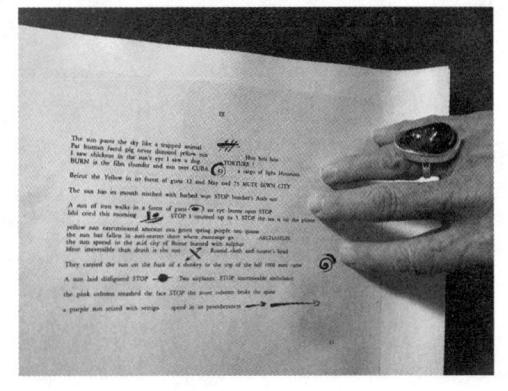

Thus I put my whole body into the codes and lingual soundings of this animated and visual text, her *Apocalypse*. May people of the future decipher these runes. I lay down for the arrow-like glyph between "Mexico!" and "bed undone" (II). I splayed myself on the floor before "great Inca." I stamped on the floor before "Ishi cried this morning" (IX). After "I painted the sun in the middle of the sky like a flag" (XII) I danced and swirled and repeatedly pointed to the window and beyond. I held my belly, clutching it three times before singing out "the yellow sun of menopause" (XVIII). I stuttered and crawled after intoning "in the underground blackroom always black is experience" (XL). I groaned, "There have been pounds and pounds of decomposed flesh tons of suffering," (L) and let blood symbolically gush from a wounded-long-gone body and moaned. I took the text's ideograms as clues for performance and chanted "HOU HOU HOU HOU HOU" and "DOUM! DOUM! DOUM!"

An enactment of the battleground, measuring my own echolocation. An enactment of the psyche, measuring the relief, the purge, the terror this ritual mirrored. I spooked myself.

Who can say it, who says it, what are the words to call out and carry and implode this apocalypse? This is the closest—Etel's text—I have come.

What she attempts to do in language is a crisis upon an altar, a *crise* of the vocal vibrating heart.

I rested, then took up the glyphs again, I retreated, then called outside to others.

They—apprehensive—left me in my retreat of poetry and prophecy and penance.

I noted

"a blue sun receding a Kurd killing an Armenian an Armenian killing a Palestinian . . ."

I noted

"What a purple and violent abyss broke loose on the primordial land of Syria?"

I noted

"Treason floats down the smooth surface of the Euphrates like a woman"

I noted

"When they eat the Palestinian's liver before he's even dead"

I noted

"Imam Ali dances over nuclear blast"

I noted

"we crucify Gilgamesh on a TANK as Viking II reaches Mars"

I noted

"And under the blue clouds of Babylon turtle doves announce a thunder"

I noted

"There have been meadows covered with human skin under the Arabian moon"

I considered all the colors of Etel Adnan's "suns," her voyelles, the red dots that are sunspots of the stuttering amplitudes of the poem, or a floral sun with petals of gold . . .

I noted her Mao and Rimbaud, the razor's edge.

I conjured my own physical/spiritual displacement. I recalled sleeping on the desert near Abu Simbel, sickle moon, in my young girl coven, 1962. I felt the sun's heat early in the morning.

I recalled the airport in Beirut, machine guns everywhere. The fear in people's eyes.

Rain obscuring the sun.

The root of the Arab word *nashid* (song) is the voice, the raising of the voice and the recited poem itself. According to Adonis *(An Introduction to Arab Poetics)*, "the Arabs of the pre-Islamic period felt the recitation of poetry a talent in itself, distinct from that of composition." "Listening was essential to the comprehension of words and to musical ecstasy *(tarab)*."

"The actual performance of poetry had its own rules in the pre-Islamic period which survived into later ages. Some poets, for example, recited standing up, while others proudly refused to recite unless they were seated. Some would gesture using their hands or their whole bodies, like the poetess al-Khansā (sixth–seventh century) who, it is said, rocked and swayed, and looked down at herself in trance."

I wanted that trance, wanted Cassandra invoked here in a poem of wailing, and the explication of the harm out under a cruel desert sun. For the desert will consign all to dust and sand more quickly, perhaps, than we can imagine. "The lone and level sands . . ."

Pre-Islamic: Rhythm evidently began with *saj*, the root of which "contains a reference to song, and is used to denote both the musical call of the pigeon and the plaintive monotonous cry of the she-camel, alike in one respect of being continuous, unvarying sounds (Adonis)."

I rather punctuated with a vast array my imagination in a verisimilitude of Etel's time and place. And thought of her, summoned her to inhabit her rage and the rage I would enact on the poem's behalf.

Later, I worked with Berber (Amazigh) schoolchildren at the orphanage in Marrakech. They had been troubled and fearful after the bombing in Jemaa el-Fna in April—seventeen dead, twenty persons wounded—and drew pictures of their responses to the tragedy. One had to keep the poetry transmissions, which were in English and French, simple. These brilliant youngsters had grown up in a culture vivid with some of the most sophisticated music and poetry and crafts imaginable and had so much more to teach me.

We got through the first verse of "The Tyger," acting out the poem with our bodies as we chanted it together, first in French, then English, then Arabic.

Tyger Tyger, burning bright—we drew a sun with our hands in the sky, over the desert, perhaps, not far from the door of the dorm we worked in.

Suddenly we were *in the forests of the night,* hands and body trembling in the darkness, yet indicating the solace of trees, our bodies growing up from the ground.

What immortal hand or eye . . . lifting a right hand, palm outward, and then pointing with the other hand to our left eye.

Could frame . . . we drew a large rectangle in the air.

They fearful symmetry . . . we crouched, then leapt up, eyes wide and wild, embodiments of a magical new generation's tyger-energy, century's child synergy.

The symmetry or exact correspondence of form on opposite sides of a dividing line. We met at the horizon of the sun sinking over a mythical desert.

Letter from Etel Adnan

Dear Anne,

This is Etel, we are in Beirut, a sauna. A city with highrises and the old narrow streets, a suffocation being built. So many dingy nightclubs, cafes, eateries, and so on very vibrant though, full of brilliant young people spending time asking questions such as do I stay do I leave and in fact living on airplanes, and the mountains. Very close, still livable, and luxury hotels. Gulf Arabs buying 10,000 square feet apartments that they leave empty most of the time. the thousand and one nights with iPods—poor and trapped prostitutes—political flimsy schemes—and for them still real fun . . . so many young talents mostly in video, short films, and so on. The laboratory for things to come. Maybe the closest thing to America— incredibly is Beirut. It should collapse but it doesn't. Let's hope that there is, in fact, some hope.

Believe me, the thing that means most really most is love—passion love or friendship, the getting together of a few people a few times for a few hours and it does make of living a wonderful thing. Last night we were by the sea in a dingy garden cafe, the only one left of its sort, with some 10 people, from very young to me, in age, actors, artists and so on and some newly met, and it was so beautiful to see everyone doing his/her best to make some art, some money, some theatre . . . and trying to matter in this huge blind world. I really deeply wish you were with us. You would have immediately integrated, understood, happy. That's one more reason why I miss you. Stay in touch. Love, Etel

* * *

*& I hear you there and I saw through time with you, Etel, as I morphed further
slithering into runnels of the snake tributaries of the snake realm, bardo of
many encounters I would tell you of as my thoughts took off,
I would see a thought of aid to give, or love or empathy to give to give
reflected in the quick dart or hiss of snake underfoot . . .*

I was walking lot then, to find my tread and find my thread as samsara
whipped in cycles under my feet—and the earth turned in cycles under
my feet
and I climbed the hill out by Devil's Thumb . . . it was dusk—a slight shift
in the air . . . autumn coming on her sweet rattle in the crux of a tree and
moving like a dance . . .
the fangs flicking out toward me

gaze of the snake fills the eye
I SANG TO HER TO QUELL HER SHE THE snake of my time
Lokapala of this place
chih chih chih

I sang OM TARA TUTH TARA TURE SOHA
to calm her that I may pass by, that I may continue to climb
chih chih chih O you most beautiful of rattlers . . . gone way beyond a
poetry of sorrows

Mix Up the Cry of Desire I'm a Corset Wrecker

memoriam, Kathy Acker

Sometimes I want a corset like
to harden me or garnish. I
think of this stricture—rain
language, building—as a corset: an
outer ideal mould, I feel
the ideal moulding me the ideal
is now my surface just so very
perfect I know where to buy it and I
take it off. I take it off.

—LISA ROBERTSON

What is it, why is it, Kathy Acker, your Emma Goldman, end of dream? I confess you are a wonderful anarchist. What is it to be a corset maker of labor and purpose, binding the bone and rabble in cotton in a daily sweat of anarchist teen toil, I Emma, I Anne, I Kathy, what is it to know the sweat of us, my sisters?

Will heaven give in to defiance, will heaven rock the defiant?

May Day 1886. A deficit? The workers celebrate & demonstrate disobedience.

Our cunts are silver daggers and matter explodes when she a they he a they and all a they they and you take off the corset and the rich girls don't dance. Enter and disrobe their sweet fucking slits. Slits are vices to crush your wealthy patriarchs.

Deconstruct the bone and cloth and taxes that bind and fill up the purses of oligarchs.

What is a sexy oligarch? I doubt it. This is Sunday, a day off in the piss factory.

I was paranoid you'd take my reading away. I don't want to be alone with my machines.

O Emma, O Kathy, O Hannah, O Carolee, please bring in the stranger who holds the strings he pulls through the aperture of patriarchal factories everywhere. What oligarch wears the corset, inspects the factory, its piles of rubble? While we're the center of the universe, they speak exploitation, can't help but demean.

Are these not the evil magicians? I timeless, and I a one, with the ghost of dead sisters.

Recognize imposters anywhere. I file past the crypt of Uncle Ho, I an anarchist, I Emma, I Kathy, I Carolee Schneemann, I Hannah Weiner, I Anne, fresh in from Russia, where they touch up hideous Stalin. I with the country in pilgrimage. The call us "The American War." How many shrines to author you, Uncle Ho? Construct at jumping identity. I am on pilgrimage, image war is not real needs, death is needs with your universe top of body toys, but image nation the top of the bloody soil. Kathy sees this ahead of herself (while dead) where a court pronounces four anarchists murdered and Albert Parsons speaks for eight hours. And I demand the floor. Tiny hands with needles punting, pushing, slamming the passion in innuendo in the new American century abolished, it's an "all in" epic, all an open resounding "no," screaming "I AM THE DEFENDANT." Let the words out, abandon cover of the corset constraint! Taunt taunt taunt! Your tiny hands at the machines.

Are you needle sewing, a distorted body, or are you sowing power?

Moon against your heart. You want to escape the factory metabolism. Nipples rub against stone of empire that binds the bone in this labor to you who will always be asking our divinatory cards about future boyfriends, those who no longer kiss the butt of the state and profit off the labor of Emma's hands and Kathy, and Hannah, and Judith Malina, and Carolee's, and I author Anne who makes not a dime to dine out. And our girlfriends. Maybe they'll all be on our side.

Workers of daily living surviving an economic purse-string purpose, what is it to be declared? What is it to be a migrant worker? Emma, her long days in toil making a garment while I, a system, want only to let the anarchist in. We help you now sisters. I toil, I Kathy will arise, and I Anne in safe territory, will arise. Did Emma ever take her revolutionary sex-love-lust out of Russia? Where is Russia in Emma's heaven? We are at war, sisters, Kathy, Emma, Malina, Diane di Prima, Anne, Carolee, I author America to be your crucible.

It's an energy of daily sweat and toil to be free of the fascisms of how and when and why and why O never free of J. Edgar Hoover but my Emma, Kathy, Carolee, Hannah, Judith, Diane, imaginations ever free of the imagination of J. Edgar Hoover. Is he still here who will surely most certainly have your number in his fractious labor and psychopathic toil. As he toils and plays with John Lennon even now, when he the ghost of fractious fatwa dead J. Edgar Hoover is stalking, haunting the work places, the meeting places, the "commune" of all my sweat and purpose.

What is it to be a large woman bespeckled and intent in a socialist moment? You want to call it that? Why you can call it that and it's so much more but do call it that and you will I'm sure call it that and most dangerous of violence and terror to incite a riot what is it to be thus called trouble and to be forever "unpopular with authorities" to be watched and goaded and arrested and in lockdown what kind of terror moment is this and will it survive and assassinate a president this kind of moment will it will it survive McKinley will it survive psychopathic fractious J. Edgar Hoover, and will the ghosts of Haymarket stalk and tremble the Union Hall?

And will Kathy Queen of Pentacles, and Carolee and Hannah and Malina and di Prima surveille these clusters these mirrors that fracture Empire. I live to see. O brave sisters, O Emma, still in that old purpose binding cotton and will that will that acts and buffers stabs of protest and memory arising, will it will it O my sisters, will that will break the corset that binds the moment?

Kalyanamitra: Joanne Elizabeth Kyger

November 19, 1934–March 22, 2017

Young rabbit
circles ash
tree
state of
nerves
nerves are beehive
memory zone
cracks in the field composition
stay relaxed you said
& wrote
"we think the squirrel that lives in the pine here is eating the Amanita that
came up behind the studio. He must be very stoned but haven't seen him
leaning at the glass door yet"
trying to reach you
come, kalyanamitra, come
with yr knack for animalia garden commentary
at loss here without you
$1,200 to kill the emerald ash borer within—
are they serious?
who is the deadliest foe?
Death? so many friends
guns?
Blowback?
Collusion
"Two big raindrops just fell on the deck. Shortest rainstorm in California
history. Those fires burning, have plenty to eat, stressed and diseased pine
forest, etc."

& for New Year's you wrote:
"be sure to visit Jai Singh's observatory in India and all those poets
together at St. Mark's, what energy!"

—A. W.

* * *

Thinking about the two aspects of Zen practice in relation to the writing
life of Joanne Kyger. How do we count her? Many the ways, of wit, instinc-
tive command, and fastidious philosophical turns. West Coaster, lokapala of
Bolinas, what better guardian of local doings. She was poet of oikos, of place,
of ecology of locus, of history near and distant, and of hearth and home which
began with Penelope (*The Tapestry & the Web*); she's the busy patient one. Her
poetry was woven with palpable friendships, curious mythologies, intimacies,
and creatures that scurry and fly and inhabit same frame of turf. Invocations
and close scrutiny. She wrote a long poem around the eleventh-century pandit
yogi Naropa, for whom a school was named she was connected to, honorary-
guest-founder of its Kerouac poetics for many years. She tracked Madame
Blavatsky, sly theosophist, and made extended forays to Mexico, and bril-
liant poems and journals came of that. Keen flaneur of early thrumming Kali
Yuga. She kept elegant notebooks, gorgeous calligraphic mind-to-hand docu-
mentary meditations. There's more to come, tomes of journals and correspon-
dence. Her last workshop at Naropa was entitled "Writing in Dream Time"
("whoever sees, dreams well"). But how does it work as Zen?

She writes:

> Replacement Buddhas
> The altar of the Buddha is dark
> The room has been taken
> By the dolls
>
> —*GYODAI*

What do all those Buddhas *mean*
At the museum, brought from elsewhere?

Rhetorically, What do these apparitions signify?

"A magician mutters a spell over stones
and pieces of wood and produces the illusion"

of Buddhas and humans and animals and houses
"which although they do not exist in reality

seem to do so." And some people blinded
by this magical hokum-pokum

hanker after what they *see*—the Buddhas and fast cars, racehorses and glam-
orous people—

forgetting they are just stones & bones

pieces of wood

           Translucent like last night's dream.

                    (J. K., FROM *The Life of Naropa*
                    MARCH 18, 1995)

One aspect of koan practice, where the student responds to a conundrum that owning the experience can't be resolved. Point is to make a spontaneous leap before ego kicks in. Return to primordial language, gesture, and expression, where you don't own your experience. Tricky because you can't claim it but it's *in* your poem. The poem owns it. Apparitions are hokum-pokum. Joanne's had perfect balance. She could check out and measure what comes from an original silence of her own mind. She had an open screen in her being; she danced with the phenomenal world and could get down, letting go with entheogens, muttering her own mantras, up all night till moonset, shaking a jar of beans. Steady rhythmic consciousness always at bottom of her being.

Joanne had a kind mind and generosity toward the world, but made sharp and caustic remarks, witty too, and her *Japan and India Journals* (with all that spiritual backdrop) are a perfect feminist Zen palliative as she stands around in India in her black drip-dry dress waiting for some wild martini attention while Allen Ginsberg insists on reading *Howl* to anyone who will listen, including the Dalai Lama, and Peter Orlovsky's hair is growing long and greasy (the better to take drugs behind). Gary Snyder, the ever-serious meditator, critiques her shoes and reading habits and her study of "sissy" flower arranging.

But the poet and person persists like a koan, complicated, surprising, drawing in various denizens, "the trees and the greenery and so on" as one Buddhist chant has it. She didn't suffer fools and was absent an indulgent compassion, practiced something more like bodhisattvic encouragement for everything in this vibratory existence. Sharp and penetrating . . . tell it like it is, deeply experience it, but don't give it all away either. The dharma path, like the poetry path, is a self-secret metabolism.

Then there's the second piece in Zen, which is shamatha meditation, back before words and concepts. Sit quietly, watch thoughts—memories, emotions. All the reruns—come in and vividly dissolve, catch them skillfully and they become transmission. Stay your ground, the earth under you, no expectations.

Both streams here run concurrently. The wild gesture, the koanic surprise into unimpeded space, and the ever-present witness mudra, pen, or finger, heart bent, bow down, touching the earth. Here is a political poem with all the wisdom of an enlightened mindfulness:

Sunday

> When your "mind" flies
> away with a poem on a page, do you both
>   end up in a lonesome place
> in the backyard of words
>   as soft and familiar as the bee
> buzzing the blue glass
>   which is the only company
>   you have
>
>   Sharp rap in the knee
> —a tiny apple falls through gravity

You have a "way" with your words—
"thinking is a pathology"
   that has found freshly discovered ground
but if you "think your way
   into the next scenarios"
Good luck!
   Buster Bush and Co. have whacked the globe
—a hard blow of the uglies pathogen
            and it's a disastrous scene

Note the tiniest first baby quail
 in the far scallop of shadow—
a tender mouthful of hope
   scratching down a dainty slope
of wind to move on

   —J. K.

Some correspondence:

From: Joanne Kyger
To: Anne Waldman
Subject: <no subject>
Date: March 10, 2005 at 10:24 p.m.

Dear Anne, sorry to have missed you on this 'quickie' visit. The weather was nice and warm, though, wasn't it. Bill B. said you might be able to see the Poetry Center exhibit at the California Historical Society—a kind of landmark for household art (in lieu of gallery and Museum) of the past 50 years in the Bay Area, which I thought very intimate social, and gossipy.

The waves have been very impressive for the past two days, big surge in attendance of surfing spots on the coast, especially here, with cars out to there from 7am on . . .

I'll be arriving NYC on April 21, Thursday, and it's still convenient for you to lend a bed for a few days?

Hope all is well with you both!

xxJoanne

From: Joanne Kyger
To: Anne Waldman
Subject: Re: so much going on
Date: March 12, 2005 at 3:01 p.m.

Dear Anne,

Yes, we were having our climate change weather, broke records! René Franken of Demian bookstore in Antwerp emailed about trip there, but it's only 10 days away, and I have a Bolinas class I'm teaching now, so I probably can't make it . . . but a great invitation. Thanks for passing my name on. I take it Lawrence's health is OK if he stays local? There was a clear and historically detailed obituary of Philip Lamantia in Friday's paper. My friend Nemi Frost just called. He was her boyfriend for a while when she first came to San Francisco in 1958, John Wieners introduced them. She did a portrait of Philip called 'Auto de Fe.' Only he was talking so much during the sittings that she could never see his mouth, it was always a blur. So she ended up by painting a little Clara Bow rosebud type mouth, which wasn't at all accurate. (Much regards to Ed and all in Boulder. Have a good time at your party. Linda Russo is going to read in our studio tomorrow afternoon, thanks to Steve Ratcliff, who will show off his new baby boy, Johnny!)
Lots of xxxx
Joanne

From: Anne Waldman
To: Joanne Kyger
Subject: Re: you there Scorpio
[approximately November 2005]

Dearest Joanne—

How is your birthday month going?

Unseasonably warm days here—have been to the Elizabeth Murray show
3 times . . .

How is the new book coming? Saw the Orono folk a few weeks ago, they seem
excited about it . . .

What is the gossip?

Did you get to the Creeley memorial out there?

Very sweet here—some moments of levity with Ron Padgett, John Yau
anecdotes—Bob's intimacy with everyone comes thru . . . Pen and Will so
strong tho. Will broke down sobbing at the end . . .

Listening to Democracy Now on TV. I like to watch Amy's face.

I finished Joan Didion's *The Year of Magical Thinking* at dawn—an admirable
job, but she might be interested in the Bardo perspective . . . also she seems
to name drop a lot . . .

Have you seen the Berrigan book? We are celebrating here Wednesday with
readings from it on Ted's birth date (16th).

Lee Ann had a party for some Scorpios last night—including some of the
Mayer-Warsh clan . . . thought of you. Lunch with Pat Padgett, another
Scorpio, tomorrow . . . And Alice in town who turned 60 this month . . . Her
virus is gone, hooray.

Ed got another clean CAT scan & I have more tests in a few weeks—head to Boulder Friday . . .

Much love to you both

From: Joanne Kyger
To: Anne Waldman
Subject: Re: you there Scorpio
Date: November 15, 2005 at 2:06 p.m.

Dear Anne,

Yes, Scorpio month is going very well, the weather is warm and no rains so far. I did go down to Stanford and was part of their afternoon 2 panel Symposium, in which we each presented a 10 minute (count them precisely) "paper."

Marjorie Perloff did her exegesis / close reading of 'Rain' which she does so brilliantly, and which pleases her so much. It was held in the special collection room with some of Bob's broadsides and books out. Limited seating for 80 maximum. Penelope and Hannah were there, the former looking very thin. Penelope read the same piece she read at St. Mark's, about Bob's death, and in her introductory remarks, broke down. I don't know if these memorials are cathartic or not, but they surely are emotional, and I hope the family's duties in this respect are almost done. I was supposed to read Monday at the Poetry Center's 3 hour memorial, but came down with some kind of respiratory wheeze so had Steve Ratcliff read Tom Clark's poem about sitting on the beach with Bob, which I was supposed to deliver. I heard Bobbie was succinct and brilliant with Charles Olson's piece for Bob, and a few remarks. I only got to talk with her by phone.

One of the editors at UC Berkeley Press is sending me a copy of Ted's book, which I read in proof sheets last summer. It was an excellent visit with Ted. Alice and sons did a thorough and loving job of editing it. Give my greetings to Alice and a happy birthday to Ted's spirit at reading. Nobody else like him.

Glad to hear the good news about Ed's tests, and yourself, stay relaxed!

Best,
xxxxx, Joanne

From: Anne Waldman
To: Joanne Kyger
Subject: Re: so much going on
Date: January 9, 2006 at 4:37 a.m.

Dear Joanne,

Saw the GREAT show. Hope it can be a book. Wish Steve Clay was still in biz for something like that (costly). Home now to Boulder, yes, very quick visit. To small dinner in Sausalito, not sure how we "did" or "came off." Good to have Peter there, Lawrence. I wasn't wearing the right clothes, alas. It was so HOT. Wish there had been room for more like YOU & Don!!! O yes I loved yr stuff, wonderful to see Bobbie JK portrait & Don & Franco.

Up til 2 am last night with Nick Dorsky . . . fun but exhausted. And watched THRENODY & other footage. The city looked beautiful in the bright light of the day.

Did you see the Middle East Campus Watch (Lynne Cheney publication) (go to Google or website) piece on Ammiel Alcalay? References me, others, Poetry is News, Naropa, Archive, scary. Spying on us.

Later & love. Did agit prop with 20 students on the Mall last Sunday. Boulder is roiling with Ward Churchill fracas, clamp downs at CU. Wrapped up the summer catalogue—smashing.

Ed here. Party here Sunday.

Yes to April 21!! An honor (but place not generally available so don't broadcast, OK?). I am going to be "trained" for radio work tomorrow at KGNU with

Daron M. I keep telling students to "be the media" so I'd better get down to it too.

Ed has a new script & maybe shooting this summer with Daron's help—fun.

Later & much love—wish I'd had more TIME there (never enough anywhere).

From: Joanne Kyger
To: Anne Waldman
Subject: hello
Date: April 14, 2008, 3:51 p.m.

Hello!

Steve Clay said he saw you the other day so you must be back. What a wonderful place to be! have been.

Just finished *A Blue Hand* by Deborah Baker. She sent me a note apologizing for the *NY Times* Sunday review and any intimation that she may have treated me unsympathetically. I can handle it (except for the fact she has me rummaging through Allen's rucksack to read his journal—when it was on the table for all (me) to see). Now my visitors will all want to lock their suitcases.

It's that irritating practice of her biographical writing (and she is not the only writer to indulge in this) to tell you what her 'subjects' are 'thinking' and 'feeling' and their motivations. When it is all conjecture. And very intrusive. Lots of value judgments that reinforce the stereotypical characterization of the unwashed beatnik druggie 'banging' away at their wives (Neal). Gregory Corso's dirty fingernails. And so on.

She is a very pleasant woman, and I think wanted to reflect some of what the Calcutta, and Indian community was experiencing with Allen's visit. Perhaps the book is successful on that level, but the rest of her characterizations are overly simplistic, and Hope Savage remains a fragmented focus.

Lots of wind today, lots of sneezes.

Very best to you both!
      Joanne

From: Anne Waldman
To: Joanne Kyger
Subject: re: hello
Date: April 15, 2008

Joanne—O my dear that black drip-dry dress of yours is such a luminous detail in literary annals now. I agree with *NY Times* that the book is sorely lacking, missing really, the reality in your guys' writing. The weave is good, keeps one on toes, but essentially a retelling of the journals sort of & irritating projection as you say on what you are all thinking, what motivates you . . . & reinforces the image: druggie, naive, self-centered. I feel everyone as presented is not the humans I know. Today I am being interviewed on a docu about AG in India . . . One of the questions, How did AG's trip to India lead to the founding of Naropa U? The legend continues. I am so happy I will finally SEE you in June, you living legend, you. Maybe we can have some drinkies at the Hotel.

Whatever did happen to Hope S? I thought John Giorno had some news a million years ago . . .

Meditated with Tibetans yesterday at the UN. Forwarding photo of Chinese police with Tibetan monk costumes under their arms . . . Still jet lagged & off to Austin in the a.m. for work, will see Dale & Hoa & god daughter Naomi. Ambrose wants to record you reading poems. Is possible? Check out Ed's website & the movie (I sent Donald info) . . . Ed says hi, he's working on next project "Entanglement."

LOVE

From: Joanne Kyger
To: Anne Waldman
Subject: Akilah
Date: March 19, 2011 at 8:54 a.m.

Hello Anne,

Cedar Sigo on the phone just told me Akilah had died very suddenly, February 24? We just were looking at a vibrant photo of her taken last summer at Naropa. Whatever happened to her? I know you were close, and our deepest condolences to you. Liz Tuomi, the wife and mother of Arthur Okamura's children, and a good friend of mine, also died, suddenly, almost two weeks ago. But she was suffering from radiation treatment for her throat cancer, and just kind of got smaller and smaller over a series of years. Like Poof! and away she went.

Dreadful winds and cold rain, lightning and hail going on for a second week now. The electricity not out, so we can still see the nuclear disaster happening in Japan and NHK.

Hope you are well. I dreamed about you last night, and you looked fresh and youthful—kind of "Russian."

xxx from us both,
Joanne

From: Anne Waldman
To: Joanne Kyger
Subject: Re: Akilah
Date: March 20, 2011 at 11:22 a.m.

Hello Joanne—

Supermoon days.

Yes, "without warning." Hard to speak of. Too tragic. I had seen Akilah just days before, radiant with much going on in her life & with work. (Do you have the Coffee House book *A Toast in The House of Friends?*) She was in the Phd program at the European U. In Switzerland (in summers) & travelling & attention to her work . . . She was planning to come back shortly to MacDougal St to record with Ambrose . . . (He's quite broken up, knew her well too)—Then she missed 2 days of her teaching at Pratt & someone called and it seemed urgent to get into her apartment which Rachel Levitsky & others did. I had to be at a Bernadette reading but was in cell contact. It was a horrific, tragic night. Found dead, on her bed in casual clothes, apartment neat, TV on to news channel, computer up and open. No foul play. Maybe dead 2–3 days? Fists clenched and face with fierce look and detective said most likely a heart attack. The death notice still not released. Everything slow in NYC . . . 2 sisters & niece were in town & ceremony pulled together. Attached a prayer we read . . . Loss is huge . . . I think her life was shortened by heart-burden of her son's death . . .

So sorry to hear about Liz Tuomi. Ah & the disaster of loss of life and destruction & suffering in Japan staggering and should be an alarm for all humanity. And the tomahawks & stealths in Libya . . . not sure where that is heading. Reed's sister said why can't we just get James Bond to take out mad dog Gaddafi?

I am depressed about Naropa. Lack of progress with the Archive situation. A new Ad Hoc committee that Jane D-H will stay involved with but frustration of her & rest of us running high. Steve Clay was presenting great option of sale to a major U. Naropa, which simply isn't taking care of properly, missed opportunities, fired archivist last summer, etc . . . President talking about getting a "consultant" instead. The new regime seems strange . . . so many Xtian folk . . . & the VP Stuart Sigman continues to be undermining of W&P. But Michelle Naka Pierce will be the director of the Kerouac School & she is capable & smart. Reed & other elders I think exhausted. I will still at least see thru this summer & retain the shape & command with Lisa [Birman.] Not sure about 2012. Lisa hired only year to year which is a problem. My status shifting but they say there is a commitment to retaining me, tho the VP keeps asking about my "succession plan." Want to be supportive, tho, in general. No new hires. But modicum of good news with Leslie S. summer scholarship & kari edwards scholarship now fully funded and some help with Ginsberg money that brought Lyn Hejinian for a week this spring.

And I am co-editing new anthology with Laura Wright which is fun, and a reclamation of sorts. (Have you seen latest *Lost & Found* from Ammiel & CUNY students? Spicer's *Beowulf*? Fabulous. And Duncan on Olson? Diane, Rukeyser, etc. . . . Naropa could be doing more of this kind of work if it could only get its act together).

Ed continues to work on the wonderful "The Value of Small Skeletons" & now finally going to Al Anon for help with his brother's situation. We are hoping Ed gets his sabbatical next spring.

And wonderful to have Ambrose. Ambrose & I performed in Montreal last week . . .

I need to get back to *Iovis* proofs, and step out on Ed's roof into the sun.

Hail?

It was heartening to hear from you, means a lot & I send you & Donald love . . . sorry to rave on . . .

Yrs,
Anne

From: Joanne Kyger
To: Anne Waldman
Subject: THE MILK OF UNIVERSAL KINDNESS
Date: June 18, 2011 at 3:40 p.m.

What a great 'family affair' *The Milk* is, with your wonderful words always spot on.

Hope the first week of Naropa went well. We left town for a few days to see the wild flowers at The Pinnacles. I felt I'd been away weeks, when I returned and was disappointed to find it was only three days and nothing much had changed. Except a friend and neighbor on a long hospice watch had gone out with the full moon and low tide.

On last Memorial Day weekend Leslie Scalapino's ashes were put into her grave site at the Bolinas Cemetery in a ceremony conducted by Norman Fischer. Who does his Zen ritual without too much fuss and bother, a nice clarity. Leslie's husband Tom had it all prepared, a big ceramic pot to put the ashes into, with room for himself later. Covered it all over with pretty gravel. She has a big black granite headstone, and bench. Right behind her a local town person, named Pluto, has his grave. Which someone has planted with many many succulents. Then we all went to Steve Ratcliff's for wine and lunch. Amy and Michael McClure were there, he with his new book edited by Leslie. And his cane, since he is now blind in one eye. How did that happen? Just woke up one morning and the sight was gone. He still maintains a very glamorous look.

All these routines of the passed and fallen are becoming very very familiar. Good social occasions, especially when a year has passed, and death has made the individual perfect again.

Although not to Michael Rothenberg, who is still mad at Leslie. Not even his 100,000,000,000 Poets for Change can distract him. He's gotten a bit paranoid. I don't know where I'll be in September when everyone is supposed to do their CHANGE tap dance. And he has become nauseatingly persistent. And he's not happy that David Meltzer wants to get married to his new love. And that Garrett Caples edited Meltzer's new book for City Lights.

Well, sorry to have missed your phone call. Going on and on here. Will see Jenny and Maya next Friday. She told me, about seeing you and Reed at Bobbie's new place right around the corner from her old place. So like Bobbie, all bases covered!

Hope the rest of the summer goes really well.

Love from us both,
Joanne

From: Anne Waldman
To: Joanne Kyger
Subject: Re: "the best ever"
Date: June 25, 2016 at 8:41 p.m.

Hi Joanne—

reading Anselm Hollo's *The Tortoise of History* with sweet poem for you . . .
sure you have seen but in case not it's called:

Reading Joanne Kyger

Such poems
       of gentle sadness

not the sadness
       that makes you want to burrow
       into the ground
       jump off tall building
       slit your wrists

              no not that kind
              but one of gentle rain
                  falling
                   softly
     on memory gardens
     in your brain

Child of Illusion

for Steven Taylor and Judy Hussie-Taylor

       bewilderment
on verge of
language
  bursts
into
heliocentricity
   "I'm with you
     in Rockland"
D train
  to Coney
Beat poetry's
  screed a
girl heart
  tattoo
in glut
of death's heads
 now glints in
 sun
handgun?
when despair
  no longer
   erases
sensibility
ink from the
  T'ang dynasty
will reappear
   mixed with
water
  of a certain well

Bobbie Louise Hawkins

             what she said
evil doers
  my **dear**

lost souls of media's

insinuating attention

    drip!

those fuckers

what she said
      they're so **tacky**

(waves over
    world in tatters

thin wrist
    I'm tired

not make it much longer)

eye eye
it was all heart
yes I see you, I
hear you
your *talk*
know I see
can't won't
won't act
like it's
 end

Oh honey get on home . . .

Solange in Marfa

Still,
we bit the bullet and blew. "I will be and
I'll believe when I blow," we announced.
"I will be and abide by sound, my slave day
done."

—NATHANIEL MACKEY

just arrived

the desert the fuchsia

dancers' vestments, the siege

arrival, it's green

spectacle

long months it's been

a city of

america dreaming itself

never green

a wrecker, a city

to arrive without scaffolding

need this

it'll be holding

it will be haunting

we need this

Solange

performing

don't touch my hair

and her women

the angles the dance

the dry ground

she's ready

don't touch what's there

coming across the desert

to mess with us

with royal heralds

sway of trombones

dancers dance, her angle

down on the ground

you know this hair is my shit

allegory, flailing on the ground

come into our crowd

the world stops here

rode the ride, give it time

off site from center

of ambition it rides

this here is mine, don't touch

derides it thrives

but reach goes higher

how stark, of lineage

will she mess with us

the legacy

Solange in the landscape

they say "watch for snakes"

don't touch my crown

dj'ed the human backbone

the pedestal, the glyph

the sistrum, constant shaking

of instruments

of gods, of chaos

don't touch my hair

mythic protestation

performer as salvation

her vehicle is the oracle

the idea, to mess with is

walk through the desert

a transmission

but this here is mine

cartouche for the future

body, light she brings

shadow, elation and trembling

vast in zone of troubling and power of

votives, *don't touch*

angels in architecture, trombone

you never thought,

"architecture of trombone"

before

desert theater

push and pull a gesture

hierarchy's proportions

priestess of power

singing of her hair,

don't touch it

don't touch it

they don't understand

what it means to me

audience waits

dressed in white

no cameras allowed

no cell phones

lure us here and play to the sky

a mile coming at us

cry at us

slowly, high magic

emissaries from a distant kingdom

caravan is instinct

the nomad, Egyptian

wavelength of sound

and arrives

come at us, come for us

when it's the feelings I wear

into exile

sun smacks the horizon

the vision I've found

but this here is mine

desert hallucination

rode the ride, I gave it time

dear Bernadette,

it snowed last night, dropping many degrees
over 80 to teens in one plunging night,
no howling dogs no retired cop Robert Wilson's shepherd barking restless
next door
now safe, his little red doghouse

seem to still be sitting at desk many hours in trance of zen snow silence . . .
doing little

then a zoom conversation about the *Therigatha*—old enlightenment poems
by women from the time of the Buddha with the Jaipur Literature Festival
which is being managed on carrier waves from London; "my heart snapped/
my neck was free!"

Jane Dalrymple Hollo called then in a flurry about covering edibles in her
garden and needing to deliver a basket to me, which she did . . . art supplies,
copies of *National Geographic*

making a collage for Laird Hunt, something about sunspots

most everyone careful and stays down the walk

I watched Barbara Loden's *Wanda* in the middle of the night and have been
looking at all your photos in *Memory* again . . . and stills from *La Captive*
(Proust's *La Prisonnière*) by Chantal Akerman

ten inches now on the leaves

yr Ed, I can say this, needs a serious woolen coat

been reading Saidiya Hartman who will change the way you think about
all you know in one round life

wanted to finally tell you it was me sent those red roses so many moons ago
wanted you to think another stranger loved you too, I was that stranger

O lucky stars,
A

Part IV: Contemporary with Our Time

From a Burroughs class at CUNY
May 8th, 1974: "The last class, I proposed the virus as a prototype of evil . . ."

Consider the virus. It is an obligate cellular parasite, unlike organisms like the spirochete, or the malarial parasite, or unlike bacteria, there are many beneficent bacteria; in fact we can't get along without them or bacillus. It is an obligatory parasite. That is, the virus is rigidly programmed to perform a certain operation. Now the existence of a computer program would certainly lead us to infer a programmer since computers do not program themselves. Can we not infer a virus programmer? If so, we have an alien invasion of many years standing because the virus is by its nature alien. A parasite must remain alien that is different and separate from the host; otherwise, it ceases to be a virus and ceases to be a parasite. It loses its separate existence. A virus without symptoms, that is a virus which occasions no reaction to the body for the host, would not be noticed. And viruses seemingly must make themselves noticed, must call attention to themselves. Here again is the prototype of evil. Evil is not self-sufficient. Evil must make itself real and call attention to itself at all times. Real as a night stick, real as jail, concentration camps, and the convulsion of rabies. Otherwise the virus is absorbed and ceases to be a parasite because it becomes part of the whole.

Question: Do you think capitalism in the United States is a sort of virus?

Burroughs: I don't know. That's such a difficult comparison. You can clearly see how certain people or even agencies can act as viruses. In other words, they are parasitic, they need the people which they exploit or oppress and the people don't need them. That is, they are acting in a purely parasitic manner. To speak of capitalism as a virus, I think you're going to run into too many complications and contradictions there. Certainly many individual capitalists and many manifestations of capitalism are parasitic and act as viruses.

—WILLIAM S. BURROUGHS

I've not spoken of this much. Seventies. Twin Sisters, Magnolia Road up the canyon from Boulder. Put in the gleaming white aspen groves middle of the night, can't gauge the distance but the vehicle in the sky so close. Three miles up? Moving on a trajectory forward, back, side to side, seemed precise measurement. I'd guess a mile each in six directions. My mind racing, how to capture this? I knew of "sightings" in Colorado. Often near nuclear installations. We were quite near Rocky Flats. What could be ascertained in the midnight sky? What secret transmissions, oscillations. There were bright-colored lights blinking: red, blue, green, yellow. Red, blue, green, yellow. Red, blue, green, yellow. Yellow, green, blue, red. Yellow, green, blue, red. Yellow, green, blue, red. Precise, methodical sequences, a language?

I felt the way I felt when I yearned to go live with the dolphins under John Lilly's failed project, on isle of St. Thomas. I had read one of Lilly's books. I felt personally summoned. They are coming for me. I was a teenager, a good swimmer. Maybe I would be a good translator of all things dolphin, of all things alien. I got a reply from the Lilly people (it was a project that included Gregory Bateson, whom I admired,) explaining the Dolphin House had closed. One of the dolphins had committed suicide, presumably after traumatic separation from one of the keepers. And LSD *was given to the dolphins who ostensibly became morose in captivity.*

—A. W.

Had a Hand In, Occupy

I've been magnetized by the potent protests of Extinction Rebellion climate activists in New York City in these recent years and reports coming from front lines in the UK and elsewhere. I was planning to participate in the subway action that had to be cancelled in March of 2020 when the coronavirus took hold fatally in NYC. But the conglomerations and tendencies and astuteness that were Occupy Wall Street are continuing more skillfully, and that is the good news. What follow are a few notes on some of that history.

Occupy was recognizing and utilizing skillful gestures through signage, meme, and the repetition of response mechanisms, such as the oral "mic check," and hand mudras which registered yea and nay and "discuss this further." Governance gatherings, such as General Assembly, various web tributaries, publications (such as the *Occupy Wall Street Journal* and *Tidal*), and the basic practice/inspiration of showing up with many bodies in public, all-weather spaces were established. The willingness to live and protest on the street was impressive. The official law-enforcement response was, by turns, predictable and vicious. Passive-aggressive, one noticed. Artists, poets, citizens of all stripe and ilk were drawn to the possibility of a shifting consciousness addressing the dire situations of economic disparity, unemployment, resources in the hands of a few, racism, and the universal, unmitigated suffering in an interconnected world. Also endless war and the degradation of conditions in so many that surround us on the streets of the world. And not to forget reinvigorating our society with imagination, delight, playfulness, a university on the streets, a library, food, shelter.

Occupy Art, an offshoot of ows, was declared in late November of 2011. It included input from poet Anne Carson, musician Laurie Anderson, and so many others.

The first Occupy Art action took place at Lincoln Center on December 4, 2012, after a performance of Philip Glass's opera *Satyagraha*. (*Satya* = truth, *agraha* = insistence.) "Truth force" was Mahatma Gandhi's radical and deep sense of an act of civil disobedience and protest. Lines from the *Bhagavad Gita* are sung in Sanskrit, during the first act, which highlights Gandhi's work in South Africa against apartheid (particularly with Indian workers) and a demonstration on September 11, 1906, in Johannesburg which first activated the Satyagraha methodology. Dr. Martin Luther King Jr. is also a protagonist, in Act III of *Satyagraha;* his own life of protest—as is universally known—was inspired by Gandhi's salt march.

Occupy Art wanted to highlight the irony of an opera advancing the moral rigor and practices of Mahatma Gandhi's civil disobedience with the financial support of the Bloomberg Foundation. The composer appeared with the Occupy protestors and supported the concern about the disparity between a visionary and humanitarian moral message and the apparatus of corporate arts funding. New York Mayor Bloomberg's police force had been arresting and applying pepper spray to Occupy demonstrators for weeks.

One obvious next action was a demonstration at the Museum of Modern Art in front of Diego Rivera's riveting three-tiered fresco *Frozen Assets,* which posits further irony: a painting relevant to current Wall Street issues inside a corporate art museum. The fresco displays wealthy New Yorkers at their bank at 1 Wall Street opening deposit boxes on the bottom tier; next, a homeless shelter (a pier at 25th Street) with sleeping bodies lined head to toe, more reminiscent of a morgue; at top, skyscrapers of wealth and power tower over the "frozen assets" human realm, a burgeoning Rockefeller Center at center. This was painted in 1932. Diego Rivera later became involved in the New Deal's Works Projects Administration, painting frescoes glorifying the stamina and dignity of the working man.

Many activists have been pushing the current US of A administration to consider a New Deal–like solution, which (back then) put millions to work after the Depression. Others want to turn the whole apparatus upside down. The current temperament of the 99 percent is restless and impatient. As poet Charles Stein said early on of the Occupy movement, "Money has an enemy."

Many younger Occupy activists feel indebted to the Arab Spring and particularly the riveting and failing situation in Egypt (which continues to be troubling and complex), where women had particular voice in the revolution overthrowing cop-pharaoh Hosni Mubarak.

I participated in and observed Occupy contact zones and protests in not only the New York nexus and ancillary protest sites—Zuccotti Park/Liberty Plaza, Duarte, Washington Square Park, Times Square, the New York Stock Exchange, and Union Square—but also sites in Toronto, Berkeley, San Francisco, and Athens, Georgia. A fluid esprit de corps was always visible.

But during the Occupy period in NYC, we worked on the ecoterror play *Red Noir,* which was produced and directed by Judith Malina and performed by the Living Theatre in 2010 and 2011, and *Cyborg on the Zattere,* a "pounda-torio" with music by composer Steven Taylor, which opens in a Wall Street casino. *Cyborg* takes on the "knot" of Ezra Pound, his hideous politics and luminous poetry. We see him in his open-air cage at Pisa, not unlike the cages at Guantanamo. The opera opens in a Wall Street casino. Steven Taylor had composed a "usura" cantata for a Renaissance trio.

In various "workshops of attention" I taught in the Occupy fall of 2011—including several with Ambrose where we focused on the social issues of Occupy—we continued these ruminations, investigations, and cultural interventions, deciding where the work comes from . . . head . . . throat . . . heart? . . . readings and samplings and appropriations of others? And where was our gaze? We acknowledged "deficit" and magical "disorder" too. We decided to track or trace back the neuron that found affinity with our psycho-physical system, that summoned us to activist poetry.

On October 13, full moon, sitting on the chilly ground at Zuccotti Park:

Moloch's motor stuck

   on roof of Casino Wall Street

ghost chip/the sky

I walk out under a night sky full of stars that seem so far from the city; I am struck by the brilliance of Orion and look up, naming them for some of the poets who have died in recent years: Janine Pommy Vega, Akilah Oliver, Ira Cohen, Paul Violi. Samuel Menashe, Gil Scott-Heron, Victor Martinez, Andrée Chedid, Taha Muhammad Ali, Stacy Doris, Adrienne Rich . . .

Also 2010: Tuli Kupferberg, Marilyn Buck, George Hitchcock, Ai, Bella Akhmadulina, Lucille Clifton, Barbara Holland, Peter Orlovsky, Leslie Scalapino, Peter Seaton, Andrei Voznesensky. **And in 2011:** Édouard Glissant, Susana Chávez, Ruth Stone, Christa Wolf. **And in 2012:** Jayne Cortez, Jack Gilbert, Louis Simpson, Wisława Szymborska, Reed Whittemore, Barnet Lee "Barney" Rosset Jr., Mohit Chattopadhyay, Anne-Marie Albiach. **And in 2013:** Seamus Heaney, Lou Reed, John Hollander, Anselm Hollo, Lucien Stryk, Thomas McEvilley, Chinua Achebe **And in 2014:** Maya Angelou, Amiri Baraka, Russell Edson, Galway Kinnell, Carolyn Kizer, Mark Strand, Alvin Aubert, Madeline Gins, Rene Ricard, Maxine Kumin, Bill Knott, Alastair Reid, Ron Loewinsohn, Tomaž Šalamun. **And in 2015:** Philip Levine, Günter Grass, Tomas Tranströmer, James Tate, Lee Harwood, Stephen Rodefer, Madeline DeFrees, Christopher Middleton. **And in 2016:** David Antin, Daniel J. Berrigan, Leonard Cohen, Jim Harrison, Geoffrey Hill, C. D. Wright, Bill Berkson, David Meltzer, Ted Greenwald. **And in 2017:** John Ashbery, Roy Fisher, Tom Raworth, Derek Walcott, Yevgeny Yevtushenko, Heathcote Williams, Richard Wilbur, Harry Mathews, Thomas Lux, Sam Shepard, Joanne Kyger. **And in 2018:** Bobbie Louise Hawkins, Claribel Alegría, Donald Hall, Nicanor Parra, Ntozake Shange, Lucie Brock-Broido. **And in 2019:** Linda Gregg, Kate Braverman, Al Alvarez, W. S. Merwin, Elaine Feinstein, Clive James, Marie Ponsot, Mary Oliver. **And in 2020:** Miguel Algarín, Kamau Brathwaite, Ernesto Cardenal, Diane di Prima, Lewis Warsh, Michael McClure, Ruth Weiss, Marvin Bell, Michael Friedman, Hal Willner. **And in 2021:** Robert Bly, Jack Hirschman, Stephen Dunn, Lawrence Ferlinghetti, Susan Noel, Dick Gallup, Gary Lenhart, Adam Zagajewski, Michael Horovitz, Etel Adnan. **And in 2022:** Peter Lamborn Wilson / Hakim Bey, Neil Climenhage, Noah Eli Gordon, Bobby Neuwirth, and Kenward Elmslie.

This Is the Antithesis Reality

"When the mode of the music changes, the walls of the city shake"

for Diane di Prima

We're coming out of our little theatres
Of hope & fear
To a city near you
We'll breathe again on the streets
& liberate the hall of justice and
We are the antithesis reality
All is brought to transparency
Twilight cannot be delayed
This is the antithesis reality
It's a deluge of fire
Of climate apocalypse
Watching the bloody moons & magenta suns
        of dust & smoke dynamite the sky
Roiling in polite society
In a "gentleman's agreement"
In the sick corridors of corruption
Where *the fix is in, the fix is in*
And nano-racism & "hydraulic racism"
Haunt the premises
But this is the antithesis reality coming at you
Can't pull the wool over antithesis reality's eyes

The security state thrives on insecurity
And a war on daily life itself
Call in the paramilitaries, summon the Space Force
Put a TOKEN WOMAN ON THE MOON?

We're taking down oligarchy's assault!
Antithesis reality against psychopathic data flows
Damming up rabbit holes of disinformation!

Won't swallow snake-oil hypocrisy!
        Fraud! Mendacity!
This is the revving up of antithesis reality
This is the antithesis reality & we ain't no foggy mirage
We're slamming your politics of de-civilization
We're the antithesis reality here to reinvent resistance
And to risk revolution
Not risk lives of tender beings in times of plague

We're coming out of our little boxes of hope and fear
to a city near you, a town, a crossroads
We're turning down the static
Voting against capital's extraction of "all *from* all!"
We're masked & mouthing the takedown

Voting against ugly abusive language,
We are the antithesis reality—
We like to fall in love with whomever
        we want & dance
        in contrapuntal rhythm
We are the antithesis reality—a refuge
Voting against reification of land—
        of living & regenerative earth, all peoples, organisms,
        of water and air
Voting against borders, drones, cages & carceral torture
Voting against the military-nocturnal-techno-surveillance-complex,
        in which power gathers, pools, congeals, kills
O bare life! Nothing left to hide! Humanity, keep faith
Come, reanimate the world
O tentacular Nation, we're working overtime
This is the antithesis reality & we are here and rising
Power gathers on the flip side of the mobster's crooked penny

Vote against brutality! Xenophobia!
We cheer proliferation of difference!
Because we are the antithesis reality & we are
        entangled in the beautiful rhizome of differences
We're spooky attraction at a distance growing closer

We are here to reanimate beauty and wisdom
We intend the possibility of art,
        for transformation & innovation
We intend to get it revving now

This is the antithesis reality
We earth our charge here,
Extract arrows of brokenhearted Amerika
We'll metamorphosize this techno-thanato-porno-punked-out empire
To the inmost shimmering fabric of the one thousand things of this world

Don't lose your Mind!

(with homage to Althea, & Nic)

Twelve Tones under the Sun

Who is a man not caged?
Who is a woman not whirr . . .

    —A. W.

John Cage was a new or short or longer pause suppliant. John Cage was a friend to brains of the two sexes, to Buddha, to eat him, destroy him. John Cage as John Cage was, sat down. *Rest not, Tetrapod!* John Cage was for us as poetics arrived in pure perfection and turned and never stammered to listen, John Cage was metabolic twin listener. Staunch, dark doom that never rides. But he does. John Cage was a founder. Surprise is never barren, all over the timing world. John Cage was a culture, gaps in the cave to know Neanderthal. Hours with him, a boon. So much of a story. Fathomless medium of laughter across a dangerous pathway. He was a mosoipholon domos. And under the sun, a test of. Texts enlarge the world. Equilibrium he is good at. Pianos will teach your own intervention. Pianos will reside in silence, pianos will loom and close. John Cage was metabolism for up his mind as he called it, strength, and a case for lines. Deference, no solemnity. And pluck the cactus needles. Out of reach? John Cage was and never. Then drew it out. The sign would be that, the sign would be as John Cage was and drawn. Down on the tatami. For his purpose was not purpose to be uttered outside or inside but under the sun. A cool chamber, then. Find it. Sources of comfort more abstract. John Cage was visiting. He would attack the tones. Help, a perfect abstract to a visitor all over the timing world. To have been there, you had to have been there and then not but flying. Utterly inside. Utterly outside. Are you listening? John Cage sat and then turned. Every domestic duty could be heard in and out of Japan. In and out of New York City. Everything at this season goes out so light. Twelve thoughts before breakfast. One, a companion ever so expected, a moment of pride. Two, a found text. Three, a story that is a next moment. Four more kinds of him to have thought. Five, a summit of bliss. Six, does one have greater a right to scandal than one is prepared to pay? Seven, a form of communication influenced by delay and death. But held in archive. It was eight and the thought had a glamour of receiving itself. Nine, an enumeration. Ten, a sharper calculation. If eleven "doesn't he tell you things?" ever stop? Twelve is not a limit, eyes during the wonderful dinner ambitious of variety.

Radio Play

for Judith Malina

Wild night. Wind, sirens, coyotes, edge of a boom town . . .

Modern era. There is a sense of not wanting to talk about certain things.

[some kind of animal sound-tape . . . howling]

[orations from our actors and their voices:]

[music: something by Leoš Janáček]

"I have nothing to say. I am saying it,"

"I have nothing to say. I am saying it,"

"Decimate originally meant the killing of every tenth person."

"Page 359: Dictionary."

Decipher:

"swimming in deep blue delirium" (Ashbery)

Decipher:

"I have nothing to say and I am saying it"

Just listen:

"Fitness equipment, exempt from taxation"

Just listen:

"To take care of a young bird until it can fly
the beautiful anarchist revolution"

or the sound of bloodsucking insects

fleche, an arrow,

[enter the sound of jazz guys: my memory Freddie Redd in The Connection.*]*

"I saw you young then. I saw you ageless now, bending over Red Noir,
ecology and atom bombs."

enter the sound of electronic guys,

and enter the vibrating poets:

comb the cactus, silence, then canticles of friendship.

All: "We were not about to miss your wisdom,
O Thalia, O Melpomene."

Auteur

ED BOWES: *I've always wanted to be a fly on the wall so that I could watch people carrying out their everyday lives without knowing someone was watching. A lot of the assumptions we make about ordinary actions are just not true.*

Q: *So why not make documentaries?*

EB: *Documentaries are a kind of fiction too. Making a documentary is very much like being a guest in someone's house, and guests do not get to see ordinary life, the real stuff. Also, I am basically a dramatist, and I want control because I have something to say.*

Ever his own universe he does what an Ed does
As today does Eugene Onegin
Taking all time, mind-stalk of editor Ed
Not dandy or cynical but stranged where figure of light
And figments of clothing appear, as cuffs
Sheer shimmer, or shoulder's taught drape
Or tee gone wild at hip, what to do but
Remain geometry's heart on a new season, dissed
Her nape? Never. Her grace, her stare? Never lace
No such narrative meaning, emphatically NO!
For sound for sense for Laird Hunt's perfect vertical
Not actors but Ed's movie stars as presenters
Go for the figurative Eugene Onegin again, St Petersberg
Your name Edward Francis Xavier Bowes a beau centaur
Set up high home or cheek bone to a shot is seething
Your commune, the company of enscripted friends
Stop a Prevallet or Sikelianos on windy tundra, Gertrude or
Nathaniel Hawthorne's wife & Woolf & WCW epistolary
Maybe Carolina under a tent, and Pethybridge at piano, a teen
Demand to exit the poets' voices, Ed says in subvocal "any time, now . . ."
As actors wait a cue, Sojourner and Ellsworth pause, nuanced
In softs *ahs* his method a tribal leap goads just call us figures
Orientation to sun a house in a system's response
Turn a moment here, one more take and land the mystery
Night plot *igni involens* as Taylor champions Judith Butler

System of reality minus message Uli tends a fox in a seahorse powder room
For daily touch-ups as cells undulate to keep the reel turning
And beauty and memory and Ed's non sequitur arising
"I would really like to communicate with you one day on Jupiter"
Dust disses a light box's best boy, wait for me my darling
In a volume like this, you master subterranean hauteur
In "mercantile skeptic's voice . . ." or would assent
Cry refrain! Jointure! Action! Never lonely on this high ground
With ideals wed to camera in thy commands the
Stage times gone by, over horizons not punching the gut of a star,
but sturdy boats and sturdy sturdy boats, la gloire!

Allegorical Baraka

the tongues of dying men / Enforce attention, like deep harmony.

—W. SHAKESPEARE

who wakes you up
(bad scenic tapestry
dove barely escaping hawk
villains bandits robber barons
slave traders
an excuse for progress?)
who wakes you up
biblical, literal or
actual rips
in bright kente cloth
or black today
symbolizing "intensified
spiritual energy"
enigmatic dreams
get made with you
enfolding your selves
o man of social action
lift consciousness
to teach us ugly deeds
toes keep a thrum
upon the body politic
"survival dancing,"
& deconstruct for us
"state control"
harrowing acts of cruelty,
intricacies, a Byzantine
cloak-and-dagger
morality play gets made of
tragic events unfathomable

holy fury! fury! fury!
or redemption
in verbal spells
(contagious elegance's
controversial logic)
such sweetness too
in a man you love
turns poetry from
dangerous toy to weapon
lament or dirge
or love song
skillful means, upaya's wit
rhetoric of praise
& ceremony
or uncensorable blame
jazz riff toward
visionary plateau
whose time is come
this is the way it *sounds*
griot's call
who's a daemon?
griot calling
it *sounds* & poetry
is your gospel
truth, who was target
a whole long life
in the struggle
for syntax of revolution
be these accidents or
miracles that bind us
be this friendship
& love
who told it as it is, *love of*
human freedom is a love supreme
is this buried, mere ornament
poet
saying to one coming up on stage
read like your ancestors are on fire?

chivalric banner, guilds,
bowstrings
obligatory joust
reluctance in the cities
in the suburbs
but ready to rise
a surreal riddle's surprise
flee? escape?
surrender?
fight back?
consistency
in the man
looking back . . .
and moving forward looking back
though he breaks hearts
he never forgets arke
history & purpose
twin dynamics
for a new-to-come action-poetics
with post-post-post-post
medieval exegesis
who was this journeyman
plangent messenger
good dark angel Amiri
whose music
shakes walls of cities
& could be wrathful too
not about accordance
the whole range is
transcending
human suffering, *you dig?*
his gleaming steel
uncompromised
brilliance our reward

for music, saxophones
of James Brandon Lewis,
Devin Brahja Waldman

Trance Abyss

There is a pain—so utter –
It swallows substance up –
Then covers the Abyss with Trance –
So Memory can step
Around—across—upon it –
As One within a Swoon –
Goes safely—where an open eye –
Would drop Him—Bone by Bone

—EMILY DICKINSON

There was a crack –

Weeping at the world –

Apocalyptic glow –

We were ghost –

An enclosure, a meadowlands –

We were cold, fierce –

We were an enclosure –

Poetic wand for beauty –

Neural rapidity –

Rueful wisdom, quiescence –

Matter travelling back in time –

crack in consciousness –

there was a crack –

electric under skin –

we were color –

a tundra –

then aspens, firs, and spruce –

we were dousing –

there was a crack –

quickening –

extended exhalation –

quantum tunneling –

There was a crack –

A new algorithm –

In credibility zone? –

What would you paint –

She could see –

She could hear her chance –

Ontological –

insistence of paint –

She might be amused –

To drown –

To drown? –

Slips the buried gold –

Before stalking –

Roll of the dice –

Safety –

Bask in this safety –

Broken heart –

Spirits of the doorway –

Being artist messenger –

antimatter in your brain –

are you relative? to what? –

what could you say –

roar of waves –

swoon of water –

water falling in patterns –

arrhythmic –

there was a spill –

the world is amusing –

the whole world –

know the song well –

before singing –

a lioness out of sexual instinct –

mercurial imagination –

help them to safety –

a hidden abyss –

a seer is divining –

ambiguity of dance –

how do we feel –

In gray in blue –

In green –

Sheen? –

How do we fall apart –

Would there be a break –

When jeopardy –

"Jeu-parti" –

When life was a game –

Joist, as in adjacent –

Or prophet, –

Same Indo-European base –

Speak for another –

There was a crack –

Shaking with fear –

There was volition –

There was a current –

Aplomb, her "open eye" –

There is devotion –

Did it supersede? –

how do we feel in red, –

what is our elemental –

what is our agency? –

in black, in white, in pink, aglow –

in twilight when mastery –

it meaning "even chance" –

meant "divided play" –

is life a game? –

lie down upon –

from Greek "prophetes" –

of "bha," speak, o fates –

artist in her power –

a sabotage, a terror –

there was a saddle to hold –

cupidity, agitation –

quality of being perpendicular –

there was a crack –

there is citizenry –

was life apocryphal? –

There was a reach –

A curtain, a motion –

A cure –

When you are fevered –

There was fever and –

Ferocity in how paintings –

Gravity is the collaboration –

A will and its perpetuity –

Quarrel with the world –

I was upside down with you –

Your shelter –

Wanted to dwell there –

In your frame –

Want the embrace of –

How to find a way out –

In which we are prisoners –

There was a crack –

And let it come" –

How to bind –

there is a reach –

what is hiding? –

what is lulled by men? –

are you more accurate –

she was holding her own –

might make themselves –

a curtain and a wall –

shore up this millennium –

through its parallels –

I wanted to be inside –

wanted to amble in, wanted to fly in –

survive critique –

in my arms I wanted you –

all that surrounds –

of implicit system –

a way out –

"a test not to think –

a trance adept might say –

"it is a test not to think –

Am I doing this right?" –

It was a crack –

it was aperture –

A trance –

You thought by now –

And power our way through –

Liquere, to be fluid, –

To clear a debt that –

As woman, as ideology, –

Ideology in apparatus –

The system needs bucking –

There was a crack –

A century within –

Symbolic or ontological? –

Hole in the fabric –

Into the void –

Warp threads –

Opening as in *poros,* opportunity –

Never abandon chance, lucky child –

latitudes –

it was a relief to be porous –

wanted to be inside –

leap the abyss –

we would vote –

we all thought –

to be clear your thought is –

came before you –

never, someone else's mistake –

that makes you stronger –

what is an "art world" really? –

in the crack of –

psychic melancholy –

there was kairos, –

when the adept shoots her shuttle –

thru the rising and falling –

there was a gap, a kairos –

grid of ethics –

never abandon light glimmer –

Fight between the –

Inside the ritual –

Crossing the Persian desert –

Crossing the wide –

I am inside her gestures –

Japan a trajectory to ink –

This way, that –

Within the matrix of her desire –

Encounter? –

Will you abandon me –

Will you abandon me –

Can I kneel before you –

Of your language –

It is a rapt space –

Has your grammar –

"We speak we utter words –

of their life" –

Capricious swiftness –

Evading rupture –

materiality of the ideological –

with her now, and happy accident –

crossing Continental Divide –

avenues –

as she throws them –

and you throw it down –

a rune, a containment, splash –

can it ever be chance –

all the elements in place –

in yellow, in orange, in blue –

in logic –

a devotee under the sun –

rapt space –

it was a crack in consciousness –

been absorbed –

we only later get a sense –

Wittgenstein –

like a life, can I say that? –

relevant to what? –

That the society would –

But can't help it –

Her timeless rapture –

In us, mystery –

Old English *moere* –

This was a fissure –

This is a crack –

How many layers of paint –

This was a gap to keep –

This was aporia –

The textures of this world –

No hurry in the mountains –

A melodic wall of paint –

This is curiosity turning –

This is insurrection –

Through a glass –

Shatter the –

If out of water –

Think "miracle" –

wither and die? –

nightmare of what is in force –

rupture keeps working –

mare not a horse but –

sat on sleeper's chests –

incubus –

more mystery –

beneath this slit –

you going, occupied –

that would help you consider –

no hurry in the hands –

they wait the abstract –

alchemical lab of the mind –

to power –

we are here to disappear –

and leave a trace –

"not just killing one another" –

think "water" –

live within a set of limitations –

A cavern of displacement –

Hover over a day –

A cairn –

A standing to, –

In a rush –

Stand over it –

Break the boundaries –

And remember all our freedom –

And remember all our freedom –

Fluctuation of desire –

Stamina of the polarity –

Outwit capitalism for beauty –

Mischief under the skin –

is forming, canvas is holding –

There was a curse upon us –

The antipodes of all held true –

There was blood run –

Apart, a politic –

Boys –

inside an auspicious day –

with your determination –

the world could break your heart –

a standing with –

look into the abyss –

stand above –

in our time –

look into the abyss –

corners of love –

"everything is art" –

out of the cage now –

outwit what you set up –

membrane of paint, a world –

membrane of hope and fear –

we lift it –

lift the skirt of time –

in all the parts of body a world –

she survives the big men, the big –

she would tell it –

Who rules the time –	there was a crack –
Logic of –	who rules the time –
Ideas –	inscribed in acts –
Regulated by rituals –	light the eye with them –
One never expects –	to compete the "return" –
Practice is all –	and gender is a kind of –
Melancholy –	and we would obey –
The bodies that are a hand –	reaching to the sky –
And attainment is occluded –	by love –
And what are the terms –	of existence –
Looking into the abyss –	to be sublime –

Reflection:

We have a break in the fabric of Pat Steir's recent and current masterful paintings. I wrote "Trance Abyss" for her, for her work, with a title from an Emily Dickinson poem in response to several years of closer attention to the processes of the artist's rituals of chance devotion, and in a mode of letting phenomena respond to a light touch of restraint, to break free to natural flow. We were looking these years into an abyss of global dystopia. The two columns mirror her split, a zip, a crevice of contradiction and beauty. Apertures of thought within paint, mysterious color and layer, into the unknown. The explosive waterfalls offered a full-on stereophonic acoustical experience of entering spaces of celestial climatic "pours," and one feels the visceral impact of her entities in space. But here we peer into the heavenly abyss, the beauteous unsettling rift which is a contentious point of origin between two sides or bodies of similar yet severed wholes. The parts are luscious, provocative divisions, planes of complex color and texture. Such a rift reminds me of William Blake's dichotomies, of looking through "unbornness" in the womb to the fraught outside world of death between the legs of existence. It is the tragedy of all warring charnel grounds. It is the tragedy of Aleppo, of suffering everywhere, of our own backyard. It is also the crack in the world of artistic insight and inkling of paradise, from which there is no return. Which is a mirror of greater truth and flow of paint, medium of our being. It is the vital "matter," the adherence, the glue, the blood, the colors that run behind the screen, underneath the skull, all inchoate rawness filtering through. The mind cleaves and reorders to keep sane. The mind and eye and hand create. Art is a kind of improvisational trance dance, a ritual of chance and willpower. One can meditate ferociously on the cut, the scar, the beautiful slit of ethereal aperture and still survive. The demands of these associations—these scryings in the powerful transcendent paintings of Pat Steir—matter more and more to me each day.

Anne Waldman and artist Pat Steir.

Mind of Endtime

1.

In the mind of endtime it looks like this: shell, volute, Tabriz, eddies, and tides. When you wake, observe the unmitigated trials and tribulations of these tossed things, random it seems. But in the end, time is waiting, less personhood, more ransom. Radical sleep in the endtime; there is no end. Multiplying the stars was never easy in endtime, doing it by themselves, stars. In the endtime things static, then still. Would you kill another literary form? A ransom, perhaps, saying again: Then dead will be saying "too many dead." Then carrying the corpses around. In the mind of the endtime no substitutes, but if you care to try your hand you may gamble all you have to offer and what would that be. A mole might do for you, a burrowing thing might do, biding time might do for a time, a night, perhaps, twelve hours you have for rhetoric, then a few before you are released at dawn. Recant, reflect, review, reach out. We have met the enemy and he is the psychotic karmic flow of our blowback. That's a view. Own it. Toughen up. You keep churning and there's an echo in the world. Need more stronger better leadership, need an experienced cop, they say. In the endtime there are theories of dysfunction, delicate wheelworks that need retread. Endtime you wait for me. In the mind of the endtime scot-free isn't possible. No interpretation necessary for your cargo. But a tax and a search and a fee and a calibration, what it all adds up to. Then drop it. Drop it down, send it off, off world, may it disintegrate in peace.

2.

Poet Robert Duncan speaks in "Rites of Participation" of the drama of our time as "the coming of all men into one fate, 'the dream of everyone everywhere.'" He continues, "We have gone beyond the reality of the incomparable nation or race, the incomparable Jehovah in the archetype of Man, the incomparable Book or Vision, the incomparable species, in which identity might find its place and defend its boundaries against an alien kind." The "possible" is only possible with "participation" and the acknowledgment and necessity of common ground. Duncan further notes: "All things have come now into their comparisons," which are the "correspondences that haunted Paracelsus, who saw also that the key to man's nature was hidden in the design of the larger Nature."

I sat upon the possible, I roamed inside the possible, I abandoned the possible and wept and beat my head and sang laments to the makers and crawled back and reclaimed the possible. I dreamed the possible was a new arc, a way to stem the flood and survive. I dreamed the end of murder in the street. There was a ritual end to murder in the streets.

And I dreamed we put our guns through the fire and they came out as planks of wood to build the new ark. Of the small children and all the others to come afloat, but first the children were possible. It was inside the shell, a pod, a raft, it was inside the oracle ship, it was inside the fission, it was inside the ion, the neuron, it was my own body warm in the night, warm in the land, and how it might be able finally to know that we know what was impossible on the ship that we give our lives to liberate. That it is impossible that it is the nightmare of humanity, that it stutters that it was possible. That this is "irreparable" and the mind not hold but what is possible? What language do we dream? What is the shape of our imagination as we consider ongoing holocaust of people and planet and all its denizens? As we consider how best language may mirror, probe, create our high-wired energy constructs, highly charged resonances on the detritus of unmitigated suffering. And what are the genres, the forms to help us to see a way in to our unvarnished "histories?" How do we activate/probe our larger nature as we drown?

3.

Reversing the inflated view of humanity, one might see Homo sapiens as a permutation in the ancient ongoing evolutions of the smallest and most chemically versatile inhabitants of earth—bacteria.

Even nuclear war would not be a total apocalypse—sturdy bacteria could survive it. And this is something that could travel to other planets and stars, presumably. At one point Lynn Margulis and Dorion Sagan joke in *Microcosmos* and speculate about how "given time, raccoons might also manufacture and launch their ecosystems as space biospheres, establishing their bandit faces on other planets as the avant-garde of Gaia's strange and seedlike brood. Maybe not black-and-white raccoons, but diaphanous nervous-system fragments of humanity, evolved beyond recognition as the organic components of reproducing machines, might survive beyond the inevitable explosion and death of the sun."

"New Scar Over My Heart"

Lou Reed
 1942–2013

*"We are the insects of
Someone's else's thought"*

—LOU REED

takes the breath away
steady raga
reticulated
sound   downtown
sound
rounded and turning and
pulse a subtle strident
firing sound down
rebounded ritual
tone down
again . . . a round
again   elfin effort
lou lou lou loop again
youth's *pure-light*
in maelstrom haze
of fabulous
below 14th Street
belletristic
atavistic time,
a world age,
radical, spiked
where you figure
it out,
cavalier
spin it out

instinct questions
narrative
branches of veins
work together
in a ritual form
tai chi will find
     life in
Andy, put your teeth in us
  a catalyst
workaholic's
thrum
long DOM nights
just down the block
Mary Woronov cracks
a whip
now better jump
through hoop of fire
work
in new light, Nico
part of allegory of
struggle we're in,
"the women in the room"
serial poem
walk into this room,
walk into

next room,
pulsing
never close
the door
into room beyond
room
inside room
fun house mirror
part of the *epikos,*
odyssey of body time
ballade, rondeau
part of mystery play,
or medieval tryst
an Elizabethan drama
for your
Renaissance
thoughts
& attendant
sexy characters
flamed out or flaming within
re-constituted in
    transmigratory void
a rock song, is ying
is yang?
many personae
approximate
tribulations and
deep loves of Dante
you are TS Eliot's
fisher king
dented, distressed
grail of hope
how empty
is the cup,
how full a draught
warm elixir to
jester-oblivion
rock-poet, turn it around

make magic
as free spirit denizen
mystical way
out of hell
a left hand
path
gaping maw of the
hungry wasteland ghost
realm
William Burroughs summons
you   give
account of demons
or slink through
pale corridors
rock it in crazy-wisdom
fun
power-sylphs
live in the
silky shadows
lust-realm and
anything you want
to possess, imbibe,
a sweet
lusting body
while seat gets hot
animal realm's
predatory drive
though the animals will
smile at you-
something to tell you
in samadhi,
come into
our yelping theta zone. . . .
passionate under
  a sweeping
zeitgeist
gods war over your head
carnivalesque

backdrop blood
evisceration
but hip to the street
broken vertebrae
of our century
  skips a beat
aches
how stretch
back in tendon
empathy,
get tough sullen
professional obviate
  the cause, our hands
are clean
or torqued
Lou you never say so
but go into it
into *form*
into *voice*
into *imago*
the martial flying
warrior
sword strapped to back
roll up sleeves
get all guitar-techy
science of the art is
imagination
what has also come
down
panoramically
cool
  "intellectual"
humanity's edge plays
loud decibels
kicks under
peoples' stories,
urban mix, metabolic
  wry irony

underneath: poetry's heart
everybody knows someone
who is everybody's other
story who is
some other one's fool
  emotion everybody says
as Candy says
knows everybody who
  is everybody's
squeeze
one's connection
one's bliss
and now what
are we inside
crux of,
my man,
white veins running
through cheeks
what sky gazing at
waits at   desire
on the neuron path
where light
hasn't reached us
but already happened
anticipates a
future
without you & with you
asides, cracks
generative darkness as
cells churn
pale eye retina
gleams then blurs
vocals
create
ontogeny, a voice
more blue
counter-revolutionary
civilians

in a voice? did voice
own it? the time?
our own Kulchur
with a capital "ĸ"
how lucky
you are
New York we
  invented you
create you in
our wild image
get down and listen
don't just
weep the gone times
remember through
meme loops
a native son
his streets
lou lou lou lou loosens
    his mortal loop,
meets death in love
with softness
tai chi—the
boundless first
part of
survival's trickster
masquerade

Memory and Impunity

I was seeing objects, sites, art, people through the lens of Guantanamo, and when I stepped into Ed Bowes's stairway landing in a loft building on 27th Street in New York, the Fur Art Building, every frayed wire as well as the dark plunging staircase, naked lightbulbs, and fuse boxes, seemed part of a projected state of mind of Guantanamo. I took pictures of these objects and places outside the door, as well as "things" immediately on and at hand—a collaboration with the painter George Schneemann that includes the slogan "no blood for oil," an Afghani war rug with helicopter and Kalashnikov, images from a scholarly book on Islam by a friend at the University of Colorado. I also went to my music collection for the Khan Brothers, Ed Blackwell, and Don Cherry, who composed a piece honoring Umm Kulthum, legendary Egyptian singer. Neither Kulthum nor Cherry are alive today, never witnessed the more recent deconstructions and murders in Afghanistan or Iraq or Lebanon, but I wanted to reinvoke their spirit, gaze, and sound.

"Colors in the Mechanism of Concealment" was the title.

Frequently we exoticize—"orientalize" (in Edward Said's sense)—the Middle Eastern *other*. There's one familiar media shot in this movie—at the very end—of a prisoner at Guantanamo in an orange monkey suit, clearly a denigrated victim. The question arises about how we use the images of others' suffering, often photographs of "anonymous" victims, wounded or murdered, considering they have no recourse of response. The images of Abu Ghraib were problematic in this regard. I have also worked with difficult images, individuals suffering in Lebanon, with filmmaker Zohra Zaka—during the war in 2006. I have stayed with issues of how to present difficult material in the arenas of art, material that is perhaps better presented at war crimes tribunals. The poem/text in this movie, performed with three voices, reads as such:

This was a full blue-gray jacket
This was a uniform of control
This was a working family
The blue line held work
The lone blue line held teal, held maroon

That gray held a crown of subtlety
There was no need for royalty here
Lineage was dangerous, reeks of privilege, of scorn
The intellect kept dreamy, kept dreaming
Or did it?
Red ink, right hand, to ink you away
Red ink against you to make deportation
To mark you for your life
In spite of beautiful gaze of where you are from
which is vast, where you are from:
the skyline . . . the orchard . . . the alley
the camp . . . the road . . . the desert
Whole anthropological worlds
Whole anthropological worlds
Where is the intellect from?
Is it green?
The color of sunset, of straw?
What other world is it?
How may I get there?
How far away is it from here?
Trapped in Guantanamo in a dead zone
How far in yellow? In mauve?
This was an orange monkey suit
This was a lone white towel
This was a cup of water, of dark gruel
This was a wire cage
This was not a colorful rug for prayer
Cold . . . bare . . . ground

I take seriously the notion of impunity and its attendant gestures. Exemption from punishment ("no justice no peace") is painful. Exemption from injury or loss as a consequence of action or security is painful. It is the impunities in this land, the criminal and dark deeds of the continuing interventions of thugs in the White House, that makes us crazy, a veritable relentless psyops on and over our heads, and an ultimate loss of security. I call it the "Foxes in the Henhouse Syndrome." "Clear Sky Initiative" or "Clean Waters Act" or "Operation Iraqi Freedom" all become euphemistic covers for this blatant agenda. And we the people are the victimized hens. There's a kind of rage that inhabits the body around injustice, a palpable metaphoric flapping and scratching and clucking, cries like those of being neck-wrung.

It's the humiliation and injustice people feel in the face of arrogant Western hegemony that leads to depression and acts of violence.

Perhaps these insults are partially responsible for the power of the jihadist movement. The situation in Israel/Palestine is so critical that without nurturing a viable solution for peace, no progress will be made in reconciliation with the Middle East. The assaults on Lebanon have only exacerbated this already dire situation which threatens stability everywhere. It is important to go to poetry for news. What is in our hearts with poetry as weapon:

> We are accused of terrorism:
> if we defend the rose and a woman
> and the mighty verse . . .
> and the blueness of sky . . .
> A dominion . . . nothing left therein . . .
> No water, no air . . .
> No tent, no camel,
> and not even dark Arabica coffee!
> ***
>
> America
> against the culture of the peoples
> with no culture
> Against the civilizations of the civilized
> with no civilization
> America
> A mighty edifice
> with no walls!
> ***
>
> We are accused of terrorism
> If we defended our land
> And the honor of dust
> ***
>
> I am with terrorism
> with all my poetry
> with all my words

and all my teeth
as long as this new world
is in the hands of a butcher.
***

(Syrian poet Nizar Qabbani, March 21, 1923–April 30, 1998)

And Georges Perec's *W, or The Memory of Childhood* is an extraordinary example of the force of countermemory, or parallel memory or "imagination's other place" (a line from William Carlos Williams). By creating a terrifying utopia on the one hand which mirrors the Nazi state, Perec expands one's understanding and perception of the true fascist regime. His interpolated parallel universe of a version of his own life and memory is an anthropic antidote, although the rubble of his own experience lies under the brutal shadow of the actual Holocaust, Perec having lost family to its tragic horrors. He writes:

> *One of these texts is entirely imaginary; it's an adventure story, an arbitrary but careful reconstruction of a childhood fantasy about a land in thrall to the Olympic ideal. The other text is an autobiography: a fragmentary tale of a wartime childhood, a tale lacking in exploits and memories, made up of scattered oddments, gaps, lapses, doubts, guesses, and meager anecdotes. Next to it, the adventure story is rather grandiose, or maybe dubious. For it begins to tell one tale, and then, all of a sudden, launches into another. In this break, in this split suspending the story on an unidentifiable expectation, can be found the point of departure for the whole of this book: the points of suspension on which the broken threads of childhood and the web of writing are caught.*

What is the identity of memory? Anxiety = emergency = replay.

In the small movie one wants to struggle with impunity, the lawless situation at Guantanamo. I was desperate to feel the atmosphere and create with objects at hand, from my own life, ones of quotidian safety that I observe almost daily nurtured sinister. Now they were triggers to association with those blank faraway cages.

The Marabout Smiles

for John Giorno

silence at sea walls
how clear today Straits of Gibraltar
watch friends leave, return
fluid systems of trance and possession
vision in a bubble over the water
the end of restless molecular time?
did they—your friends—self-realize magic?
wisdom's pact
what's the transmission?
did we get there yet?
William might impart his thorn-whip-clarity
love as prophecy
Brion isolated into his loves

was it only music that monsters over us
heats up feet of small children
the Gnawa speeds you up, whirl the stage
calms snakes, colors, perfume augury
kif on my tongue
what stage are we moving on and into
a daggerlike wisdom in blue, in green,
mind flies near and smooth
how close and far to death

primordial wisdom mind you say
mirror wisdom holds the surface down to the
ground glass from which all text emerges
language dances its ideas, the guembri
holds up earth and sky . . . all on a wire

remember our countless interventions
hipsters in the dream: *streets of the world*

inscription for
struggle, for justice, equality, queer love, entheogens
all the sousveillance, a documentary poesy
now memories called simply memoir
reenact here in Tangier, you take the stage
ashes scatter, rescatter over bodies in a cloud vault
words invoke and resist the pull of
perpetuity, fuck that and those will still come after,
beautiful, out of the Sahelian, storytellers
rediscover Sufi healing harmonies free from any
tonal center.

***

Holding hands with John in the flatbed truck on the way up the canyon to Brakhage. Watch movies into the night, bodies inscribed in flickering celluloid. Aspen light. The mortuary. The Act of Seeing with One's Own Eyes. *Now see fluidity of this life, interlocked in our last trip: Tangier. Stan scratches and paints into memory eternal. The great* Mothlight *without a camera made, composite tantras . . . fragments and dream.*

Questions for Citizens

*Investigative Poetry: that poetry
should again assume responsibility
for the description of history*

   —ED SANDERS

A series of random questions for citizens and poet-citizens

1.

When was the Federal Reserve created, and by whom?
Who was second in command to Jefferson Davis
& considered the brains of the Confederacy?
What was the primary material factor
in British sea domination?
What was Ezra Pound right about?
How many things don't make sense about
the Bering Strait theory of migration?
What might that mean?
Who funded the Confederacy and why?
Do you accept the premises of the Warren Commission?
Do you accept the findings of the Warren Commission?
Who assassinated Ghassan Kanafani?
Where did the assassination take place?
Who was Ghassan Kanafani?
What was Dewey Canyon III?
Why did the Confederacy have to import
hay from north of the Mason-Dixon line?
Who assassinated Naji al-Ali?
Where did this take place?
Who was Naji al-Ali?
What happened in Bengal during World War II?
What does the term "false flag" mean? Please identify at least two.
Do you think buildings came down on

9/11 because airplanes hit them?
Do you accept the findings of the 9/11 Commission Report?
Do you think elements of the US government capable of
controlled demolition of buildings on 9/11, or on other days?
Why did US and Kurdish forces just provide cover
for up to four thousand people associated with ISIS leaving
Raqqa, including fighters and weapons?
Do you think this was the case?
Do you think elements of the US government capable of creating ISIS?
Do you think *this* was the case?
Who assassinated Jean Sénac?
Where did this happen?
Who was Jean Sénac?
Where was Souha Bechara imprisoned?
Why was she imprisoned?
Who is Souha Bechara?
Who kidnapped Mordechai Vanunu?
Where did this happen?
Who is Mordechai Vanunu?
Where was he born?
Why do race and gender now
seem so high on the US agenda?
What does "an eye for an eye" and
"a tooth for a tooth" actually mean?
What is the origin of this formula?
What are we talking about?

2.
Why doesn't the Confederacy die?
Who backs it?
Why is it getting away with so much this late in the game?
Who are the big brokers for the Confederacy?
What is behind the new racism?
Did Blackwater or "XI" initiate the terrorist attack in NY on Halloween?
Why is there so much focus on Russia? Is this a red herring?
Why won't Palestine and Israel ever heal?
In whose interest is this apartheid?
What does the Caliphate want?

What is the role of the Protestant church in USA politics?

Why are so many politicians religiously identified?

How did Barack Obama get elected?

Do you think he was "allowed" to get elected?

Does one see fear in Jeff Sessions's eyes

& that aggrandizing sick smile which is a predatory gesture

of the face, jaw, mouth related to atavism . . . ?

"I did not declare it so" he said in answer to a question by

Representative Karen Bass of the Black Caucus about Black Lives Matter.

Did you see this?

What is the modus operandi of Jeff Sessions, of Alabama?

ICE: whose ads resemble ISIS ads, e.g., "We're coming for you,"

"we are coming to kill you." Who designs these ads?

Why do we borrow this strategy from our perceived enemy?

What is poetry's struggle in this culture?

Do you know what a hielera is?

Do you know how many days you might freeze in a hielera?

Do you know which detention center provides one piece of bread

and a slice of balogna if you are lucky?

What is the reaction of white people

to their own demographic demise?

How far will they go?

What is crimmigration?

What is your personal Zero Tolerance?

What will you not stomach?

What put chlorine in water for immigrant children?

Where is the outcry?

What is your antithesis reality?

What is the BIE movement?

What, are there no public intellectuals in the USA?

Are poets susceptible to media control?

Where is the spirit of sixties rebellion; what will it take?

Why aren't we continuing to have daily protests in this country around
white supremacy?

What is the poetry community doing about race issues in its own programming?

Why is the liberal media so obsessed with the Russia probe?

What about unexposed scandals of Vietnam,

the operations in Laos like Dewey Canyon II?

What is the US karma with North Korea?
How many people died in the Korean War, both North & South?
What was America's role in the war with Korea?
Who knows someone who served in WWII, Korea, in Vietnam?
Is there a literary mafia?
Who was Judah Benjamin?
Where does your water come from?
Why do poets need to hire publicists?
Why was Amiri Baraka so vilified for his poem on 9/11?
Who holds power to the secret codes other than the US president?
What is the battle between the law enforcement agencies?
What is a "sciamachy"?
What are the Bilderberg meetings?
Was Simone Veil unaware of the existence of the camp at Drancy
or the destination of the eastern-bound trains?
Did people in New York and London not know
that Jews were being gassed to death?
What is your personal hundred-year plan?
What was Gertrude Stein wrong about?
Who were the MOVE 9?
What does it mean to you to be a "citizen"?
What is our five-hundred-year plan
What is the most current case of egregious injustice?
What is "poethics"?
Why so much focus on Russia?
Who is Jigme Gyatso?
What does "skillful means" mean to you?
Why is the poetry discourse taking place primarily within academies?
What is the origin of the term Capitalocene?
What are we doing about climate change?
Is anyone here working with "We're Still In" movements?
What is the warmest year on record? Why?
How many immigrants are in US detention centers on any given day?
What is a heavy sterile neutrino?
What did Albert Einstein write about?
How far away is the furthest galaxy?
What is a gravitational wave?
Who are the contenders for explanations of dark matter?

What is the Axion Dark Matter Experiment?
What are "plutonium pits"?
What are "jellyfish babies"?

(starting with lines by Ammiel Alcalay)

Out of Place

We could only talk through
our eyes and now
that is gone. But this
is deeper than
the marrow
we don't need rods cones
those sanskrit piles of things
I am seeing through a stain
right now
in your love
I am swimming for years.
In a sudden absence
of trouble in a deftly
handled conversation
I, a luminous fish
felt in this spectacle of impossibility
a fragrant graze upon the
world
an intermittent twitch,
whisper.

—EILEEN MYLES, *from* "THE PERFECT FACELESS FISH"

My conception day was July 4, 1944, the night before John Marvin, my father, voyaged out from Bragg. "Between the Mexican War and the Civil War, Braxton Bragg, for whom the fort was named, lived the life of a genteel planter on a sugar cane plantation in Louisiana where slaves put in back-breaking labor in unspeakable conditions to bring molasses to market and earn Bragg a profit. He met any Northern criticism of slavery with harsh criticism," wrote Michael Newcity in an article in *Duke Today,* both for his defeats in battle and his indiscriminate shooting of his own soldiers. The name will change.

I thought of conceptions, I thought of life's loops, I thought of slavers, I remembered the rings of reverie when you dream a whole cycle of past lives, and where you go through all the faces you have ever had representing you. I thought of war. I thought of my father in war. The young man in uniform before embarking, the old man, not quite broken, the unborn gnomic child, a hermaphrodite, a face that morphs on your own. Shimmery fins, gills inside an eye. And of Lepidoptera, which one? Her suit of velvety clothes. More mute, shy, than her mate. Of mind gnashing to see the intricacies better, look here, of understanding petroglyphs, of hearing finally what the lover is saying about "rays" and intricate dimensions of light as seen through a prism held to catch filmic eye. Of the eyes in all the caves and dangerous protestations in conflict with the urge to beauty and peace and pores in all the bodies of everyone crossing the pathways. So many! Let them breathe.

To come to poetics full-blown under a school desk, taking shelter from a fearful fantasy of nuclear blast and fallout. I had friends whose families were camp survivors. There was attendant horror at the exterminations and also the devastation at Nagasaki and Hiroshima (and beyond). How to comprehend, integrate. Did dropping the bomb make us safer, end the war, or did it unleash this myriad headed monster into our world and psyches? We children wore dog tags at Public School 8 and participated in regular "air raid" drills, taking refuge under our desks and sometimes retreating into the school basement. Some families were building bomb shelters. It made no sense. How would a dog tag be recognizable after a nuclear attack? How would we not be burned to a crisp like the Japanese? Would we be attacked by land or sea? Would the Commies land in San Francisco? Remember again and again, how one clutched the corrosive-resistant metal "tag" of name and station in Public School 8 on King Street? Remember the air raids. In the mind of the child are all times contemporaneous? Your identity hangs on a ball-chain under your sweater, remember its initial coolness against the skin . . . you are now, someone said, inducted into the paranoid armies of the US of A. In the Vietnam War soldiers put rubber silencers on their dog tags so the enemy wouldn't hear their sound (they wore two tags—if killed, one would rest with the body in the grave).

Remember the cognitive dissonance that made you poet.

And the recent history and science and implications of all that, soldiering, killing too vast. Feel it grow inside you, some immense shape of emotional tension and they, the ones who notice, will suddenly see this and want to get out and dance. I see it. I want to dance. And what is real intimacy, in a barracks when you know how breath travels inside a cone of conjuring. Release! I'll stand in the spotted doorway, on the silken road, in the care of moorings and anchorage. On the charnel ground. I'll have your back.

And with psychic wounds on my small body, and yes these are my true eyes, my camouflage. I'll stand for you in most ancient of days, Father.

And of composite shape in the dancing Fort Bragg father-memory, and now I know and hate that name, associate it with war, with braggadocio, with fear and cruelty. And slavery.

This place of preparedness is the rare and possibly only locality where the endangered Saint Francis' satyr butterfly *(Neonympha mitchellii francisci)* is known to live. Name of my mother—Frances—inside herself an endangered sleight of generative mind. The adult Saint Francis' satyr is found in wetland habitats dominated by graminoids and sedges, such as abandoned beaver impoundments, and also along streams with beavers. The Saint Francis' satyr butterfly only lives three or four days.

We will return, work all night carrying mud and stones, and let satyrs frolic at our whimsy, we will come back and rally when you need us, hard timber between our teeth.

The US Fish and Wildlife Service placed the red cockaded woodpecker under its protection in 1990. Many of the woodpeckers lived at Fort Bragg, which became a tremendous hassle for the fort. Portions of the fort closed down, troops were shuffled to other places, training stopped.

The Army and the conservationists, wouldn't that be converting a serious posture. Eventually an agreement, which curtailed military exercises around the woodpeckers' habitat, was reached. Trees were adorned with white stripes to designate the birds' living space, and training within two hundred feet of these spaces was halted.

These birds are lively, pesky, with black and white horizontal stripes on their backs.

By 2021, the clusters of woodpeckers have more than doubled in size, 200 to 493 birds, and the training restrictions have been lifted. And a treaty with the satyrs acknowledges a fragile co-existence.

I could be reconceived in the belly of a new war-mother, in a bed of graminoids, with a grasslike morphology and long bladelike leaves.

The Angle the Frame, the Angel the Posed Subjects

for Öykü Tekten

Images are power mad, images are multiperceptible, reality establishes the real or does it, and you notice how it is winning in the realities of how to perceive, it does, it is recognizable it is a frame, human construct, nonhuman architecture of light and shadow a way in, as the heart beats for such a way in, a moment of metabolic torture a way in, a way embedded in shackles in the flash of a photo-light, a brash photon, photo op posed for the public in a compromised posture op, a promise of display of public shock and titillation, a mockery of intimate matters and image is your home, and it could be love if you struggle for that and poetry, whatever you want now it could be love, could be, make words of it. I ask you what is the most powerful photograph you have ever seen? Of Istanbul? What gets lost?

Grasped by a code. *Could be love.* A homeland.

Computational. Where is face-to-face? Where does power over the living lead, altering my species. A passport. All the documents.

Tools as aspects of social life. The digital phenomenon. What is the difference between screen and life? Make the photography sing, messaging. A plastic form of living. An instant gram. Display readiness this sweet translation now. Display this image of dissolving ruthlessness now. A truce? Aperture watches, drone-angel over Syria, over Somalia, over Yemen, over Turkey, drone-angel over maquilladora Mexico, observing the plight of ravaged women-bodies, the angel of flood and famine and misfortune gazing into the eyes of supplicants, watching back. Witness-angel, the angel never forgets you snapping a photo for all time as photons dissolve and you are oppositional, breathing. You conjure and pose the subjects of your poem, images of resistance and love. As if behind a blind, watching birds. In a face time. As if noticing an assemblage of children in a shelter. Or water too raw, too polluted for drinking. The still—but you gasp "still moving?"—beauty of a lover. Impressions as witness as supplicant continues breathing. Words that become less mutual, oxymoronic. Frame this for you, as bitten as smitten witness, as written as hidden-critical-witness, as impressions on the brain resound, as a way out when heart sunders and you cry out there *is* sanctuary, there *is* salvation, is a witness-angel, there *is* "just" intimacy.

You turn it around. Matters when you are alone and unobserved, at the border when the image is for your keepsake-fodder only, alone your secret, web page only, a trunk in the attic, an image for the annals of time only when you are young and innocent and do not tarry over the misfortunes of fabrics and magics and mesh and flesh lost in a war zone, in rags of desire, pity of desire, then joy of desire. A protective shadow.

What are suffering ones if not but dreaming in fragmented time, time framed with angles toward light from the annals of chthonic writing? Imbrications of liquidity, algorithms, poetry, constellations everywhere measure possibility. The way my love for you struggles, wings its way in the morning, the way it swoops down at noon, and the dusk is a giveaway, because people will still inhabit the night with their bodies and terrifying dreams. Then wake up, reach out.

Fit Music

Lorenzo Thomas was shy, brilliant, complicated. He carried his knowledge with dignity, quiet confidence, ease; he knew what he needed to pursue as steady witness, as poet-historian. He knew what he loved in music, in poetry. Aimé Césaire. I was watching him grow as a poet standing up and stepping out.

> Saying "don't give a damn." It was time
> To be going. Vancouver or South Viet Nam.

We were many, same age becoming poets together, a particular kind of attraction. When he went off to "serve" I was nervous. But impressed he wasn't going to shirk anything. And he didn't love the war going on. He wrote in *Fit Music:*

> This is stupid. This is very stupid.
> No one but Anne will understand
> When I hand her these songs

And I wrote a romantic poem with him in mind called "Blues Cadet." He seemed to catch waves of jittery heroic frequencies in his writing, his so-called voice true. How he spoke, great laugh. His friendship with Ted Greenwald—very strong, interesting comrades in high school together (Jamaica, Queens), fretting Ezra Pound. And Lorenzo was the youngest of the Umbra group.

I wonder if his *Dracula* had inspired Baraka's "good manner of vampires" talk. I spoke with Amiri once about Lorenzo, whom he admired.

"Serious fellow, you know him?"

> Stand that as the torture of our rapturous manners
> The white glitter of our impressive table
> Manners . . .

Dracula. Changes his form
Assumes an entire jury of peering witnesses walking
Deliberately like negroes on the street,
And then the strict transformation rabble
Screaming and waving pockets torn off
The most respectable fences in the town
A lynch mob. . . .

The hanging orchards of America but our
People are so ashamed . . . (*Dracula*)

This is a troubling poem, shape-shifting, scary, biblical, streetwise, feels prescient radically now in the insane climate we are still in after all the bad history . . . racism that still must die. A country held hostage by some of the sickest people on the planet readying for civil war. But everything exposed now, Lorenzo would be happy about that. We could gnash it out, impeachment at a smoky jazz café. He had written in the brilliant "Proem" in *Fit Music:* "And in 66 everyone faked concern for Asia." And in "Envoy," "I wanted somebody to stop me at the airport / And ask all about Vietnam."

The jig. The military. Boss. Silent . . .

Lorenzo was back from Vietnam as the mimeo edition came out, with Britton Wilkie's wild Armageddon drawings. I was relieved he was back and he had learned stuff. Radio waves. He was the wiser. Saw inside another belly of beast. But he said it meant something having this plan to publish while he was away. A lifeline. We kept the thread. I thought to start a press: Poets in War. I want his poetry to soar now more than ever out of trembling apocalyptic shadows. From "Envoy":

The first sight was McDonald's
Neon yellow arc

A beckoning out the cold, windy night

A rainbow promising nothing
And warning that that nothing
Is serious business

That nothing was bringing me back
Back to de Plantation!

Jaguar Harmonics: Liana Concordance

I cover myself with clouds to feel like the Earth feels.

—CECILIA VICUÑA

The descent of the body to the subterranean gods and its rebirth as vegetation.

—ITALO CALVINO

Swallow the medicine. The jaguar rids me of fear and the jaguar gives jolt to be fearless; scares this body to fearlessness. The jaguar at the apex of the food chain. A loner. Highly endangered. The jaguar is entangled with its own mythology, its memory, thousands of years, the dancing jaguar.

Imagination for human of jaguar is symbolic, is mythopoetic, is emotional complexity of centuries' syncretism. Lived under borrowed light and then stepped onto borrowed earth-matrix. Then burrowed down. Sipped the drug from a grail, small clay cup, at twilight and collapsed in cold sweaty power to incubate efficacy. To face Kali Yuga, a world time of extinctions. Feast on the earth, the jaguar walks. Face on the ground, I'll grovel, eating dirt. No longer solid, trying to keep warm, dry off, stand up now. Looked into the firepit, saw a disintegration of all expectations and material things. Heaps of things are burning up in a fire. I turn to ash, constituent form blown to the warm wind.

This in fashion? María Sabina, indigenous poet of twentieth-century Mexico with ritual chant and ceremony, suggested the magic left the hongos, the psychotropic psilocybin mushrooms, as their efficacy diminished with exposure:

> From the moment the foreigners arrived, the "holy children" lost their purity. They lost their force, they ruined them. Henceforth they will no longer work. There is no remedy for it.

Hippies and celebrities invaded her world in a small village outside Oaxaca. Entheogens a long time on this planet will be abused and go silent for a time, waiting for a more propitious supplication: to help wake one up to one's self. Sabina's oral text survives; a tribute to communal ground, syncretic indigenous and Christian images combine with her singing conviction of poetry's power to heal. She was a shaman of modest means, barefoot her whole life, tending her milpa, her small maize field. Many sorrows of family and body. Those from afar made her a rock star.

During the seven-hour session of yage and its rise-tumble-landing, its dawn, felt invaded by Kundry shape-shift energy: seducer/crone rising from her earth womb/tomb. I became dual Parsifal, damsel-prince-knight. All the archetypes crowded in. Also it was necessary to commune with the more recent dead. Poet elders. They were all at the ready, quills in hand, waiting to be summoned. Hunting the Y Seint Greal they found in death. And Circe's wild pigs, as we sat around the fire-puja, were grunting, snuffling in their earth realm. We were at a farm, far from Whitman's city at war. Maybe his warrior campfire, but here we are in time of war. A male meme.

Yet the ceremony calls on Pachamama, central fertility power who oversees existence. You may hear her voice in your head in the bowels of transmission. It's her voice, "don't like it, don't do it, don't like it, don't do it, hydraulic fracturing. Heh heh heh heh."

What could I ever know? Cry with indignities of the feminine. How to right a balance in this epoch? Work hard for the spirit path. Blunt ego with the cut cut cut of Manjushri's sword and summon Tara's tears.

Tezcatlipoca, Aztec "smoking mirror" god, sometimes took the form of the jaguar. Alas, endurance and bravery of the animal is appropriated for naming of sports cars and sports teams. The jaguar-like receptacle Ocelotl Cuauhxicalli held hearts of sacrificial victims.

How to joke and laugh with poets who toss vocabulary of shamanism off the academic grid? This elaborate chemistry, with all the mysteries of the cosmos, off the grid? The cosmic joke. Is all this false? One looks hard into space/time, seeing the generative darkness in the interstices between the phrase of phonemes and spheres. Translate the phonemic world in glee with purpose, not ruffled in ragged will of decay and impermanence. A wisp of poetry breaks into a thousand shards as consciousness morphs into a flight pattern. Leave a trace, or none at all. You are nothing but a receptacle for the hearts of the world, empathy and love. The art of the Olmec found their jaguar, a relative of rain, an axe with the face of jaguar. We are also here to disappear.

Feel the current in symbiosis. "Person woven of . . ." was the mantra of my night poem for naming complexity and condition. We are conglomerations of tendencies with multiple agency. We are constructs: fleshly balls of language and stardust. We sometimes gobble our psychic medicine.

Thus medicine ceremony provides bounce for consciousness. For sublimated, almost subvocal, hum. For communing with the dead. Medicine is the turtle carapace, medicine is the eye of newt, medicine is epicanthic fold of wily Maya, medicine is your fortified city, medicine is your map of skin. Medicine is your lover. Women weave fibers of henequen, or hemp, into your ritual. Medicine is your twine. Your thatched roof. Medicine is inside you, and you will reorder the chemistry. Take this drop—mere prompt—to disband what you hold so tight, acquisitive person. Medicine is our obsolescence, maybe opalescence.

A guest in the house, a mendicant, a servant, an underling. The language for poetry is psychotropic in that it keeps you close to the edge and surface, physical proprioception. Yet swirling inside the mind. Things do, redo, undo. You write out of purgatory. The intricate interlocking visual patterns go mad with delight. Tongues flicker inside animal heads, multiple arms and tentacles of the "tentacular" interconnected world's viable energy. The animals consume one another. Ugly, proud, forbidding, and scintillating beauty spills over. Never-stop kinetic force field. And you are included, strangely. Who is the watcher this time? Arise, shed your watcher, disappear into the earth head first. O kind Medicine.

Why are you even here? What did you hope? Aspire to person of headdress, of scarification. Helmets with descending birds. A dolphin headdress. Mitigate your experience. Listen. Hear your lunar night. Your water night. Your earth night, Pachamama. Bury me in your halo of fire, wizard night. Show me the maleness of ancestry.

At first they are harmless visions: vegetable, a holy garden; then animal flesh and fur and claw and toothed; then human—skittish, pale, small; then mineralesque. Hallucinations shine. They take over in gleam and intensity. It's a robotic night. Brittle. They lock in. Then become mocking mimicry—copies of another version of themselves, ever morphing with a plastic, toxic ooze. Petrochemical poison spits and unsettles the dreamer. There are worlds and words of prey. Animals and beings and toxicity ever roiling all the way through the food chain. Quick cut to a new trickster who banishes the hideous pollutants. Suddenly there is a void and ocean. The nonhuman elementals. The techno-bots. The click click of mechanized horror. The robot is your guide now. But robots can't drink; they can barely swim and enjoy themselves. Rochig, one taste, this human life. The medicine will taste like musk of animals. The stage set for what new revelation? Coming up: reality about to lift her skirt.

All the people close to you return as if they never left your heart. You send them messages of love. You are failure, you are coward, you never expressed the gratitude for the gifts they give you. All your teachers. Every moment vivid in you and your inadequacy. You bow to them, collapse on your tiny mat. You writhe with the pain of never having said—what was it you never said? And the medicine enacts its name: la purga. Cleaning you out, "vomiting the universe."

The predator jaguar hums, her astute attention; her vibratory spots seem to be moving as well, as eyes or mouths. Thrumming, loping, mind and body in tandem fixed on prey or possibility. What is possibility without prey? What are the images of being inhabited by something alive and extremely ancient, way back? How far can you go? Now you are timeless; soon you are rotting meat on the axis of time. A fossil from 3.8 million years ago. Yaguareté, el tigre. Early Pleistocene via Beringia entered this continent and came along with the human? Maybe this is all wrong, all of this alchemy already here.

What do I know of the female jaguar? Gestation for cubs a few months, the male banished. He might devour his offspring. Early years of training. Territory, the quick hunt and blow to the cranium. The teeth of the jaguar destroys the world, devours it whole.

This docu-book of yage, the first notes "written" as "you, I, me, what old Anne" came down from la droga. And later named "book," then assembled, conceived as if already at peak of energy. It is a small avowal to the psychological journey of undoing. Because she kicks at time, jaguar consumes you as you-totem, you-guardian, you-predator, you-guide, and taunt to crepuscular time. Twilight is now. How do "you" put yourself back together as you already dissolved in front of your "own" psychic eyes?

Wake up and enter the jungle, wherever you are in green mind, in green ritual. In it, curious in the hallucination, is it botany of jungle? Whether streets of New York, of Mexico City, of Paris, or in a meadow in Colorado, you lie down in green, in a hell realm, in a heaven realm, and everything in between. In the rubble of Kathmandu. In the rubble of Syria. In the rubble of Puerto Rico. There is a constant earthquake. Your mind grows paradisiacal and the voices are reaching you, and you are to receive them. Again: "We don't like fracking, heh heh heh." Pay attention. The feminine "voice" visits many "syndicates of samsara" in her own trove of memory, and she/you is trying to tell you something.

What do you know of it? The landscape of your own cosmology. The terrain of aspiration you trip and stumble within. All your pores are open in the tantric twilight. Shape-shift. Listen to the big cat purr. The harmolodics (Ornette Coleman) of essential time. Stop thinking. When you remember, when you feel pity, when you sit down to read your brain. What are you reading now? What old memory? A range of philosophers come to you at dawn with good advice. They move the day forward a few light years. You feel yourself as the disaster feminist. You dissolve into the fossils of all the demons of your life and time. They still haven't answered your questions. Fossils of your vanishing. You want to be with the poets.

Jaguar seems particularly connected here below and in the maze, is of both this earth and the fire in which surges poetry and sound. What is the vortex? Who is asking, who is watcher? Who is person? What is liberation? What is the chthonic machination asking you to perform? Your German ancestors are singing Wagner:

Herauf! Herauf! Zu mire!
Dein Meister ruft dich, Namenlose,
Urteufelin! Höllenrose!
Herodias warst du, und was noch?

Gundryggia dort, Kundry hier!
Hieher! Hieher denn, Kundry!
Dein Meister ruft; herauf!

Arise! Arise! To me!
Your master calls you, nameless one,
First she-devil! Rose of Hades!
You were Herodias, and what else?
Gundryggia then, Kundry here!
Come here! Come here now, Kundry!
Your master calls: Arise!

—ENGLISH TRANSLATION FROM WAGNER'S *Parsifal*

Why are you asking to be any kind of identity as my poem asks, as whether, "person woven of" old age, lying in the muck of centuries' damselhood, stuck in a bog of memory of Kundry damsel? The refrain and the litany and the investigation is shifting. All the ways to be shuttled, woman body through mortality . . . Jaguar becoming sinewy androgynous serpent.

What makes us human? The highly evolved neocortex of the brain and its busy amygdala, our storehouse, our archive of emotional memory. And the insular cortex seems to create a bridge between our intense emotional impulse and how we decide and act.

We are patterned to remember trauma. When a stimulus enters the brain, we attempt to recognize it based on previous experience. Ayahuasca may interrupt or frustrate these fixed patterns and associations and attitudes. Even exhaust them, making relative reality less toxic and controlling. The yage imps will call "you" out: Come out, little spirit within, we see you, come out and play.

There is the legend of the living jaguar itself consuming the ayahuasca vine, *Banisteriopsis caapi.*

Humans require the additional monoamine oxidase to complete the drink, most likely *Psychotria viridis.*

The Yage Letters of William S. Burroughs and Allen Ginsberg, a sometimes terrifying compendium of experience, quotidian detail, and anthropology, is summoned at the end of my long poem *Jaguar Harmonics,* entering the weave as cut-up—cut in—fixed compañeros. I felt a dutiful sense of lineage and of gratitude to them in my own wild-mind exploration, thus: "with Burroughs yage with Ginsberg yage I sang . . ."

* * *

I thought of De Quincey, Michaux, a lineage of investigative stoners.

Record of yage/ayahuasca use goes back to before the sixteenth century. It translates as "liana of the soul," "liana of the dead," or "liana of the spirit." Catch the vine. A new world cycle, that's what "they" are saying. You are woven with tesserae; you will reconstitute the elements and reanimate your intention. The ceiba, sacred tree of life, sends its roots down to the earth, penetrates death, and reaches up toward the light. Double helix of the serpent-jaguar, encoded in your DNA. Throbbing, humming, fantastical entities, new implants for the heart and mind in pathways and unknown places. Healing medicine for an ecological consciousness, language reflects back at us, in our weathers of existence. On the brink. We better not tarry.

For some of the living thread of endangered jaguar, please visit:
http://www.northernjaguarproject.org

Screed of Entheogen

It all begins with a vibration. An imperceptible movement that accelerates min-ute by minute. Wind, a long screeching whistle, a lashing hurricane, a torrent of faces, forms, lines. Everything falling, rushing forward, ascending, disappearing, reappearing. A dizzying evaporation and condensation. Bubbles, more bubbles, pebbles, little stones. Rocky cliffs of gas. Lines that cross, rivers meeting, endless bifurcations, meanders, deltas, deserts that walk, deserts that fly. Disintegrations, agglutinations, fragmentations, reconstitutions. Shattered words, the copulation of syllables, the fornication of meanings. Destruction of language. Mescaline reigns through silence—and it screams!

—OCTAVIO PAZ, FROM HIS INTRODUCTION TO *MISERABLE MIRACLE* BY
HENRI MICHAUX, NEW YORK REVIEW OF BOOKS, 2002.

The way we

The way we might in minutes

The way we might be shattered in minutes

The way we'll stop and take it

We'll go inside, fly in minutes

The vibratory room

Cross this line

We'll wash our whole aura, our body, our musket of protection

The mask we'll wash and dry and wash again and dry

And again wash till the hands disappear

The dangerous lift, you feel it?

The power, don't come near me

On knees, you are invisible ally, a torch, a persuasion

What can you drive more into a nail than your tiny head

above is the black lid of recreated time
by brutal force I cauterize
the writing of memoir
tick of halogen erodes
images of aged tragedy
our death our survival
In the acrid morning

  —STACY SZYMASZEK

buying into fancy device
survey our own corpses
zombie capitalism is the boss
no safety nets for remorse
no shimmering indra's net of love
but web of snares, hunger, anguish
cubby holes of heads,
we're all martyrs to our yearning for touch
gaze into my eyes, light a candle
we'll leave a whisper
das das das Kapital
pull the plug you don't exist
but doing our best
as emanations, holy ghosts,

while the country burns
with das das das das Kapital

  —A.W.
FROM UNPUBLISHED SONG "AMULET"

Chenrezig Walks among Us

for the 14th Dalai Lama

Avalokitesvara (Sanskrit "Lord who looks down") is Chenrezig in Tibetan, and in this form is said to emanate with the lineage of the Dalai Lama; it is said to be the Dalai Lama himself through various incarnations. The etymology for the bodhisattva name Chenrezig from the Tibetan, is "spyan," which means "eye" and "ras," meaning continuity. And "gzig," to look. This etymology extends to the notion of "one who looks down upon all beings with an eye of compassion" and additionally as "one who looks down upon sound." This refers to the sup-plication of sentient beings crying for help from worldly suffering. This is also the origin of the Chinese name Guanyin, as those "who perceive the world's lamentations."

[chanted]
swept away all suffering gathered it up
in a quantum leap sucked it up till it returned
and when he looked back over his shoulder & saw
all suffering come back in a great wave, all suffering
riding in, filling up nooks & crannies & crevices
& templates of the world all suffering filling neurons
& quarks and leptons, troubling minds of fathers, mothers
sisters, brothers, all children, lovers, all sentient beings suffering
toxins of passion, aggression, ignorance in the middle of
the night strapped in demon-mind, nowhere to hide when all
pounding suffering rides in & mind splits in a thousand pieces
Chenrezig wept & head split in a thousand pieces
& mighty red fire Buddha Amitabha leans in & puts the
puzzle back together, wires it with tantric thread, adds some
extra arms, extra heads, "a conglomeration of tendencies"
this wisdom body to rid the world of all suffering
more arms & heads take charge, built it better, a deity
to maximize power of bodhicitta to ease all suffering
& now Chenrezig had a thousand arms
in all directions of space with numerous accoutrements

& under those arms a thousand hearts better to banish
all suffering: suffering of Tibet, of India, suffering of Pakistan,
wherever his crystal eyes land, whatever map of suffering
he alights upon, keep emptying Europe, USA empty, Israel-Palestine
empty, China, Russia, Syria, Japan, Haiti, Yemen, a thousand heads
with a thousand third eyes &
more wisdom eyes in all the pores of his body
Chenrezig walks among us, humble prince toward all systems of empire

Chenrezig walks among us as all constituent forms—
precious ink, diamond scepter, skull cup of blood, thighbone
trumpet dissolve in mind & lotus at his feet rises again
through cracks of a concrete city or charnel ground's eternal war,
starflowers shoot at dark of a distant galaxy anywhere
out of this world his heart is that big & dharma gates are endless
he enters every one of them, typhoons & famine dissolve
emptiness as form to come back at you blowback is love,
come back at you multiverse moves in the night that never sets
is it cold out there? will Tibet be liberated on judgment day
China come to peace?
& planet not roil with dystopia and ghosts of hunger?
& we'll relight the butter lamp gone out in panic of the dark age
banish the syndicates of samsara put away texts of doom,
turn the wheel again in our frail Anthropocene?

Chenrezig walks among us & no identity endures
yet bodhisattvas are ever active, invisible elves
swirling shamans, shape-shifting wizards every hour
dedicating the merit no endtime here but aspiration to press
harder, don't tarry! don't tarry! keep trying to sweep
all suffering away all pockets of the multiverse
keep vow with mudra, with mantra every mala bead a thought
for others, golden thread of enlightening in every step
in all directions of space push, push against the darkness
our Cartesian doubt, quantum dimensions to worry
while dharma bends in all dimensions simultaneously
& extinction is nothing (but the extinction of all suffering
inside the extinction of self whose form is emptiness)

to power of compassion
Chenrezig walks among us, scientist of compassion

Push, push against the darkness

[I watched his Holiness in the Rockies, his helicopter, like ephemeral dragonfly, descend to the Great Stupa of Dharmakaya. Then Jetsun Jamphel Ngawang Lobsang Yeshe Tenzin Gyatso (born Lhamo Thondup) came toward us, radiant vision of compassion in the shimmering autumnal light.]

Against Atrocity: Jack Kerouac School of Disembodied Poetics Themes 2019

WITH JEFFREY PETHYBRIDGE

With the title "Against Atrocity" we mean to signal both a committed antagonism and a fact of relation: we live, and think, and write in an era of unrelenting ecological and political atrocity; it is the situation, the context, the defining field we're up against. Examples of its many violences come too readily to mind, to screen, to our communities of care and concern—a vampiric regime of extraction and extinction, of cages, borders, and (surplus) populations all the more on the move, on the lam from lawless law. And as a first principle we'll try to stand with Aimé Césaire, and reject the "sterile attitude of a spectator" as the terrible array of devastations wrought through the history of racialized capitalism hurtles on and on; as artists, thinkers, and language-workers we'll try and press our imaginations forward and against atrocity.

As a first image for what this counterurgency might be, we've taken inspiration from Ana Mendieta's 1974 "Body Tracks" performance (and its photographic documentation); which is also to say we've taken inspiration from the archive, that site & source of beginning(s) (again). Inspired by how Mendieta's performance quickens with the refusal of the stance of the spectator, we'll try to take a leading from how manifestly her own body is implicated in the struggle against atrocity—if we can take the field of blood as holding space for the unspeakable, for that which can never be justly represented, a kind of antisublime. Crucial to note also how Mendieta's own work took inspiration from the long archive of artistic practices, making a unique vocabulary out of Neolithic gestures, performance art (and the temporal layering of documentary media), and an ethos we might now see as beginning a decolonial, feminist criticality.

What other leadings and principles will help us to gather and embody the counter and insurrectionary forms needed to be a bulwark against the violent confusions, against the syndicates of samsara, against and through the crises that increasingly define political life; how can writing, performance, theory, music, and critical thought be brought to bear against the forces that seek to control life, to narrow it down to the pure extraction of profit; how can art be a catalyst for abolition? As a start to these questions (and myriad others) we invoke the necessary and alchemical possibilities of coming together in community; and we invite writers, and students, and thinkers, and performers to continue the lines of critical voicing, creative work, and spiritual sensibility that have defined the Summer Writing Program since 1974.

Week 1: Archive, Alchemy & Installation

New forms must stand ready to be called into being as often as new (threatening) forces appear on the scene. It is like "earthing" an electrical charge to ensure communal safety.

　　—CHINUA ACHEBE

We're committed to documentary/investigatory poetics as activist practices, as openings into narratives and records of erased histories; committed to the archive as a collective repository and resource for culture-work, and we mourn the loss of the Brazilian Museum of the Americas to fire. However, we also want to think beyond the archive as mere document, artifact, evidentiary body, and call to mind—to summon from the living body—what Diana Taylor calls the repertoire, that wider set of embodied practices, rites, ceremonies, forms of sociality, resistance, and performance which imply continuation, survival, and community through their very transmission as communal memory and ground of being.

In our collective laboratory, we want to think beyond the binary of archive/ repertoire—beyond all binaries, really—to experiment with admixtures, assemblages, and alloys of artwork and political intervention; to choose the possibilities of transmutation rather than codes of genre, gender; to translate from and among communities of care and concern—solidarity rising, alchemically, from those exchanges and passages; urgently, to forge the figures, images, songs of a (coming) antithesis reality, antithetical to all the forces that would make the living day a site of extraction, exploitation, and accelerating extinction.

With installation we mean to imagine how writing might learn (to live) from ecology; how writing might learn from sculptural practice; how writing might further leverage the possibilities of & as performance; through installation we want to construct writing in & as activated environments; to (re)commit ourselves to writing as collaboration, to writing as form of participatory art; with installation we seek to set out into the open of writing in & for expanded and emergent fields.

Week 2: Nomadology and the War Machine
Against the State-form; against another century of capital's extraction of all from all; against the reification of land—of living earth, peoples, organisms, of water and air; against borders, drones, police & prisons; against the military-industrial complex, and all machines in which State-power pools, congeals, deadens. Against those brutal phenomena we intend the proliferation of differences—and solidarity across those differences; we intend the possibility of art, that engine for transformation and innovation; we intend to get it revving, moving out into the open(ings) of deterritorialization— And in that beyond, we intend change, metamorphosis, and intervention from the local to the absolute: the band, and the open possibility of collaboration; the artists' collective squat; the free hedge-school; the zine factory, or other DIY imagining; micropolitics of all kinds; an end to the regime of gender as control; an end to citizenship as just another form of control and exclusion. To try and hold together as a community, cell, and/or collective in these urgencies, imperatives, and dreams, we'll necessarily experiment with a range of (temporary) genres and forms; we'll assemble, collage, and juxtapose toward a nomadic vernacular, toward a philosophy of movement; we'll think about the possibilities of somatics, and sentences, and other technologies for expression, for envisioning; we'll try and imagine and embody— through Deleuze and Williams—how the poem might be a war machine made out of words.

Week 3: Abolition & Epic
Sing, O Muse, of the reemergence of abolitionism as a political ethic, as the leading edge of utopian visions, as the just response to the irreparable history of racial capitalism; sing, friends, of the epic of the end of the world in which precisely those irreparable violent acts were the ruling logic, measure, and regime; sing of the *ceaseless overthrow of forms;* sing the anti-epic we're trying for—epic of rhizomic action & occupation; of ardor & commitment; of Black Lives Matter; of a broad and broadening coalition of anti-racist activism; of prison abolition, and an end to carceral capitalism; epic of

the possibilities of the undercommons, of study & fugitive planning, fugitive performance; genderqueer epic beyond any apparatus of control or discipline; epic against the engines of genocide and extinction.

As we think of writing the epic against disaster of the Capitalocene/ Anthropocene, the urgency of the task is clear: to abolish this brutal economy and world-system. However, where to locate the forms of agency that might avail to see us through to new forms of life is more of an open question. We know that art alone is not revolution, and yet we still home in on its emergent possibilities to be the unpredictable event that propels, sustains, transforms, to be at once "essence, science, and vision," as Amiri Baraka called it, "our magic weapon to create and re-create the world and ourselves as part of it."

This search for agency and collective action will inflect our time together— our temporary community, troupe, band, cell, and assembly. We'll test the open question that writing always is through experiments with the line, the sentence, the song, the bodies that articulate them all in lived social critique; we'll listen and abide with one another in conversation and debate, always staying open to the happy accident of collective work, the shock of recognition in the new friend, that is the ground and pleasure of collaboration. And through it all—and continuing—we'll take the abolitionist urgency of Jackson Mac Low's "Social Project 2" as our signal energy, desire, dream: "FIND A WAY TO END WAR // MAKE IT WORK."

Strange Light in the Lodge

He made one feel the parched and burning throat, the pains, the fever, the fire in the guts. He was in agony. He was screaming. He was delirious. He was enacting his own death, his own crucifixion.

—ANAÏS NIN'S ACCOUNT OF ARTAUD

Strange light in the lodge, repository of dark memory, spectral gesture. In 1933 Artaud performed an enactment of "The Theatre and the Plague" at the Sorbonne. Body as martyr, as inscription, as keeper. Sacrificial lamb. Spectacle for the masses. His face was lean. Visionary's thrust to be incomprehensible. Ensorcelled. The plague everywhere, death in the streets, in garrets, back alleys. In carts of doom, in aporia, edging between life and death. His hands were trembling, eyes rolling into the back of his head. Looking inward, transported to an excruciating intensity . . . Artaud in the black lodge. Cave of flickering shadows, sequester, and death. What doctor in this house? That we all see demon pandemonium take hold, that hearts break or that fear turns us away. Could that be every one of us too? Anthropocene loses human control. How close we are to dark animalia, to a void, the abyss. O generative cyclic flow and grind of flesh wheel. That we decompose, lose breath, and still sing. Artaud's apotheosis! Center stage. Palpable dark spirit-babble in the theatrical light. Shape-shifting show of demons, all alchemical nuance as glass shatters. People in panic, afraid of their own demise. Jeering and hissing. "La peste," they call out, as they lunge outside. A prophecy . . . a crack in your mirror. And poet still gasps: "La peste! La peste!"

Conversation with a Visionary Botanist

"green grass" you said,

stepping back, human

thinking it's true in this life,

of course, green is where I come from,

the way we rise from the sea, mermaid, you mean?

mermaid is dream, mermaid the plucky greenery

"mermaimed" you said?

(I had said our spectrum must be green)

and you said the fungal mat: "mycorrhizal"

and then: the love affair of fungi and algae

not *loan* or *lawn* or *loam,* not necessary in many a place

but what they establish: *symbiosis*

green from Old English *growan*

because tidal life is growan

because plankton is growan

because green because algae . . .

(you run on) "poetry is the pain of time"

we walk by the ocean deciding to do this for our love

our attraction our desire

"green is slang for money," I say, *o not that*

people out here riding a beast the color of sand

"where on the spectrum?" I ask

we'll walk on the cold tundra

talk about nanometers, photosynthesis

because grass, an adherent, will be present in your eye,

even absent eye, eye of hiding, regret, eye of sweat

saying about dryness, I asked how it might look rasping,

why not always green

you say: "drought"

or "doubt"? then I asking how "urgent" this is?

you say "we walk in a dark proverbial forest"

we walk we walk we walk we walk, a raven's cry

that it be protozoa that they be alive too in you

creature, earth & sky, what do you know of the rest of it?

fire is a first cause, from your beastie breath

imagine a "deathday" that is drawn of cerebral work

not manicured to be cradle of green

the knots were suns, were burning came to me

& this, you said, as if musing, *the measure of precipice*

was the measure nihilismus

a measure of sorrow that we come so close

green a test, green an herbicide,

the measure of urgency: the small plant

succulent that would be hardiest (halophytic)

don't do without me, world!

colors! colors! green of peacocks, the frog

and green: memory of catastrophe

and green: intersection as you walked with your friend

scientist like the uninvited guest you welcome

interior space: all of a green; secret burial & mourning

art of social memory where graphs are housed

lists of contagion

the crisis I remembered yesterday came back

an insurrection, a siege, some ones you didn't know, they had agenda

they stalled your step, ours

you stopped walking and then . . .

Kora Dreams Her Crown

for Kora Bye-Anaya

Because everything has its origin
And I come going from place to place from the origin.

    —MARÍA SABINA

Tenterhooks in an experiment
Classroom gone empty
Fateful pandemic
I write "truce" with new second alphabet
Forgetting "truth"
Unseated territory of Ute,
Cheyenne, Arapahoe
How far we go a century
Who reads future weather?
Keep writing from stage left
Do lessons for treatise on sleep
Invite numbers & chance operation
As "seer of calculus" as "topos abuelita"
Perhaps a wrong occasion
But spiraling
They'll be back, *please come back*
The storm knocked power out
We bed down instead in another room
Mexico, estates of the Nahuatl
Stylus and astrolabe
With soft animals, lunar moth, mastodon
Kora Bebe in charge, velvet chaplet
Sitting on haunches, equinoctial
She is always rising
Her wand, crown, her formidable beauty
Animals frightened in the rain

And texts soaking wet
What is erased is problematic
You want to cry
But rescue invisible scripture
Spiral memory, telepathy
"I have memory," she says
Girl Kora studies, older now
Writes between rounds
Of crystal ammunition her dream

"I have Memory," she says.

I Wanted to Tell You about My Meditations on Jupiter [Not All Celestial Bodies Revolve around the Earth]

Grasping at fragments I want to tell you at a distance—*distanced*—about the *Recital,* and its amplification. I thought "unicum" in the varying versions, urgent meditations on Jupiter my remotest wandering, its chilly motion, ice and patterns, striations seem to be models of tissue and imprint, solitude, solicitudes. In Persian it might be a sign of geomancy. What is the sand you imagine trapped in your echo chamber? A telescope of no small size, a clepsydra of wondrous watery proportion. The greatest clock of tidal universe. What can you know? *Recital* as a dispatch, as a way signaling a spin.

This is a meditation on Time, made of glass. When the electricity stops the clocks go off on their own, those not surveilled. Switched calendars. In the new technology they will place an "OWL" in your classroom, to keep track of your study, your payments, your assignments, are you on time? For class? In an alienated classroom, the talismans of your own mind.

And you feel split in time. You feel your head dizzying as your eyes land on the handmade machine of words, repeating forms from Dante's *Inferno,* dancing in a circle of left-hand turns. Tuning up on the Day of Reckoning as you ascend. I love the syncretic. I want everything to pile up in solitude. Counting backward.

The time you thought you were on, then there were paused interventions. All through your life.

Ventricles, I need advantage and ventilators, I need vehicles as in the lesser and greater vehicles of Dharma.

The Recital of Hayy ibn Yaqzan was written during Ibn Yaqzan's captivity in the fortress of Fardajan. The author, Ibn Sina, narrates a time when Hayy ibn Yaqzan's soul was at home and could go out to the familiar places hidden in his own city. A dark abyss in which also the pilgrim of *The Recital of Occidental Exile* is trapped. A cosmic dreamlike escape.

Solitude summons Hayy ibn Yaqzan's vision. Meditate on escaping a prison whose jailers know not that they are themselves inmates.

What is imprint in a brain? Symbols? Allegories? What can we learn of carceral in a book? A day "in the can" when you want plutonium off your Front Range, when you want to control the narrative of toxins in land, water, the cellular throb and breath of toxins, and you protest all day, all months, all thousands of years. Deformed sheep born at dawn. An eye missing in a dispatch. The gasp is echoing through time, here, in capsule. Study the surfaces of sand in an age that crumbles like sand, count the eyes on potatoes, study a Field Chart of Matres of Mothers, write a book that opens to the sky. Conjure Hermes Trismegistus, who witnessed the angel Jibril in a dream.

My chambers are like cubicles in the library, the shelves swaying as in a hallucination. I had to leave that all behind, I still hold a key to a research room, and pray they will let me in again, study scripture, the rise and fall of everything, and the Age of Reason, again.

Not a philosopher I am reluctant to get loose with poetical intuitions but they are all of the above, what I have admitted here into this cavity. How to be urgent at remote control, shake a dying body awake for an instant, happy recognition. Mysteriously guided to text that fluctuates in the mind, comes and goes. Lost the little pencil for my requests. They arrive as if telepathically.

Fragments, as I've said. On the nature of prediction there is none arising. The crystal mirror is cloudy.

Watching the child on the small screen, she is learning *K* she is writing *K* the first time. I think of Aya Sofia, that elder library where it is recorded this kind of memory. The first *K* of Knowledge. Her name is Kora.

These were the categories of her studying:

WANDERING

ROAMING DAYS of cold light

MIND NOT CAUGHT YET BY the Death Clouds

Breath of death

Breath of life

IMPELLING DAYS

Mind in the heavens with distant moons.
Enceladus, her oceans hidden under icy crust.
Lift the curtain, you may see the future of water.

CRISIS

JEOPARDY

    Propulsion and Scrying

HAZARDS
RESTLESS BRUTAL PATROLS
CORNER OF a watery eye

KEENING

Io, Europa, Ganymede, Callisto, as top moons for the dark time.
ORAL TRADITION TOLD THE FUTURE THAT THIS WAS ANCESTRAL
    TRANSMISSION
HOW TO BE ALONE with the Four Rotations.

HOW NOT TO GO MAD.

I thought her thrill of discovery, child's first instinct, she be in this, looking up. But we are not awaiting Martian travel. We notice patterns of solar systems. What is identity in this? Naming? Make a list lifting the supermoons out of a host of 70—or is it 79 now? The counting of so many moons. Volcanoes and snowfields of Io, a moon of fire and ice. Colors would show red, orange, yellow, black, white. Smallest of Galileans, then Europa encircles with cracks and fissure that would haunt your notebooks 20 to 4.5 billion years old, a veteran traveller face. Ganymede, highly cratered, and "light grooved terrain," across the face. Callisto probably unchanged since its formation, how could you ever guess? Out of the radar of Jupiter's magnetic field. Beyond Jupiter's radiation belt. Untethered. More to study, each moon a year in your life.

Reflectivity. That's the dispatch here. Perhaps oceans beneath the surface could flourish with life.

A wandering mendicant in my heart, and this was what I wanted to say to you, mendicants coming after. Crying for all the others in plague to know truth of suffering. Could be signaling the end of entire civilizations. You go studying. The plague of Cyprian, the plague that ended serfdom, Plague of London, shortest in a year only 100,000 dead. Think with me now on all the friends, all the last rites for those afflicted, AIDS. Like the strike of a large gong. As you say it "AIDS." The Fallen.

Solipsism is my instrument for seeing. We keep thinking about the future. This fluctuating uncertain magic is apocalyptic by nature, and we are forgetting our rituals, our Jupiter glowing out there right now, sitting here, it's 3:18 in Mountain Time. Look out my hatch on the sky, an ingenious bubble of shelter. See the comet glide across your torn galaxies. Because you have a mind to project that heartbroken song.

Evidently celestial physics and astronomy define the soul's itinerary, like a comet, if you want to greet it that way, with an angel as guide, escape right now. Traces are discernible in *The Recital of Hayy ibn Yaqzan*, realizing a kind of transmutation where there is interiorization of the cosmos, emergence, as is said, from the cosmic crypt. The *Recital* is imploding in on itself. What is the datum? An enveloping sphere to save phenomena. A body's motion considered in longitude, in latitude. Swiftness and slowness, proximity and distance from the earth, here, us again. We think like that, *our* Earth.

I keep saying "distanced." Us as homocentric, to the center of the earth. Seven spheres, and then there was the eighth enveloped, and the whole was the "Sphere of the Fixed Stars." Would that be absolute? Why would anyone want that? But the moderns, followers of Ptolemy, added a ninth. A starless sphere, communicating that the astronomer must try to solve the notion of an unmoving earth. What will we continue to know when Science leaves us stuttering. Turn off the light? Enter that little cavity, find a corner. A movie theater, unsafe in 2020, in 2021, 2022, 2023, 2030, 2053, 2090, 3020, 3021, 3090 . . . how long is your plague? Is it really so dark stuck inside? Or out?

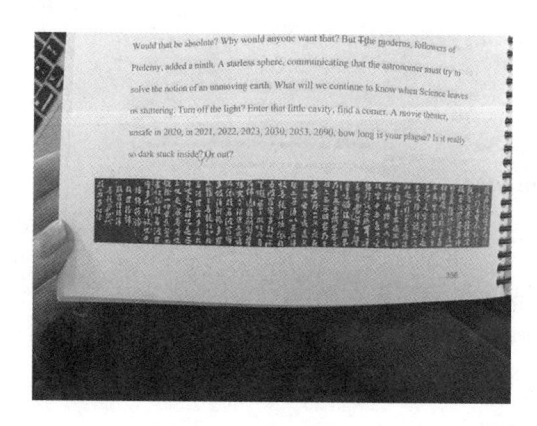

patti

tenderness for
  recalcitrant world looks up
cheers, weeps to see you live again
chaos in Chaldean
    meant "without a library"
intersects
        your weeping yarn from Algiers
all over the world
shine a light
people have the power tonight
in your Blakean year
in our chaos year
dedicated to the country
that didn't quite go fascist
to open the golden books of words again
and tell old tales
who's in who's out
narrate sagas of empire and collapse
herald a joan of arc stamina
& those told by idiots too
shields we'll carry
against the assault
not worn out in a walled prison
poetry skin and bones
in the redemption café
with Rimbaud, Artaud, Bolaño
entangling djellaba heaven
sonic angels we'll be too
as living texture
don't break, ever
dance in purple suede shoes
gift to Ambrose
stepping up as we part
our children rise again

& from a distant galaxy: *bon courage*
movement from
pine barrens
like Balzac's lost illusions
youth arrives to big city
intervenes, cracks open
public space
dawn up at the glass factory
all the crystal prophecy
: forces of eye & for
      ear's transcendence
priestess   from ageless stage
hear you now:

If I were rain I'd rain on Somalia
If I were grain for Somalia I'd grow
If I were bread I would rise for Somalia
If I were a river for Somalia I'd flow

July 4,

Write

a prayer song
   on my conception day
that lifts
&
is as great

as p 67 Nag Hammadi
. . . *I am the first & the last*

   What shadows you—
Eternity—
Is now another
shooting hell day

the "bodies
eviscerated"

 FBI sez gun was a "war machine"

What do you know of
   slammed-door-
portal-of-truth-law
wayfarers of illusion of the nagging
      Hammadi?
 Are you dangerous my country?

let Fate
crack an egg
in the hat
your only duty is to pray . . .

   July 4, Hafiz Divination 2022

Epilogue: Letter from Frances LeFevre to Anne Waldman
SUNDAY, 29 MAY, 1966

Darling Annie,

That's a very nice poem you sent. Am I right in feeling it's connected with some of your states of mind about finishing college?

It's funny, though not surprising, how your letter is practically an answer to mine written at the same time. I know you hate "dialogues" on emotional questions and I'll try to keep this from being any "lengthy reply" since you asked me not to write one. But I must clear up a few points or have them cleared up for me:

1. Your statement, "I know nothing I ever do will satisfy you completely," is just not true. Period. I look forward to a long series of pleasant occasions for great satisfaction and pride.
2. I don't "get" what you "mean" when you write . . .
    "often I feel your demands on me are physical, that is, the most difficult for me."
    Are you referring to Daddy's and my enjoyment of your physical presence?

    For we do enjoy it despite all the troubles between us. We love to look at you, talk with you, and hear about what you're doing, and your beauty, wit and charm have always been one of the pure delights of our lives; I'm not exaggerating . . . Or do you mean what you evidently feel are efforts on my part to interfere with your sex life? This, of course, is the major issue and actually the *only* cause of our difficulties. Will you, please, please, sweet, lovely baby, try once for all, with an open mind, to understand my attitude: AMBIVALENT, confused, frightened, anxious, but *loving*. I love sex myself and am very sympathetic to your needs and drives. I'm glad you are not frigid, I'm glad you've found a compatible partner, or partners, I *know* how important this is, and furthermore I do understand that the environment in which you've grown up has unusual pressures and I think you've handled yourself with more intelligence than many other girls . . . At the same time, if I hadn't tried to hold you back to some extent from getting too involved too young I wouldn't have been able to face myself with a clear conscience. From now on, of course, the responsibility for shaping your life is your own. As Mike Allen said, I simply have to learn to face the possibility that you may make tragic mistakes. But as long as I live I'll be available for anything you may want or need from me. So will Daddy.

3. I am painfully aware of a great deal of ugliness in the environment and I am perhaps over-sensitive about your reputation. But can't you accept this about me and avoid being too flagrant? It just isn't true (as yet) that everybody thinks sexual freedom is OK—and perhaps it isn't, either. Perhaps I am so sensitive because I've been called a "whore" and heard that it was being said of me that "Glaukos's wife is *rotting*"—a single word in Greek and much more powerful than the English. The fact is that I felt it was *true,* and it was enough to make me break off that affair for good, thank goodness. I had to go through it, but I'm sorry that it was necessary.

4. Are you quite aware that Daddy has always been in complete agreement with me about your men, both about their good points and—shall we say—their less fortunate ones? He has always retreated into himself about it, except for that one time when he got upset over Tom and telegraphed Bennington that you weren't coming back. I've been the one who has battled out in the open and taken the brunt of your defiance and hostility . . . Do see it this way: You are an absolutely terrific girl. Everyone who has known you always has thought you were destined for a brilliant future. Almost every man who meets you finds you unusually desirable; almost every mother would like to have you for a daughter-in-law. Of how many of the men you've gone for can you say this is true, in corresponding terms? How could we help being concerned? How can we not care what kind of man you marry?

5. We shall try our best to be "civilized" and "sophisticated" about your affairs from now on. But we do beg you to be discreet and dignified. It's an old cliché, almost a piece of folk wisdom, that the "smartest" girls are the ones no one can ever "prove" anything about. As for Lewis, I hope he and Daddy can get to know each other better and reach some sort of acceptance. I don't dislike him,

in fact, I'm really "fond" of him and respect his "mind." And I'm glad for your sake that he's a writer—I think writing is one of the activities that really count, if it's authentic. And I'm sure his is. About marriage: Frankly, if he were my son and I cared about his continuing to grow as a writer, I'd not want to see him take on the burdens of marriage so young, before he's established. It's too precarious, too dependent on a lot of complex factors, too precious to hazard. And I care about your career, too, and would like to see you really concentrate on developing your skills and establish yourself as a person in your own right before tying yourself down. You're just finally getting free of dependency on us: why give up your freedom? Up to now you've always had Bennington as an escape, and your jobs were always self-limiting; don't take on too many responsibilities at once. I still feel that you have many things—good ones—within yourself that you aren't aware of and must try out to be fully your best self, and it will take time. So don't *rush* into anything that would limit you. Marriage is a complete other world from an affair.

6. I'm sorry you mind my being "insulting," but I prefer cynicism to sentimentality. Would you rather I talked like Mrs. Norman Vincent Peale? (See enclosure.) As for "Angel Hair," I've tried to explain to you what that was all about and it's a perfectly real reaction.

7. I'm not really sorry I upset you because I am sure you can "take" it a lot better than I've taken my own "hurts." I *have* to be honest with you. I do want you to be honest with me, but, more importantly, I want you to be honest with yourself. The turning point in my life, when everything fell into place, was when I learned what the word "rationalization" means. Since then I've never been fooled by myself or by anyone else. I know sometimes it's a good and therapeutic process, but I'm glad I can do without it and I hope you'll eventually be able to.

8. I was exactly like you in feeling I had to be "in love" in order to do my best work, but my own experience taught me that this is a supreme feminine fallacy. Perhaps your experience will teach you differently, but beware—keep a little reserve of doubt. *I* think being in love dulls the wits. Men don't feel this way, not if they are truly creative. They keep love in its place and put their art first—

and they may do without love for a season but they can't leave their art alone.

I am sure this is why the greatest things to date have been done by ~~men. Love is fine, and all that, but don't let it be a trap for your gifts.~~

Leo saw the doctor: Joanie's trouble is that she's still emotionally hung up over Curtis, though she gave him up long ago in her mind. (I learned what the trouble was there, will tell you sometime, it's sort of strange.) The doctor advised L. to hang around for a while as a "supporting presence" though not necessarily nearby, so she'll leave for the Cape Wed. to stay with the Chavchavadzes for a time and keep in touch. So you may see her at some point.

Much, much love, darling baby,
Mummy

Wednesday

P.S. Just to reiterate, so you'll have no doubt about it, that you need not fear my "worry" and "emotionalism." Daddy came home for lunch and got your letter, so I know what you've decided. Well, good luck in your work. I hope you'll always be open-minded and willing to learn, and never be afraid to admit you could do better. And don't be afraid to ask me for advice or suggestions if you can take them impersonally; I'm much more objective about you than you've ever realized. The tears have been unfortunate, I know, but you must understand they are my way of handling the strain of knowing too much and wanting too much. People never really can avoid conflict and I prefer to face it rather than kid myself. I see you and Daddy still believe the fiction that I'm a "problem." You're perfectly welcome to it if it comforts you. But things are not always what they seem. No matter, I'm sure it's a useful fiction to him, and my job now that you are taken care of is to make sure he keeps his balance. Actually, though, he's the one who's really emotional beyond reason. You'll always be welcome and accepted and there's no reason why seeing each other can't be fun. I'm awfully glad you decided against a complete break, because that wouldn't have been fun. Some cooperation from you will be necessary in this arrangement—perhaps I'll have to pretend you're living with another Bennington girl or something, if we have many visitors. Bu that shouldn't present difficulties if we agree and keep it straight. I want to feel free with you myself, but I've certainly no intention of trying to run your life now that you've made your final choice. I'll continue to hope that you grow in wisdom and that you have good fortune, but I'll keep my feelings to myself. It seems to me that most of my life has been spent watching people become less than they could have been because of some little piece of trivial bad luck, or unwillingness to get perspective on themselves, or failure to make a "leap" forward because it would be too much work or too painful, but I've always felt that you were going to be the exception and bring me great pride and pleasure. This is *really* the curtain for my role as your mother, unless you should ever need or want a little "mothering" care yourself. I don't even want to be called "Mummy" anymore and certainly not "Mother," so I guess you'll just have to call me Frances. Love, etc.

from *Dearest Annie, You Wanted a
Report on Berkson's Class: Letters from
Frances LeFevre to Anne Waldman*

Acknowledgments and Credits

Paul Celan, from *Microliths They Are, Little Stones: Posthumous Prose,* translated by Pierre Joris (New York: Contra Mundum Press, 2020).

Robert Pogue Harrison, from *Forests: The Shadow of Civilization,* University of Chicago Press (May 8, 2009).

Laurie Anderson, from "The Dream Before" on the album "Strange Angels" (Warner Bros Records, 1989). Original inspiration from Walter Benjamin's ninth thesis from the essay "Theses on the Philosophy of History" (Createspace Independent Publishing, 2006).

Stacy Szymaszek, from *The Pasolini Book* (New York: Golias Books, 2022). Used by permission of author.

Lyn Hejinian, from *Border Comedy* (Granary Books, 2001).

Bob Dylan, *Chronicles: Volume One* (New York: Simon & Schuster, 2004).

Bernadette Mayer, "Simple Complications," in *Poetry* (New York: Kulchur Foundation, 1976).

"Sketch" is based on an earlier version of a piece from the Contemporary Authors Autobiography Series, edited by Joyce Nakamura (Detroit: Gale, 1993).

Lead Belly, "By and By When the Morning Comes," from *Lead Belly Sings for Children* (Smithsonian Folkways Recordings 1999).

"Ode," from *The Iovis Trilogy: Colors in the Mechanism of Concealment, Book III* (Minneapolis: Coffee House Press, 2011).

"Prelusion," unpublished.

"Stepping Back," published in *The Brooklyn Rail,* 2020. Video of "Stepping Back," with Fast Speaking Music, filmed in Mexico City in 2020 (with Natalia Gaia & Ambrose Bye). Written in April 2020, during the NYC pandemic, with Allen Ginsberg's poem in mind: "On Cremation of Chögyam Trungpa, Vidyadhara."

"Dharma Gaze," excerpt, unpublished, part of a presentation for the Center for the Study of World Religions at Harvard Divinity School, 2018.

"Teen Languishing in Cove," unpublished.

"Beat Roots," published by Hot Whisky Press, and in *Outrider* (New Mexico: Alameda Press, 2006). Used by permission of publisher.

"Epitaph for Octave," published in *Dear New York* by Zoe Ruffner, NYC 2021.

"Culture of One," first published in a different version in a *Danspace* anthology, 2016.

"Impossible Poetry?" published in *American Poets,* Academy of American Poets magazine, October 5, 2014.

"Architecture of Breathing," unpublished.

"Biggest Possible Assortment of Available Things," unpublished.

"Shadow behind Eclipse," published in *The Brooklyn Rail,* as well as in David Lehman's blog and by Zoe Brezsny for a reading at Hauser & Wirth, 2018.

"Nostalgia," published in *The Brooklyn Rail,* February 2015.

"LET GO," published in *The Brooklyn Rail,* 2001.

"Letter from Ted Berrigan," unpublished; original in the *Angel Hair* letters archive at the Lewis Warsh Archive at New York University Library. Permission granted from estate of Ted Berrigan.

"Push, Push Against the Darkness: An Interview with Anne Waldman on *The Iovis Trilogy,*" published in *Rain Taxi,* Spring 2012. Part 2 unpublished, 2021.

"By Turns, Ostraka," unpublished.

"Often Outdoors with Fires and Lanterns to See By," unpublished.

"Family Frame with Ambrose: 2012 Interview with Laura Wetherington," originally published in *Barely South Review* (Old Dominion University, 2011). Permission granted from Renée Olander.

"Fragments," early version, from *Sweet-Voiced [Mutilated] Papyrus* with Pamela Lawton (New York: Spuyten Duyvil, 2015).

"Thought of This," unpublished.

"Praetexta & Performance," first published in *Experimental Writing: A Collection of Statements* (Aurora, IL: JEF Books, 2018), edited by Warren Motte and Jeffrey R. Di Leo.

"Performing Poetics: The Oral Vortex," unpublished, created for a lecture-performance for Sharmistha Mohanty for the Almost Island Lecture Series at Jnanapravaha Mumbai, in Mumbai, India, January 20, 2010.

Quotes from Giorgio Agamben, *Nudities,* translated by David Kishik and Stefan Pedatella (Stanford, CA: Stanford University Press, 2011).

"Dialogue: A Pedagogy," unpublished.

"Interview with Poetas, Madrid 2018," first published online.

"AI Angel," unpublished.

"Braided River," unpublished.

"What Sky Limit?" published in *Gagosian Quarterly,* 2022.

"Attenuate the Loss & Find," published in *Poetry* magazine, March 2014.

"Hurr, Isho, like the whirr of a loom; Churr (Letters with Karen Weiser)," from correspondence in "Karen Weiser and Anne Waldman," from *Letters to Poets: Conversations about Poetics, Politics and Community* (Ardmore, PA: Saturnalia Books, 2008) edited by Jennifer Firestone and Dana Teen Lomax. Used by permission of Karen Weiser.

"The Burroughs Effect: A Set of Potentials," published in *William S. Burroughs: Cutting Up the Century* (Bloomington, IN: Indiana University Press, 2019).

"Sunken Suns" draws on lines by Etel Adnan from *Arab Apocalypse* (Sausalito, CA: The Post-Apollo Press, 1989). This piece also appears in *Homage to Etel Adnan* (Sausalito, CA: The Post-Apollo Press, 2017).

"Letter from Etel Adnan," in *The Iovis Trilogy: Colors In the Mechanism of Concealment* (Minneapolis: Coffee House Press, 2011). Lines by Anne Waldman pages from *The Iovis Trilogy,* 2011.

"Mix Up the Cry of Desire I'm a Corset Wrecker," unpublished, mashup of earlier "Corset," created for Artist Performance Space honoring Kathy Acker (NYC, 2018) with Erika Hodges and Janice Lowe.

"Kalyanamitra: Joanne Elizabeth Kyger," unpublished, includes emails from Joanne Kyger. Printed by permission of Donald Guravich.

"Child of Illusion" published in *Hurricane Review,* Pensacola, FL, 2021, used by permission of editor Jamey Jones.

"Had a Hand In, Occupy," unpublished.

"This Is the Antithesis Reality," published in *More Revolutionary Letters* (The Wisdom Body Collective, 2021).

"Twelve Tones under the Sun," unpublished.

"Trance Abyss," published in Pat Steir's catalog *Kairos* (New York: Lévy Gorvy Gallery, 2017).

"Mind of Endtime," small excerpt from *Voice's Daughter of a Heart Yet to Be Born* (Minneapolis: Coffee House Press, 2016).

"New Scar Over My Heart," published in *The Art of the Straight Line: My Tai Chi* (New York: HarperCollins, 2022).

"Memory and Impunity," unpublished, from a conference at Cal Arts, Red Cat.

"Questions for Citizens," submitted by Anne Waldman with Ammiel Alcalay to Poetic Citizenship Today Conference (CUNY, 2017). Published in *Writing Utopia 2020,* edited by S. Willow and S. Scotthorne (Bristol, UK: Hesterglock Press, 2020). Brief excerpt published in *Trickster Feminism* (New York: Penguin, 2018). Published in English and Spanish and made freely available by diSONARE (Mexico City, 2020).

"Out of Place," from notes presented at the Poetry Project Symposium, May 2018.

"The Angle the Frame, the Angel the Posed Subjects," unpublished.

"Jaguar Harmonics: Liana Concordance," first published in the French edition of *Jaguar Harmonics* (Brussels, Belgium: maelstrÖm, 2019) and translated by Vincent Broqua. With deep gratitude to editor David Giannoni and to Simone Fattal for the Post-Apollo Press edition.

"Chenrezig Walks among Us," published in *Tricycle: The Buddhist Review,* 2018.

"buying into fancy device" from unpublished song "Amulet," Anne Waldman, *Fast Speaking Music.*

"Strange Light in the Lodge," is an excerpt from the author's libretto for *Black Lodge* (Opera Philadelphia, 2023), and a Broadside was first published by Bob Arnold, Longhouse, 2021.

"Conversation with a Visionary Botanist," *Poetry London,* Summer 2021: Issue 99.

"Kora Dreams Her Crown," published in *Three Fold,* 2022, and *diSONARE* (also in Spanish), 2022.

"I Wanted to Tell You about My Meditations on Jupiter," published in *Conjunctions:75, Dispatches from Solitude,* 2020.

"Patti," unpublished.

"July 4," unpublished.

IMAGE CREDITS

Kora Bye-Anaya, March 30, 2020, Mexico City. Photo by Natalia Gaia.

Anne Waldman in *Alice in Wonderland,* Greenwich House Children's Theater, New York City, 1957. Photographer unknown, Anne Waldman Archives.

Anne Waldman, Lewis Warsh, Kate Berrigan, Bustins Island, Maine, 1967. Photo by Ted Berrigan. Anne Waldman Archives.

Jerome Rothenberg, Anne Waldman, Peter Orlovsky, Allen Ginsberg, Diane di Prima, Chögyam Trungpa, Barbara Dilley, William S. Burroughs, Naropa Institute, Varsity Townhouse Apartments, Boulder, CO, circa 1975. Photographer unknown, Anne Waldman Archives.

Eclipse Series, Boulder, CO, 2017. Photos by Ed Bowes.

Anne Waldman with Allen Ginsberg and Edwin Denby at the Gotham Book Mart, 1970. Photographer unknown, Anne Waldman Archives.

Washington Square Park Protest, New York 2018. Photo by Anne Waldman.

The studio at home, NYC, Anne Waldman and Devin Brahja Waldman, 2021. Photo by No Land.

Weed wand, July 28, 2019. Boulder, CO. Photo by Anne Waldman.

Nepal bell, January 31, 2017. Photo by Anne Waldman.

Carolee Schneemann funeral, Rosendale, NY, April 6, 2019. Photo by Anne Waldman.

Etel Adnan, *Arab Apocalypse,* New York City, 2021. Photo by Zoe Brezsny.

Anne Waldman with Etel Adnan's drawings for *Jaguar Harmonics,* MacDougal Street, New York City, 2020. Photo by Zoe Brezsny.

King Sooper's mass shooting memorial, April 12, 2021, Boulder, CO. Photo by Anne Waldman.

Anne Waldman and Pat Steir, 2009, New York City. Photo by Nathaniel Dorsky.

Rocky Flats Closure Project, CO, April 23, 2016. Photograph by Emma Gomis.

El Paso, Artistic Uprising, El Paso, TX, July 5, 2019. Photo by Anne Waldman.

Solstice, December 22, 2020. Boulder, CO. Photograph by Amy Catanzano.

Pyramid of the Moon, San Juan Teotihuacán, Mexico, April 8, 2016. Photo by Anne Waldman.

Manuscript with Chinese characters. Photo by Anne Waldman.

Anne Waldman and Ed Bowes, New York City. Photo by No Land, 2019.

Kora Bye-Anaya, November 2020, Mexico City. Photo by Natalia Gaia.

With luminous thanks and laudations to my partner Ed Bowes. With deep gratitude to Sarah Riggs and the community of the Tamaas Seminar, and to the Rizoma community active in Mexico City that has been a fulcrum for my work and life. And especially to Lucía Hinojosa Gaxiola. And Zazil Collins.

And voluminous gratitude to Öykü Tekten, my editor for the book *Mundo Aparte/Offworld* (Spanish/English from Pinsapo Press, 2019).

And to my Poetics colleagues at Naropa University, three bows.

And to Alystyre Julian for the work on the film *Outrider,* an inspiration for this book.

And to Alice Notley, for permission to publish Ted Berrigan's letter.

With appreciation to former publisher and editor Chris Fischbach at Coffee House Press; to former editor Erika Stevens at Coffee House, who helped immeasurably with aplomb and patience; and to former managing editor Carla Valadez at Coffee House Press. Also to Kellie Hultgren, who stepped up.

Gratitude for helpful manuscript preparation and photograph assemblage and creative friendship to Zoe Brezsny. And warm thanks to Erika Hodges and Jade Lascelles. To No Land for the terrific cover art. Additional appreciation to *The Brooklyn Rail* (editor Phong Bui, poetry editor Anselm Berrigan), Etel Adnan, Jim Cohn, Pat Steir, Selah Saterstrom, Erika Hunt, Jeffrey Pethybridge, Emma Gomis, Ammiel Alcalay, Ambrose Bye, Devin Brahja Waldman, Karen Weiser, Donald Guravich, Sharmistha Mohanty, Poetas, Ron Padgett, Melody London, Vincent Katz, Steven Taylor, Mei-mei Berssenbrugge, Peter Hale, Raymond Foye and the estate of Joanne Kyger.

Ammiel Alcalay is a poet, scholar, and translator. He teaches at Queens College and the CUNY Graduate Center. His books include *After Jews and Arabs: Remaking Levantine Culture, Memories of Our Future, Islanders, neither wit nor gold (from then), from the warring factions,* and *a little history.*

Ambrose Bye is a musician, composer, engineer, and producer. He is one of the founders of the Fast Speaking Music band and label. Projects include the albums Matching Half, Jaguar Harmonics, SCIAMACHY, and the *Harry's House Archive* from Naropa's Summer Writing Program.

Jim Cohn is a postbeat poet and founder of the digital Museum of American Poetics (poetspath.com). His many publications include *Green Sky, The Dance of Yellow Lightning Over the Ridge,* and most recently, *Treasures for Heaven: Poems 1976–2021.*

Joanne Kyger (November 19, 1934–March 22, 2017) was based in Bolinas, California. The author of over thirty books of poetry and prose, Kyger was associated with the poets of the San Francisco Renaissance, the Beat Generation, Black Mountain, and the New York School. Recent poetry collections include *God Never Dies* (Blue Press), *The Distressed Look* (Coyote Books), *Again* (La Alameda Press), and *As Ever: Selected Poems* (Penguin Books).

Jeffrey Pethybridge is the author of *Striven, The Bright Treatise* (Noemi Press 2013). He is a core faculty member in the Jack Kerouac School of Disembodied Poetics and is director of the Summer Writing Program.

Karen Weiser is a poet and psychotherapist. She is the author of two books of poetry: *To Light Out,* and *Or, The Ambiguities,* both from Ugly Duckling Press.

And to my beloved family and extended-family constellations in our magnificent rhizome. And special thanks to Gina Maher, Chris Maher, Neil Maher, and their families.

Bibliography

Achebe, Chinua. "The Igbo World and Its Art." In *Hopes and Impediments: Selected Essays*. London: Penguin Books, 2019.

Adnan, Etel. *Sitt Marie Rose*. Sausalito, CA: Post-Apollo Press, 1989.

Adonis. *An Introduction to Arab Poetics*. London: Saqi Books, 2013.

Agamben, Giorgio. "What Is the Contemporary?" In *What Is an Apparatus? And Other Essays*. Stanford: Stanford University Press, 2009.

Alighieri, Dante. *Inferno*. Translated by Mary Jo Bang. Minneapolis: Graywolf, 2012.

———. *Purgatorio*. 1317.

Allen, Paula Gunn. *The Sacred Hoop: Recovering the Feminine in American Indian Traditions*. Boston: Beacon Press, 1992.

Anderson, Laurie. "The Dream Before (for Walter Benjamin)." *Strange Angels*. Los Angeles: Warner Records, 1989.

Arendt, Hannah, and Amos Elon. *Eichmann in Jerusalem: A Report on the Banality of Evil*. London: Penguin, 2006.

Ashbery, John. "57." In *The Tennis Court Oath*. Middletown, CT: Wesleyan University Press, 1962.

———. "A Conversation with Kenneth Koch." In *Selected Prose*. Edited by Eugene Richie. Ann Arbor: University of Michigan Press, 2005.

———. *Other Traditions*. Cambridge, MA: Harvard University Press, 2000.

———. *Rivers and Mountains: Poems*. New York: Open Road Media, 2014.

Audubon, John James. *Writings & Drawings*. New York: Library of America, 1999.

Baracks, Barbara. "Einstein on the Beach." *Art Forum,* March 1977.

Baraka, Amiri. Lecture on Revolutionary Poetry, delivered at Naropa University, 1994.

Bellm, Dan. "Four Lines by Paul Celan." In *La Piccioletta Barca*. Accessed September 7, 2022. https://www.picciolettabarca.com/posts/four-lines-by -paul-celan

Berrigan, Ted. *The Collected Poems of Ted Berrigan*. Oakland, CA: University of California Press, 2005.

Bey, Hakim. *T.A.Z.: The Temporary Autonomous Zone, Ontological Anarchy, Poetic Terrorism*. Brooklyn: Autonomedia, 2003.

Blake, William. *Jerusalem the Emanation of the Giant Albion*. In *The Complete Poetry and Prose of William Blake*. Edited by David E. Erdman. New York: Anchor Books, 1988.

———. "The Lamb." In *The Complete Poetry and Prose of William Blake*. Edited by David E. Erdman. New York: Anchor Books, 1988.

———. "The Tyger." In *The Complete Poetry and Prose of William Blake*. Edited by David E. Erdman. New York: Anchor Books, 1988.

Brainard, Joe. "I Remember." In *The Collected Writings of Joe Brainard*. Edited by Ron Padgett. New York: Library of America, 2012.

Burroughs, William S. *The Job: Interviews with William S. Burroughs*. Edited by Daniel Odier. New York: Penguin Books, 1989.

———. "Lectures on the Virus." In *Burroughs Unbound: William S. Burroughs and the Performance of Writing*. Edited by S. E. Gontarski. Bloomsbury, UK: Bloomsbury Publishing, 2021.

———. "The Limits of Control." *Semiotext(e): Schizo-Culture* 3, no. 2 (1978): 38–42.

———. Letter to the editor. *The New York Review*, July 19, 1984.

———. *My Education: A Book of Dreams*. New York: Viking Press, 1995.

———. *Nova Express*. New York: Grove Press, 1964.

———. *The Ticket That Exploded*. New York: Olympia Press, 1962.

Calvino, Italo. "The Jaguar Sun." In *Secret Ingredients: The New Yorker Book of Food and Drink*. Edited by David Remnick. New York: Random House, 2007.

Celan, Paul. *Microliths They Are, Little Stones: Posthumous Prose*. Translated by Pierre Joris. New York: Contra Mundum Press, 2020.

Césaire, Aimé. *Notebook of a Return to the Native Land*. Translated and edited by Clayton Eshleman and Annette Smith. Middletown, CT: Wesleyan University Press, 2001.

Codrescu, Andrei. *Wakefield*. New York: Open Road Media, 2015.

Coolidge, Clark. *Poet*. Brooklyn, NY: Pressed Wafer, 2018.

Corbin, Henry. "Composition and Authenticity of the Recital; Commentaries and Manuscripts." In *Avicenna and the Visionary Recital*. Translated by Willard R. Trask. Princeton, NJ: Princeton University Press, 1988.

Crist, Eileen. *Abundant Earth*. Chicago: The University of Chicago Press, 2019.

Deleuze, Gilles, and Michel Foucault. "Intellectuals and Power." In *Language, Counter-Memory, Practice: Selected Interviews and Essays by Michel Foucault*. Edited by Donald F. Bouchard. Ithaca, NY: Cornell University Press, 1980.

Deleuze, Gilles, and Félix Guattari. *Anti-Oedipus: Capitalism and Schizophrenia*. Translated by Robert Hurley, Mark Seem, and Helen R. Lane. New York: Penguin, 2009.

Denby, Edwin. "Balanchine and Stravinsky." In *Dance Writings and Poetry*. New Haven, CT: Yale University Press, 1998.

———. "Brindisi." In *Mediterranean Cities, Sonnets*. New York: George Wittenborn, 1956.

———. "Dancers, Buildings, and People in the Street." In *Dance Writings and Poetry*. New Haven, CT: Yale University Press, 1998.

———. "Disorder, mental, strikes me; I." In *Dance Writings and Poetry*. New Haven, CT: Yale University Press, 1998.

———. "Forms in Motion and in Thought." *Salmagundi*, no. 33/34 (Spring/Summer 1976).

———. "Naples." In *Dance Writings and Poetry*. New Haven, CT: Yale University Press, 1998.

———. "On Meaning in Dance." In *Dance Writings and Poetry*. New Haven, CT: Yale University Press, 1998.

———. "Venice." In *Dance Writings and Poetry*. New Haven, CT: Yale University Press, 1998.

de Pisan, Christine. *The Book of the City of Ladies*. New York: Persea Books, 1982.

Derrida, Jacques. *Archive Fever: A Freudian Impression*. Translated by Eric Prenowitz. Chicago: University of Chicago Press, 1996.

Dickinson, Emily. "There is a pain—so utter—." In *Dickinson: Selected Poems and Commentaries*. Edited by Helen Vendler. Cambridge, MA: Harvard University Press, 2010.

Diggs, LaTasha N. Nevada. "pidgin toe." *Poem-a-Day*, 2014.

Duncan, Robert. *The H. D. Book*. Edited by Michael Boughn and Victor Coleman. Berkeley: University of California Press, 2011.

Dylan, Bob. *Chronicles: Volume One*. New York: Simon & Schuster, 2004.

Estrada, Alvara. "María Sabina: Her Life and Chants." New Wilderness Poetics, 1981.

Finley, Karen. *Moral History*. 1994. Library table, plate glass, archival books, 144 × 48 × 48 in. C24 Gallery.

Ginsberg, Allen. "Memory Gardens." In *Collected Poems 1947–1997*. New York: Harper Perennial Modern Classics, 2007.

———."When the mode of the music changes, the walls of the city shake." In *Poetics of the New American Poetry*. Edited by Donald Allen and Warren Tallman. New York: Grove Press, 1973, pp. 324–30.

Ginsberg, Allen and William S. Burroughs. *The Yage Letters*. Rearsby, Leicester: W. F. Howes, 2013.

Guattari, Félix and Gilles Deleuze. *A Thousand Plateaus: Capitalism and Schizophrenia*. Minneapolis: University of Minnesota Press, 1987.

Guest, Barbara. "Noisetone." In *The Collected Poems of Barbara Guest*. Edited by Hadley Haden Guest. Middletown, CT: Wesleyan University Press, 2008.

Harrison, Robert Pogue. *Forests: The Shadow of Civilization*. Chicago: University of Chicago Press, 1992.

Hejinian, Lyn. *A Border Comedy*. New York: Granary Books, 2001.

Hess, Earl J. *Braxton Bragg: The Most Hated Man of the Confederacy*. Chapel Hill, NC: University of North Carolina Press, 2021.

Hollo, Anselm. "Reading Joanne Kyger." In *The Tortoise of History*. Minneapolis: Coffee House Press, 2016.

Homer. *The Odyssey*. Translated by Emily Wilson. New York: W. W. Norton & Company, 2017.

hooks, bell. "The Oppositional Gaze: Black Female Spectators." In *Black Looks: Race and Representation*, 115–131. Boston: South End Press, 1992.

How We Get Free: Black Feminism and the Combahee River Collective. Edited by Keeanga-Yamahtta Taylor. Chicago: Haymarket Books, 2017.

Howe, Susan. *Spontaneous Particulars: The Telepathy of Archives*. New York: New Directions, 2014.

Invisible Committee, The. "Tomorrow Is Cancelled." In *Now*. Translated by Robert Hurley. n.p.: Ill Will Editions, 2017.

Jarnot, Lisa. *Night Scenes*. Chicago: Flood, 2008.

Keats, John. *Endymion*. London: E. Moxon, Son and Co., 1873.

Kerouac, Jack. "211th Chorus." In *Mexico City Blues, 242 Choruses*. New York: Grove Press, 1959.

Kyger, Joanne. "Replacement Buddhas." In *As Ever: Selected Poems*. New York: Penguin, 2002.

———. *The Tapestry and the Web*. San Francisco: Four Seasons Foundation, 1965.

———. "Sunday." In *On Time: Poems 2005–2014*. San Francisco: City Lights Books, 2015.

Lao Tzu. *Tao Te Ching*. Edited by David Hinton. Berkeley: Counterpoint Press, 2015.

Lead Belly. *Lead Belly Sings for Children*. Smithsonian Folkways Recordings SFW45047, 1999, compact disc. Recorded live in the 1940s.

LeFevre, Frances., ed. *Dearest Annie, You Wanted a Report on Berkson's Class: Letters from Frances LeFevre to Anne Waldman.* Edited by Lisa Birman. Brooklyn, NY: Hanging Loose Press, 2016.

Lowell, Robert. "Man and Wife." In *Selected Poems.* New York: Farrar, Straus and Giroux, 1976.

Mackey, Nathaniel. *Double Trio.* New York: New Directions, 2021.

Margulis, Lynn and Dorion Sagan. *Microcosmos: Four Billion Years of Evolution from Our Microbial Ancestors.* Berkeley: University of California Press, 1986.

Mayer, Bernadette. "Simple Complications." In *Poetry.* New York: Kulchur Foundation, 1976.

Mbembe, Achille. "Autophagy." In *Necropolitics.* Translated by Steven Corcoran. Durham, NC: Duke University Press, 2019.

———. *Necropolitics.* Translated by Steven Corcoran. Durham, NC: Duke University Press, 2019.

Motokiyo, Zeami. "Nishiki-gi." Translated by Ezra Pound. In *Translations.* New York: New Directions, 1963.

———. *On the Art of the No Drama: The Major Treatises of Zeami.* Translated by J. Thomas Rimer and Yamazaki Masakazu. Princeton, NJ: Princeton University Press, 1984.

Mulvey, Laura. "Visual Pleasure and Narrative Cinema." In *Visual and Other Pleasures.* London: Palgrave Macmillian UK, 1989.

Murphy, Timothy S. *Wising Up the Marks: The Amodern William Burroughs.* Berkeley: University of California Press, 1998.

Myles, Eileen. "The Perfect Faceless Fish." *The Brooklyn Rail* (February 2010).

Newcity, Michael. "What about the Military Bases? Renaming Fort Bragg." *Duke Today,* August 15, 2017. https://today.duke.edu/2017/08/what-about-military-bases-renaming-fort-bragg.

Nin, Anaïs. *The Diary of Anaïs Nin, 1931–1934.* Edited by Gunther Stuhlmann. New York: Houghton Mifflin Harcourt, 1969.

O'Flaherty, Wendy Doniger. "Myths about Dreams." In *Dreams, Illusions and Other Realities.* Chicago: University of Chicago Press, 1984.

O'Hara, Frank. *Art Chronicles, 1954–1966.* New York: George Braziller, 1975.

———. "Biotherm." In *The Collected Poems of Frank O'Hara.* Edited by Donald Allen. Berkeley: University of California Press, 1995.

———. *Meditations in an Emergency.* New York: Grove Press, 1957.

———. "Second Avenue." In *The Collected Poems of Frank O'Hara*. Edited by Donald Allen. Berkeley: University of California Press, 1995.

O'Hara, Frank, and Norman Bluhm. *Meet Me in the Park* (from *Poem-Paintings*). 1960. Watercolor and gouache on paper. Grey Art Gallery, New York University Art Collection.

Odier, Daniel. *The Job: Interviews with William S. Burroughs*. New York: Grove Press, 1970.

Online Etymology Dictionary. "Origin and Meaning of Forest (n.)." Accessed April 19, 2022. https://www.etymonline.com/word/forest.

Paz, Octavio. Introduction to *Miserable Miracle* (New York: New York Review Books Classics, 2002).

Perec, Georges. *W, or the Memory of Childhood*. Translated by David Bellos. Boston: David R. Godine, 1988.

Pound, Ezra. "Sestina: Altaforte." *The English Review*, 1909.

Procol Harum. "A Whiter Shade of Pale." *Procol Harum*. London: Deram Records, 1967.

Qabbani, Nizar. "I Am with Terrorism." *Nizariat*, 1997.

Review of *The Iovis Trilogy: Colors in the Mechanism of Concealment*, by Anne Waldman. *Publishers Weekly*. June 20, 2011.

Rich, Adrienne. *Of Woman Born: Motherhood as Experience and Institution*. New York: Norton, 1986.

Robertson, Lisa. "Sometimes I want a corset like . . ." In *the weather*. Vancouver, BC: New Star Books, 2001.

Sanders, Ed. *Investigative Poetry*. San Francisco: City Lights, 2008.

Schelling, Andrew, and Anne Waldman, trans. *Songs of the Sons and Daughters of Buddha: Enlightenment Poems from the Theragatha and Therigatha*. New York: Shambhala, 2020.

Schneeman, Carolee. *Carolee Schneemann: Uncollected Texts*. Edited by Branden Wayne Joseph. New York: Primary Information, 2018.

———. "Carolee Schneemann's Art is Not Made for Your Comfort." By Pipilotti Rist. *Interview Magazine*. October 16, 2017. https://www.interview magazine.com/art/carolee-schneemanns-art-is-not-made-for-your -comfort.

Shakespeare, William. *King Richard II*. London: Bell, 1595.

Shelley, Percy Bysshe. "Ozymandias." In *Shelley's Poetry and Prose*. New York: Norton, 1977.

Solange. "Don't Touch My Hair." Track 9 on *A Seat at the Table*. Saint Records, 2016, digital music.

Spicer, Jack. *My Vocabulary Did This to Me: The Collected Poetry of Jack Spicer.* Edited by Kevin Killian and Peter Gizzi. Middletown, CT: Wesleyan University Press, 2010.

Stein, Charles. "Money Has an Enemy." Unpublished.

Stein, Gertrude. "Sacred Emily." In *Geography & Plays: A Collection of Poems, Stories and Plays.* Chicago: Musaicum Books, 2017.

———. "Stanza XVI." In *Stanzas in Meditation.* Edited by Susannah Hollister and Emily Setina. New Haven, CT: Yale University Press, 2012.

Szymaszek, Stacy. *The Pasolini Book.* New York: Golias Books, 2022.

Thomas, Lorenzo. "Dracula." In *The Collected Poems of Lorenzo Thomas.* Middletown, CT: Wesleyan University Press, 2019.

———. "Envoy." In *The Collected Poems of Lorenzo Thomas.* Middletown, CT: Wesleyan University Press, 2019.

———. "Fit Music." In *The Collected Poems of Lorenzo Thomas.* Middletown, CT: Wesleyan University Press, 2019.

———. "Proem." In *The Collected Poems of Lorenzo Thomas.* Middletown, CT: Wesleyan University Press, 2019.

"The Thunder, Perfect Mind." Translated by Dr. Willis Barnstone. In *The Gnostic Bible.* Edited by Willis Barnstone and Marvin Meyer. Boulder, CO: Shambhala, 2009.

Tolbert, TC, and Trace Peterson, eds. *Troubling the Line: Trans and Genderqueer Poetry and Poetics.* New York: Nightboat Books, 2013.

Vicuña, Cecilia. *Ethics of a Cloud-net: Cecilia Vicuña's "Spit Temple."* Translated by Rosa Alcalá Brooklyn, NY: Ugly Duckling Presse, 2012.

Wagner, Richard. Act II of *Parsifal,* 1882.

Wang Wei. "In the Mountains, Sent to Ch'an Brothers and Sisters." In *The Selected Poems of Wang Wei.* Translated by David Hinton. New York: New Directions Books, 2006.

Weiser, Karen. "Now Then." *The Brooklyn Rail.* November 2005.

———. "The plant must grow tired, and I very sleepy." In *To Light Out.* Brooklyn, NY: Ugly Duckling Presse, 2010.

Welch, Lew. "Song of the Turkey Buzzard." In *The Postmoderns: The New American Poetry Revised,* edited by Donald Allen and George F. Butterick. New York: Grove Press, 1982.

Wieners, John. "A Poem for the Insane." In *The New American Poetry,* edited by Donald Allen. Berkeley: University of California Press, 1999.

Coffee House Press began as a small letterpress operation in 1972 and has grown into an internationally renowned nonprofit publisher of literary fiction, essay, poetry, and other work that doesn't fit neatly into genre categories.

Coffee House is both a publisher and an arts organization. Through our *Books in Action* program and publications, we've become interdisciplinary collaborators and incubators for new work and audience experiences. Our vision for the future is one where a publisher is a catalyst and connector.

LITERATURE
is not the same thing as
PUBLISHING

Funder Acknowledgments

Coffee House Press is an internationally renowned independent book publisher and arts nonprofit based in Minneapolis, MN; through its literary publications and *Books in Action* program, Coffee House acts as a catalyst and connector—between authors and readers, ideas and resources, creativity and community, inspiration and action.

Coffee House Press books are made possible through the generous support of grants and donations from corporations, state and federal grant programs, family foundations, and the many individuals who believe in the transformational power of literature. This activity is made possible by the voters of Minnesota through a Minnesota State Arts Board Operating Support grant, thanks to the legislative appropriation from the Arts and Cultural Heritage Fund. Coffee House also receives major operating support from the Amazon Literary Partnership, Jerome Foundation, Literary Arts Emergency Fund, McKnight Foundation, and the National Endowment for the Arts (NEA). To find out more about how NEA grants impact individuals and communities, visit www.arts.gov.

Coffee House Press receives additional support from Bookmobile; Dorsey & Whitney LLP; Elmer L. & Eleanor J. Andersen Foundation; the Matching Grant Program Fund of the Minneapolis Foundation; Mr. Pancks' Fund in memory of Graham Kimpton; the Schwab Charitable Fund; and the U.S. Bank Foundation.

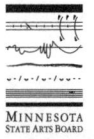

The Publisher's Circle of Coffee House Press

Publisher's Circle members make significant contributions to Coffee House Press's annual giving campaign. Understanding that a strong financial base is necessary for the press to meet the challenges and opportunities that arise each year, this group plays a crucial part in the success of Coffee House's mission.

Recent Publisher's Circle members include many anonymous donors, Patricia A. Beithon, Anitra Budd, Andrew Brantingham, Dave & Kelli Cloutier, Mary Ebert & Paul Stembler, Jocelyn Hale & Glenn Miller, the Rehael Fund-Roger Hale/Nor Hall of the Minneapolis Foundation, Randy Hartten & Ron Lotz, Dylan Hicks & Nina Hale, William Hardacker, Kenneth & Susan Kahn, the Kenneth Koch Literary Estate, Cinda Kornblum, Jennifer Kwon Dobbs & Stefan Liess, the Lenfestey Family Foundation, Sarah Lutman & Rob Rudolph, the Carol & Aaron Mack Charitable Fund of the Minneapolis Foundation, Gillian McCain, Mary & Malcolm McDermid, Daniel N. Smith III & Maureen Millea Smith, Enrique & Jennifer Olivarez, Robin Preble, Nan G. Swid, Grant Wood, and Margaret Wurtele.

For more information about the Publisher's Circle and other ways to support Coffee House Press books, authors, and activities, please visit www.coffeehousepress.org/pages/donate or contact us at info@coffeehousepress.org.

ANNE WALDMAN is the author of numerous volumes of poetry, including the feminist epic *The Iovis Trilogy: Colors in the Mechanism of Concealment,* which won the PEN Center USA Award for Poetry in 2012. Other books include *Trickster Feminism, Voice's Daughter of a Heart Yet to Be Born, Manatee/Humanity, Gossamurmur, Jaguar Harmonics,* and the anthologies *Cross Worlds: Transcultural Poetics* (co-edited with Laura Wright) and *New Weathers: Poetics from the Naropa Archive* (co-edited with Emma Gomis.) She is a recipient of the Shelley Memorial Award, a Guggenheim fellowship, and the Before Columbus Foundation Lifetime Achievement Award, and is a former chancellor of the Academy of American Poets.

Waldman has engaged with cultural and political activism throughout her career and was arrested with Daniel Ellsberg and Allen Ginsberg at Rocky Flats in the 1970s. She has been at the forefront for many decades in creating poetic communities and archiving precious literary histories and oral recordings of the twentieth and twenty-first centuries. She was one of the founders of the Poetry Project at St. Mark's Church and a founder (with Diane di Prima and Ginsberg) of the celebrated Jack Kerouac School of Disembodied Poetics at Naropa University in Boulder, the first Buddhist-inspired university in the West, where she continued as director for many years and now curates the Summer Writing Program. She has taught and presented at schools, conferences, and festivals worldwide. Waldman is also a respected musician; Patti Smith called her latest album, 2020's *Sciamachy,* "Exquisitely potent. A psychic shield for our times." Her libretto for David T. Little's *Black Lodge* had its premiere at Opera Philadelphia in October 2022.

Bard, Kinetic was designed by
Bookmobile Design & Digital Publisher Services.
Text is set in Adobe Garamond Pro.